娓娓道来
★出国考试系列丛书

U0369183

托福高分万能思路

跟名师练TOEFL 口语 & 写作

傅 辰 罗剑南 黄茜倩
◎编 著

一本能拯救你的托福口语/写作素材库

机械工业出版社
CHINA MACHINE PRESS

本书针对的是备考 TOEFL 独立口语和独立写作的同学们在冲刺之前的语言积累工作。这个扎实的提升，就是制订一个具体到每天的计划，每天搞定一个 TOEFL 常考话题。本书就是这样的一个计划，将 TOEFL 独立输出部分拆解成 30 个话题，希望同学们每天完成一个话题。每个话题都提出了大量相关问题，每个问题又给出多方面可能的回答，由大家选择自己喜欢的回答方式，建立自己的语料库。在第一部分详细列举话题问题和回答之后，第二部分将每个话题涉及的近几年的托福独立口语和独立写作的真题进行汇总，大家可以根据真题出现的频率详略得当地积累相关素材。希望第一部分的范文能够激发大家去设计属于自己的针对每道真题的答案。

　　本书适用于所有已经参加或者准备参加 TOEFL 考试的考生，也适用于想要提高英语口语和写作能力的同学。

图书在版编目（CIP）数据

托福高分万能思路：跟名师练 TOEFL 口语/写作 / 傅辰，罗剑南，黄茜倩编著. —北京：机械工业出版社，2017.11
（娓娓道来出国考试系列丛书）
ISBN 978 - 7 - 111 - 58660 - 9

Ⅰ.①托…　Ⅱ.①傅…②罗…③黄…　Ⅲ.①TOEFL -口语-自学参考资料②TOEFL -写作-自学参考资料　Ⅳ.①H310.41

中国版本图书馆 CIP 数据核字（2017）第 302466 号

机械工业出版社（北京市百万庄大街 22 号　邮政编码 100037）
策划编辑：苏筛琴　　　责任编辑：王庆龙　苏筛琴
责任印制：孙　炜
保定市中画美凯印刷有限公司印刷

2018 年 1 月第 1 版·第 1 次印刷
184mm × 260mm · 22 印张 · 1 插页 · 481 千字
标准书号：ISBN 978 - 7 - 111 - 58660 - 9
定价：52.80 元

Preface 前　言

　　本书针对的是备考 TOEFL 独立口语和独立写作的同学们在冲刺之前的语言积累工作。由于大部分中国学生的英语是哑巴英语，擅长输入，不擅长输出，因此学习再多的展开套路或行文技巧，在考场上就算有思路，也不能用语言顺利将准备好的思路表现出来。通常，当且仅当同学们曾经写过或说过一个句子，至少是类似的句子时他们才能够顺利写出或说出这个句子。因此，我们希望备考前期的同学能够吸取别人的教训，不要再走别人走过的弯路。与其花三四个月训练所谓的 TOEFL 口语、写作技巧，不如扎扎实实地进行能力上的提升。那么，对于独立口语和独立写作，扎实的提升就是制订一个具体到每天的计划，每天搞定一个 TOEFL 常考话题。

　　本书就是这样的一个计划，将 TOEFL 独立输出部分拆解成 30 个话题，希望同学们每天完成一个话题。在每个话题中，我们都提出了跟该话题相关的大量问题，并且给出多方面可能的回答，由大家选择自己喜欢的回答方式。我们甚至希望，这些回答能够激发大家去设计属于自己的回答，可以对书上的回答进行修改，甚至彻底重建。

　　总之，对于很多缺乏灵感、缺乏语言积累的同学，我们希望能够激励他们，帮助他们脚踏实地地完成这个步骤。比如，在"运动"这个章节，我们会问一系列的问题：运动有哪些？运动重要吗，为什么？你喜欢运动吗？你为什么喜欢/不喜欢运动？你喜欢哪项运动，为什么？如何提高该项运动的能力？你喜欢哪个运动员，为什么？你会在电视上看运动比赛吗，为什么？等等。针对具体的问题，我们又设计了多方面可能的回答，并进行展开。比如，对于运动的重要性，我们可能回答：运动提高身体技能；运动培养意志品质；运动提高人际交往能力等。并且，每一项回答我们都会详细展开。

　　我们希望大家能够完成这 30 个话题，并不意味着我们希望大家完全复制这 30 个话题的回答。开始也许必须完全复制，到后来可能完全自发创造，我们的根本目的是希望基础相对薄弱的同学真正切切实实地去积累一些对考试、甚至对未来出国交流有意义的东西，而不是流于形式，整天学习所谓的"技巧""套路"等一些老师们自己都不怎么相信的东西。之所以选择这么多子话题，而不是传统上比较宏观的"教育""科技""娱乐"等门类，是因为，对于基础薄弱的同学，如果门类太大，门类下的子话题之间还是没有什么参考意义。比如，同样是"娱乐"下的"影视"，如果有的同学为它准备过素材，结果遇到了一道"游戏"的题目，平常说不出来考试的时候还是说不出来。所以，细化就是为了破除这种幻觉，即大类话题之间可以触类旁通。

最后，想嘱咐大家，语言的学习重在模仿和积累。不要总寄希望于考试时的临场发挥，平常多努力，才能有备无患。希望同学们能够好好利用此书，提高自己的英语实力。祝大家在考试中能够取得好成绩。

编　者
2017 年 9 月

本书使用指南

以第一类"运动"为例。

第一步

扫一眼Part 2所有运动类的历年真题汇总。因为想搞定一个特定话题，首先要知道ETS都喜欢出什么样的相关话题。看的时候，注意扫一下运动类题目里，最常考的话题是什么。我们会把ETS常考的此类真题放在表格最上方，以便大家了解高频话题，锁定目标，然后各个击破。

第一类 运动

真 题	题 型	年 份	话题索引
All students should attend social activities, such as joining a club or a sports team in school.	口语 第二题	2015/04/12	1－1
			1－5
			1－13
Do you agree or disagree with the statement that watching sports programs on TV is not a good use of time?	口语 第二题	2016/08/21	1－9
			1－10
			1－11
If the school received a barrel of money, what do you wish it would be spent on? A sports gym or a laboratory?	口语 第二题	2016/07/10	1－1
			1－12

第二步

扫一眼每类话题开始的树状话题拓展图。每类话题都是由若干个小问题组成的。像运动这一类，我们一共提了14个小问题，包括：运动对我们为什么很重要？你平常运动的频率是多少？你通常在什么地方运动？你喜欢看电视上的体育赛事吗？等等。所以正常情况下，大家直接从第一个小问题按顺序学到最后一个小问题即可。另外，大家在扫读树状话题拓展图的时候，也可以看一下自己对于哪个小问题的回答最没底，然后可以优先去准备该问题的内容。

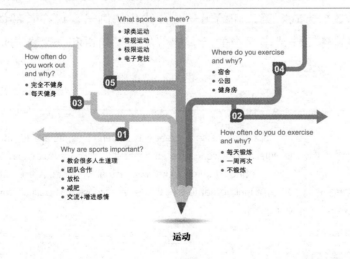

运动

第三步

正式开始学习每个小问题的素材。开始前，依然是扫读一下树状话题拓展图，看每个问题下面的回答标题。比如，第一个小问题是：Why are sports important? 回答的小标题为：教会很多人生道理、团队合作、放松、减肥、交流+增进感情。大家不需要背诵每个回答，正如前言所说，本书想给大家尽可能地提供个性化的选择。

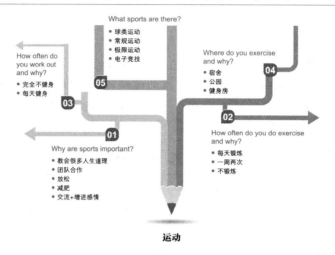

运动

运动之所以重要，有的同学可能觉得是因为它能减压；还有的同学可能觉得是因为它能让我们学会合作，增进与朋友之间的感情。那么对于前者，就直接选择学习"放松"下面的素材，而后者，则可以跳过自己不感兴趣的素材，直接学习"团队合作"以及"交流+增进感情"的素材。

如何最大化利用和学习每一个你感兴趣的素材？

在学习素材段落的过程中，大家可以选择直接背诵，也可以选择适当改写。拿"放松"素材举例：素材段落由三句话组成。第一句概括说明运动对于学生和脑力工作者来说是一个很好的放松方式。第二句给出一个具体化的例子，说在首都体育馆打场羽毛球赛，一定能缓解你工作或学习中的所有疲劳。第三句讲和一个能与你匹敌的对手大战以后挥汗如雨的感觉巨爽。

1.3 放松

Sports are also a great way to relax, especially for those engaged in[2] intellectual work, like students and office employees. A badminton game in ShouTi gymnasium[3] will ease all your stress from work or study. Also, it feels great to sweat after an intense competition with a powerful opponent.

❷ engage in 从事某活动
   ▣ participate in

❸ gymnasium [dʒim'neiziəm]
   n . 体育馆
   ▣ gym

大家可以充分发挥自己的创造力，对原文进行改写。比如，有一位同学拿到这个段落后，发现根本就不爱打羽毛球，平时都是打篮球，或者喜欢跑步。那么，完全可以把第二句的内容从a badminton game in ShouTi gymnasium 改成 a jog in the Olympic Forest Park 或者 an intense basketball match in our college student fitness center。再比如，他可能并不觉得出汗很爽，或者他压根就不大出汗。那么第三句，可以灵活改为：并且，在战胜一个强大的对手后（赢得比赛后），感觉特别爽。最终，这位同学发挥创造力后，就创出了属于自己的运动素材段落。成果如下，下划线部分为修改的部分。

Sports are also a great way of relaxation, especially for those engaged in mental work, like students and office employees. An intense basketball match in a college student fitness center will ease all your pressure from stressful work or study. Also, it just feels great to beat a powerful opponent and to win a match with crowds watching.

再比如，这位同学接着想学习"交流+增进感情"的素材。

1.5 交流＋增进感情

Sports provide us with great opportunities to bond with our colleagues and friends. For example, my classmate Jason had not been close to our instructor in his freshman year. However, because they both love to work out[6], they became best friends when Jason was a sophomore, given their frequent morning interactions at the student fitness center[7]. We all know the importance of maintaining a good relationship with our classmates and colleagues. So, it seems to me exercising is a great way to expand your social circle[8].

[6] work out 锻炼
同 exercise

[7] student fitness center *n.*
学生综合健身馆

[8] expan social circle 扩大
社交圈

我们看到素材里的例子说的是同学Jason通过健身，拉近了自己与导师的距离。而这位同学可能压根就没健身过（笔者本人也从来不健身），或者觉得与导师拉近的距离很小。没关系，他可以稍微改写下文段。改成：我通过加入游泳队，认识了很多新朋友，成功地拉近了与同学之间的距离，并且还把同学发展成了男/女朋友。

Sports provide us with great opportunities to bond with our colleagues and friends. For example, I was pretty lonely and had few friends in my freshman year. So, I joined the swimming club, hoping that I can make some friends. I met a boy/girl, xxx, who also loves to swim. We soon became best friends and in the end, he/she even became my boyfriend/girlfriend. So, it seems to me exercising is a great way for expanding social circle.

第一个小问题的学习结束了。接着，这位同学来到第二个小问题：How often do you exercise? 这时，他想到自己平时基本很少运动，如果运动，也可能只是一个月1~2次。那么在选择学习素材段落的时候，则可以选择直接背诵"不锻炼"，以及将"一周两次"改写成"一个月两次"。

2.3　不锻炼

⑤ sweat [swet] v. 流汗
⑥ intense [in'tens] adj. 激烈的

I rarely exercise. Sports just aren't the thing for me. I suck at sports. And I just hate sweating[5] all over my body. In comparison, I prefer less intense[6] activities such as reading, playing the guitar, or simply chatting with my pals.

这位同学在背诵完段落后，发现自己跟原始段落有少许区别，背诵后效果如下：

I do not exercise. I don't like playing sports. I am not good at sports. I just hate sweat all over my body. In contrast, I prefer less intense activities such as reading, playing the guitar, or chatting with my friends.

这时，他把自己背诵出来的文段跟原文段落进行对比，一句一句、一个单词一个单词地标出了区别。首先，他可以通过这个方法纠正语法错误。比如第四句，对比原文后，发现与原文的区别在于谓语动词hate后面的sweat，原文写的是sweating，而自己是直接跟了个动词原形sweat。这时，这位同学可能会很疑惑动词hate的使用方法，于是去翻词典，发现hate的用法有两个：

- [+ing form of verb]
- [+to infinitive]

那么，发现自己犯了语法错误，应该改成sweating或者to sweat，这样就学会了动词hate的用法。以后在口语和写作中就会注意该动词的用法了。

下一句，对比后发现原文使用的是In comparison，而这位同学使用的是In contrast。查词典后发现，这个替换其实没有问题，可以保留。

所以同学们在背诵时，也可以自己灵活调整，比如上面一个文段虽然第一句说的是"我平时不运动"，但原文说的是很少运动，这样的一些改编，只要自己说得顺口，都是可以适当调整的。其次，同学们可以通过比对原文，来丰富自己的语言表达方式，比如第二句，这位同学的语言习惯可能是I don't like sports，但是通过比对原文发现还有sports just aren't the thing for me 这样的表述方式，所以可以借此机会吸收一些地道的表达。

如此反复，大家便可以将剩余小问题一网打尽。简单总结一下，我们拿到任何一个文段（素材）后都可以选择直接背诵，或者适当改写同时吸收素材中的好词、好句、好细节。如果选择背诵的话，一定记得背诵完毕后跟原文一句一句进行对比，查找语法和用语地道性的问题。如果选择改写，依然还是要做到内容充实具体，并且没有语法错误。若有特定单词的用法不确定，勤查词典。推荐《剑桥英英词典》，用法写得很全，条理性也好。

另外，再推荐给大家一个准备素材的好网站：Wikipedia。比如，我们学习运动素材中的第14个小问题"你最想学习的运动是什么？"时，我们看到回答有滑雪、骑马、篮球。但这时有的同学喜欢乒乓球或者台球，但素材里并没有写，怎么办？到Wikipedia上去搜索这些运动。比如乒乓球，查词典后得知是ping-pong或table tennis；台球，查词典后得知叫pool或pocket billiards。这时我们登陆Wikipedia首页去搜索这些关键词，即可得到相关信息。比如，我们搜索pool得到以下结果。

Pool (Cue Sports)

Pool, also more formally known as pocket billiards (mostly in North America) or pool billiards[1] (mostly in Europe and Australia), is the family of cue sports and games played on a pool table having six receptacles called pockets along the rails, into which balls are deposited as the main goal of play. An obsolete term for pool is six-pocket.[2]

There are hundreds of pool games. Some of the more well-known include eight-ball (and the variant blackball), nine-ball (with variants ten-ball and seven-ball), straight pool (14.1 continuous), one-pocket, and bank pool.

There are also hybrid games combining aspects of both pool and carom billiards, such as American four-ball billiards, cowboy pool, and bottle pool.

通常百科里都会给出这个运动的基本规则、发展历史、装备，以及一些著名的球星。TOEFL口语和写作里有时会需要我们给出一个具体化的人物例子，比如像这道口语题：

> Some think that natural talent and ability is more important for an athlete; others think that hard work is more important. What do you think?

这时如果你只是说理的话很难说出令人信服的答案，最简单的解法其实就是找例子证明。比如，你说丁俊晖，9岁开始打球，15岁就拿到世界级比赛的冠军，这不是天赋是什么？并不是所有人努力就可以成功的。

如果你想拿丁俊晖举例，就去Wikipedia搜索Ding Junhui，出现以下结果：

> Ding Junhui (Chinese: 丁俊晖; pinyin: Dīng Jùnhuī;[5] born on 1 April 1987) is a Chinese professional snooker player and the most successful Asian player in the history of the sport. He began playing snooker at age 9, and rose to international prominence in 2002 after winning the Asian Under-21 Championship, the Asian Championship, and becoming the youngest winner of the IBSF World Under-21 Championship at age 15.

那么，这道题的回答我们就可以说：

> Of course, natural talent is more important for an athlete. Take Ding Junhui for example. He is the most famous pool player in China, and he started to play snooker at age 9. I'm not denying that he did practice very hard, and he did practice like crazy. But he rose to international prominence in 2002 after winning the Asian Under-21 Championship. He was only 15 at that time. It is an honor that many would never dream of. My point is that not all of us have the potential to rise to such heights, even with practice.

这时，如果段落太短不够撑够45秒，我们完全可以举两个例子，再搜一个林丹的例子加进来。搜Lin Dan就会直接出现结果。

另外一个很好的网站是YouTube，因为YouTube上有大量的优质视频资源，比如crash course，里面包含了很多不同的系列，现在该频道中最火的几个系列有：世界史、美国史、哲学、物理、电影制作、电脑、生物、文学、化学，等等。其实学习和准备托福素材是个很有意思的环节，如果你不着急短期内出分的话。笔者推荐大家一定要将学习和兴趣相结合，这样才能最大化我们的学习效率。Remember, learning English is fun.

如何将所学习的单个素材串起来，回答真题？

下面我们来说一说，学习完整个"运动"素材后，应该如何将所学的单个素材串起来，回答真题。比如看这道题：

> Which of the following qualities do you admire the most (or would you be most interested in getting)? Art skills, language skills or sports skills? Use details and explanations in your response.

三选一的题型，我们就选sports skills来答题吧。题目问的是你最想掌握的技能是什么？这时可以重新扫一眼这一类话题的树状话题拓展图，发现第1个小问题"Why are sports important?"和第7个小问题"What's special about sports?"正好可以派上用场。我们现在可以使用的素材有：教会人生道理、团队合作、放松、减肥、增进感情、增强体力、增强灵活性、增强手臂力量。这时，我们随意组合，即可轻松凑够45秒。

比如我想用"增强体力"和"放松"来组成一个文段。可以这么说：

> The quality that I admired most is sports skills, because I often get sick lately. For example, if I get trained in running and start to run every day, I'll have better stamina. I would have to run back and forth constantly. At first, I might feel out of breath. But weeks later, I will feel more energetic. It's in fact a very good cardio exercise that can prevent sickness. Also, sports are a great way of relaxation, especially for those engaged in intellectual work, like students and office employees. A badminton game in ShouTi gymnasium will ease all my pressure from stressful study. When my pressure is relieved, I am less likely to get sick.

以下是刚才回答中用到的两个素材：

❷ engage in 从事某活动
  同 participate in

❸ gymnasium [dʒimˈneiziəm]
  n. 体育馆
  同 gym

1.3 放松

Sports are also a great way to relax, especially for those engaged in[2] intellectual work, like students and office employees. A badminton game in ShouTi gymnasium[3] will ease all your stress from work or study. Also, it feels great to sweat after an intense competition with a powerful opponent.

7.1 增强体力

It builds stamina. You have to run back and forth constantly. At first, you might feel out of breath. But weeks later, you'll feel more energetic. It's in fact, a very good cardio exercise, which helps with weight loss.

再来看一道独立写作题。

Nowadays, children rely too much on the technology, like computers, smartphones, video games for fun and entertainment; playing simpler toys or playing outside with their friends would be better for the children's development.

独立
写作题　2016/2/28

这是一道对比题。如果写同意的话，其实有两块内容可以展开，即小孩都玩了什么游戏，以及到外面玩耍可以怎样对小孩发展更好。游戏部分的内容，可以参考书中的素材章节"游戏"。我们现在先尝试把在外面玩耍，即运动的部分，写出来。这时，扫一眼"运动"类话题开始的目标，看看哪些素材可以用到。然后发现在运动地点里可以写在公园慢跑（第4个小问题），好处可以写增强体力、增进友谊（第7个小问题）。最后发现素材中第13个小问题就是专门针对这道题的素材，可以直接拿来用，运动和游戏哪个对小孩发展更重要？将这些素材拼凑衔接以后，效果如下：

Research shows that children who constantly participate in sports tend to attain higher heights and healthier than those who do not. Parents all wish their children to be at least 6 feet high and be vigorous and outgoing. Playing sports is a perfect way to achieve all the wishes of parents. For one thing, sports stimulate the growing of bones and muscle tissues. For another thing, playing team sports would naturally teach children how to cooperate and communicate with others. Both are vital skills for children's future success.

Also, sports are also a great way of relaxation, especially for those engaged in intellectual work, like students and office employees. A badminton game in ShouTi gymnasium will ease all your pressure from stressful work or study. Also, it feels great to sweat after an intense competition with a powerful opponent. Another example is that I like to go jogging alongside the edge of the park in my neighborhood.

For one thing, the air quality in the morning is extremely refreshing. I am extremely picky when it comes to air quality. ~~When air quality is bad because of smog, I would even try my best to avoid going outside, not to mention exercise.~~ Everyone knows that air quality is terrible in dorms when your roommates spend the entire night smoking while playing video games. Breathing fresh air freely after a quick run just feels great. For another thing, the beautiful scenery lightens my day. I also have this thing for enjoying the green color from trees and grass. I always feel pumped up after a short run.

对于这道题，我们完全可以直接将第13个小回答的答案拿过来当作我们的第一个主体段。一个词都不用改写。在这段里，运动的好处有促进小孩骨骼发育和教会团队合作。到第二段时，我们可以将"放松"素材和"公园慢跑"素材拼凑起来，合为新的一段。为了切题，中间稍微改写一点"公园慢跑"素材中关于空气的部分。原文说的是公园雾霾的时候，一般就不到户外跑步了。但这样直接拿来用，与现在的题目并不搭，所以需要进行适当改写。现在改成为了呼吸新鲜空气，避开宿舍里打游戏后污浊的空气，而出去慢跑。这样，我们轻松运用三个素材将这篇独立写作写到了265词。后面再参考本书中的"游戏"类话题，写游戏怎么不好，文章基本就可以结束了。

以下是刚才范文中用到的三个素材：

4.2 公园

I like to go jogging[1] along the edge of the park in my neighborhood. For one thing, the air quality in the morning is extremely refreshing. I am extremely picky when it comes to air quality. When air quality is bad because of smog, I try my best to avoid going outside, not to mention[2] exercising Breathing fresh air after a quick run just feels great. For another thing, the beautiful scenery lighten my day[3]. I also have this thing for enjoying the green of the trees and grass. I always feel pumped up after a short run.

❶ jogging ['dʒɔgiŋ] *n.* 慢跑

❷ not to mention 更不必说

❸ lighten my day 开启我的一天（点燃我的一天）

1.3 放松

❷ engage in 从事某活动
   ▣ participate in

❸ gymnasium [dʒim'neiziəm] *n.* 体育馆
   ▣ gym

Sports are also a great way to relax, especially for those engaged in[2] intellectual work, like students and office employees. A badminton game in ShouTi gymnasium[3] will ease all your stress from work or study. Also, it feels great to sweat after an intense competition with a powerful opponent.

13.2 运动更重要

Research shows that children who constantly participate in sports tend to attain higher heights and better health than those who do not. Parents all wish their children to be at least 6 feet tall and be vigorous[1] and outgoing. Playing sports is a perfect way to achieve all the wishes of parents. For one thing, sports stimulate the growing of bone and muscle tissues. For another thing[2], playing team sports naturally teaches children how to cooperate and communicate with others. Both are vital skills for children's future success.

如何利用本书积累托福词汇和地道表达?

同学们看范文时，通常喜欢关注词，特别是难词、长词。但是，地道的语言远不只是几个看起来高级的词汇，甚至不是所谓高级的词组。本书范文中会推荐很多值得学习的语言现象，都以变色的形式凸显出来，可能是词语和词组搭配，可能是句型、逻辑词的使用方式或语法现象。

每个文段中的重难点词、词组、句型或语言点都在笔记区进行了解释，有的还提供了口语替换词或表达，以方便同学们在口语和写作中自由切换。

1.5 交流＋增进感情

Sports provide us with great opportunities to bond with our colleagues and friends. For example, my classmate Jason had not been close to our instructor in his freshman year. However, because they both love to work out[6], they became best friends when Jason was a sophomore, given their frequent morning interactions at the student fitness center[7]. We all know the importance of maintaining a good relationship with our classmates and colleagues. So, it seems to me exercising is a great way to expand your social circle[8].

❻ work out 锻炼
🔁 exercise

❼ student fitness center *n.* 学生综合健身馆

❽ expan social circle 扩大社交圈

Contents 目 录

Contents 目 录

| Part 2 | TOEFL 独立口语、写作真题索引

Part 1

托福高分万能思路:
跟名师练 TOEFL 口语/写作

TOEFL 独立口语、写作话题语料库

TOEFL

独立口语、写作话题语料库

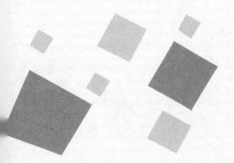

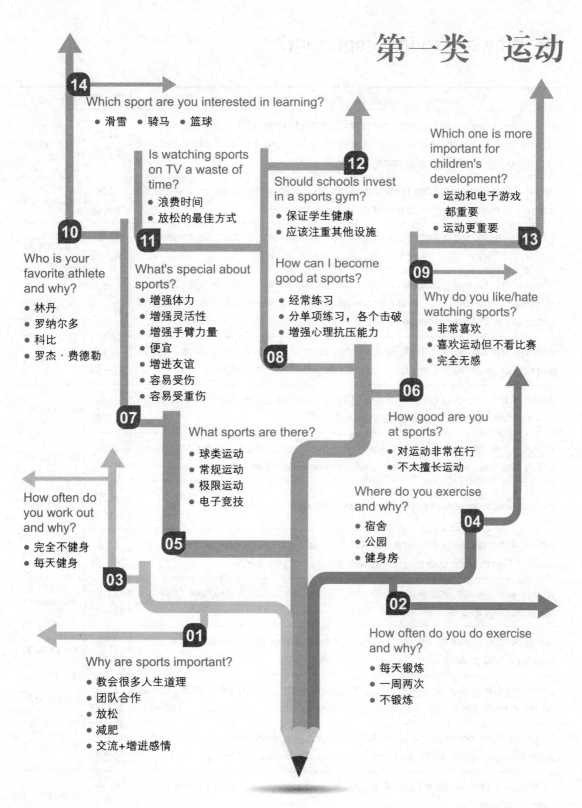

14 Which sport are you interested in learning?
- 滑雪
- 骑马
- 篮球

Which one is more important for children's development?
- 运动和电子游戏都重要
- 运动更重要 **13**

Is watching sports on TV a waste of time?
- 浪费时间
- 放松的最佳方式 **11**

12 Should schools invest in a sports gym?
- 保证学生健康
- 应该注重其他设施

10 Who is your favorite athlete and why?
- 林丹
- 罗纳尔多
- 科比
- 罗杰·费德勒

What's special about sports?
- 增强体力
- 增强灵活性
- 增强手臂力量
- 便宜
- 增进友谊
- 容易受伤
- 容易受重伤

How can I become good at sports?
- 经常练习
- 分单项练习，各个击破
- 增强心理抗压能力 **08**

09 Why do you like/hate watching sports?
- 非常喜欢
- 喜欢运动但不看比赛
- 完全无感

06 How good are you at sports?
- 对运动非常在行
- 不太擅长运动

07 What sports are there?
- 球类运动
- 常规运动
- 极限运动
- 电子竞技

Where do you exercise and why?
- 宿舍
- 公园
- 健身房

How often do you work out and why?
- 完全不健身
- 每天健身

05

04

03

01 Why are sports important?
- 教会很多人生道理
- 团队合作
- 放松
- 减肥
- 交流+增进感情

02 How often do you do exercise and why?
- 每天锻炼
- 一周两次
- 不锻炼

运动

01 Why are sports important?

真　题	题　型	年　份
Your city is planning to spend more on one of the following three projects. Which do you think is the most important? Expanding tourism, building city parks, or improving the public transportation system?	口语第一题	2012/03/18
Which of the following three activities would you most prefer to do on a weekend afternoon? Play a sport, visit a friend, or cook at home?	口语第一题	2012/07/28
Which of the following three activities would you most prefer to do on a weekend afternoon? Play a sport, visit a friend, or cook at home?	口语第一题	2012/08/19
Which of the following qualities do you admire the most (or would you be most interested in having) ? Art skills, language skills or sports skills? Use details and explanations in your response.	口语第一题	2012/09/02
Which of the following is the best way for a student to make new friends: joining a sports team, volunteering for a community activity, or traveling?	口语第一题	2012/09/23
Which of the following do you prefer? Doing exercise every day, or only when you are free? Explain your choice in detail.	口语第二题	2012/10/14
Which of the following activities would you like to do on a weekend afternoon? Doing exercise, watching TV, or spending some time with family?	口语第一题	2012/10/28
Playing sports teaches people more important lessons about life.	独立写作题	2012/12/15
Which of the following activities do you think is the most beneficial for a child's growth? Doing team sports, talking with others, or traveling?	口语第一题	2013/01/13
Which new skill do you want to learn? Playing a musical instrument, flying a plane or playing a new sport?	口语第一题	2013/01/14
Some people prefer to do team sports; others prefer to do individual sports. Which do you prefer?	口语第二题	2013/09/29
Some people prefer to watch a sports game from the audience seat; others prefer to be in the sports field and compete with others. Which do you prefer?	口语第二题	2013/10/20
Some students prefer to join school clubs, such as sports teams, right after they enter college, while others wait until the second semester. What do you prefer?	口语第二题	2014/06/15
All students should attend social activities, such as joining a club or a sports team in school.	口语第二题	2015/04/12

（续）

真 题	题 型	年 份
Playing sports teaches people important lessons about life.	独立写作题	2015/06/14
Your school used to offer three after-class activities: 1) sports, 2) art, 3) volunteering, but this year, the school's extra money can only offer one activity. Which one do you choose and why?	口语第二题	2015/06/27
In their free time, young people (aged 14 – 18) spend time taking part in different activities, such as music lessons or competitive sports. Some young people divide their time between different kinds of activities. But other young people will spend most of their time focusing on just one activity that is important for them. Which approach do you think is better?	口语第二题	2015/07/4
Your school used to offer three after-class activities: 1) sports, 2) art, 3) volunteering, but this year, the school's extra money can only offer one activity. Which one do you choose and why?	口语第二题	2015/07/11
These days, children spend more time on doing homework or participating in organized activities related to school or sports. However, they should be given more time to do whatever they want.	独立写作题	2015/07/12
If the school received a barrel of money, what do you wish it would be spent on? A sports gym, a laboratory, or a scientific research facility?	口语第一题	2016/01/24
Nowadays, children rely too much on technology, like computers, smartphones, and video games for fun and entertainment. Playing with simpler toys or playing outside with friends would be better for children's development.	独立写作题	2016/02/28
If the school received a barrel of money, what do you wish it would be spent on? A sports gym or a laboratory?	口语第二题	2016/07/10
The university will spend money on the dormitory to improve the students' quality of life. Which of the following do you think is best? 1) providing a room for quiet study; 2) building an exercise room; 3) providing a movie room	独立写作题	2016/09/25
It's a good idea for first year students to join a sports team or any other kind of campus organization.	口语第二题	2016/10/29

1.1 教会很多人生道理

Sports teach us important lessons about life. The participants become stronger both physically and intellectually. They become less inclined to[1] give up when they're struggling. One would often learn from jogging that we should keep running especially when we feel tired, because once we pass a certain threshold, the uneasiness will pass. A sense of happiness follows immediately. In real life, we should keep moving forward as well even when we run into challenges, because everything will get easier if we persist.

❶ less inclined to 不太愿意

1.2 团队合作

Sports promote a spirit of teamwork. In my own experience, almost all my friends who thrive in teams love team sports such as basketball, soccer, and volleyball. In these games, team members have to cooperate to win. Otherwise, even if you are extremely good at the game, you still cannot beat a whole team all by yourself.

1.3 放松

Sports are also a great way to relax, especially for those engaged in[2] intellectual work, like students and office employees. A badminton game in ShouTi gymnasium[3] will ease all your stress from work or study. Also, it feels great to sweat after an intense competition with a powerful opponent.

❷ engage in 从事某活动
   📖 participate in

❸ gymnasium [dʒim'neiziəm]
   n. 体育馆
   📖 gym

1.4 减肥

Sports help me keep in shape. I couldn't help but notice that my belly was starting to emerge when I looked at myself in the mirror last year, and it did not look great. So, I started to exercise every day in order to keep myself in shape. I have been performing 50 push-ups[4] and 50 sit-ups[5] daily, and my belly is under control, at least for now.

❹ push-up [puʃ-ʌp] n. 俯卧撑

❺ sit-up [sit-ʌp] n. 仰卧起坐

1.5 交流＋增进感情

Sports provide us with great opportunities to bond with our colleagues and friends. For example, my classmate Jason had not been close to our instructor in his freshman year. However, because they both love to work out[6], they became best friends when Jason was a sophomore, given their frequent morning interactions at the student fitness center[7]. We all know the importance of maintaining a good relationship with our classmates and colleagues. So, it seems to me exercising is a great way to expand your social circle[8].

❻ work out 锻炼
📖 exercise

❼ student fitness center *n.* 学生综合健身馆

❽ expan social circle 扩大社交圈

02 How often do you do exercise and why?

真　题	题　型	年　份
Which of the following is the best way for a student to make new friends：joining a sports team, volunteering for a community activity, or traveling?	口语 第一题	2012/09/23
Which of the following do you prefer? Doing exercise every day, or only when you are free? Explain your choice in detail.	口语 第二题	2012/10/14
Which of the following activities do you think is the most beneficial for a child's growth? Doing team sports, talking with others, or traveling?	口语 第一题	2013/01/13
In their free time, young people（aged 14 – 18）spend time taking part in different activities, such as music lessons or competitive sports. Some young people divide their time between different kinds of activities. But other young people will spend most of their time focusing on just one activity that is important for them. Which approach do you think is better?	口语 第二题	2015/07/04
These days, children spend more time on doing homework or participating in organized activities related to school or sports. However, they should be given more time to do whatever they want.	独立 写作题	2015/07/12
Nowadays, children rely too much on technology, like computers, smartphones, and video games for fun and entertainment. Playing with simpler toys or playing outside with friends would be better for children's development.	独立 写作题	2016/02/28

2.1 每天锻炼

I'm a sports fanatic[1], so I must exercise every day. My body craves[2] athletics[3]. I can't focus on any intellectual work before getting pumped up[4] by running.

2.2 一周两次

I try to get some exercise at least twice a week. But since I have quite a tight schedule, the actual number might vary. I realize the importance of continuous exercise, so when I don't have time, I force myself to do physical activities by running up stairs instead of taking an elevator.

2.3 不锻炼

I rarely exercise. Sports just aren't the thing for me. I suck at sports. And I just hate sweating[5] all over my body. In comparison, I prefer less intense[6] activities such as reading, playing the guitar, or simply chatting with my pals.

❶ fanatic [fə'nætik] *n.* 狂热爱好者
  ▣ I'm crazy for sports.
❷ crave [kreiv] *v.* 渴望
  ▣ want greatly
❸ athletics [æθ'letiks] *n.* 运动
  ▣ motions, exercises
❹ pump up 打足气
  ▣ fill with excitement
❺ sweat [swet] *v.* 流汗
❻ intense [in'tens] *adj.* 激烈的

03 How often do you work out and why?

真 题	题 型	年 份
Which of the following is the best way for a student to make new friends: joining a sports team, volunteering for a community activity, or traveling?	口语 第一题	2012/09/23
Which of the following do you prefer? Doing exercise every day or only when you are free? Explain your choice in detail.	口语 第二题	2012/10/14
Which of the following activities do you think is the most beneficial for a child's growth? Doing team sports, talking with others, or traveling?	口语 第一题	2013/01/13
In their free time, young people (aged 14–18) spend time taking part in different activities such as music lessons or competitive sports. Some young people divide their time between different kinds of activities. But other young people will spend most of their time focusing on just one activity that is important for them. Which approach do you think is better?	口语 第二题	2015/07/04

（续）

真 题	题 型	年 份
These days, children spend more time on doing homework or participating in organized activities related to school or sports. However, they should be given more time to do whatever they want.	独立写作题	2015/07/12
Nowadays, children rely too much on technology, like computers, smartphones, and video games for fun and entertainment. Playing with simpler toys or playing outside with friends would be better for children's development.	独立写作题	2016/02/28

3.1 完全不健身

I do not work out at all. I just don't get the point of running on a machine for a whole hour when you can call up a few friends to have an intense basketball game together. Or, we surely could gather a group of friends to go on a ski trip in ChongLi[1] of ZhangJiaKou, which is only a 3-hour-drive. Competition and cooperation, as well as companionship always increase the enjoyment you get from exercising. However, these can be quite difficult to get by merely working out alone.

❶ ChongLi 崇礼县（地名）（滑雪胜地）

3.2 每天健身

I work out daily. To be frank[2], the primary reason that drove me to work out in the beginning was to have an attractive body. But later when working out became a habit of mine, I started to feel that it had become a part of me, an activity that I have to do every day. Otherwise, something just doesn't feel right and I can't focus on my study/work before my workout session in the morning. Now, I have better fitness[3], better sleep quality, and better relationships.

❷ to be frank 实话说
🔁 to be honest

❸ fitness ['fitnəs] n. 健康
🔁 health

04 Where do you exercise and why?

真 题	题 型	年 份
Which of the following is the best way for a student to make new friends: joining a sports team, volunteering for a community activity, or traveling?	口语 第一题	2012/09/23
Which of the following do you prefer? Doing exercise every day or only when you are free? Explain your choice in detail.	口语 第二题	2012/10/14
Which of the following activities do you think is the most beneficial for a child's growth? Doing team sports, talking with others, or traveling?	口语 第一题	2013/01/13
In their free time, young people (aged 14 – 18) spend time taking part in different activities such as music lessons or competitive sports. Some young people divide their time between different kinds of activities. But other young people will spend most of their time focusing on just one activity that is important for them. Which approach do you think is better?	口语 第二题	2015/07/04
These days, children spend more time on doing homework or participating in organized activities related to school or sports. However, they should be given more time to do whatever they want.	独立 写作题	2015/07/12
Nowadays, children rely too much on technology, like computers, smartphones, and video games for fun and entertainment. Playing with simpler toys or playing outside with friends would be better for children's development.	独立 写作题	2016/02/28

4.1 宿舍

I prefer to exercise in my dorm room since it's more convenient. Some of my classmates choose to go to the gymnasium but it's just too far in a cold winter, especially when I am all sweaty. On the other hand, if you choose to exercise indoors, weather won't be a problem. I prefer to do push-ups in my dorm. I usually just put my feet on the edge of my bed, and support my body with my arm on the ground. Some of my roommates do sit-ups with the help of others. They often want to lose weight.

4.2 公园

I like to go jogging[1] along the edge of the park in my neighborhood. For one thing, the air quality in the morning is extremely refreshing. I am extremely picky when it comes to air quality. When air quality is bad because of smog, I try my best to avoid going outside, not to mention[2] exercising Breathing fresh air after a quick run just feels great. For another thing, the beautiful scenery lighten my day[3]. I also have this thing for enjoying the green of the trees and grass. I always feel pumped up after a short run.

❶ jogging ['dʒɔgiŋ] *n.* 慢跑

❷ not to mention 更不必说

❸ lighten my day 开启我的一天（点燃我的一天）

4.3 健身房

I prefer working out in the gym. There are quite a few advantages. First, the air quality outside is just too bad. If I run outside, it may hurting my body more than building it up. Also, there are trainers in the gym, so I can seek out training advice when I am not quite sure if I'm doing the right thing. last but not least[4], the atmosphere in gyms is way better than exercising alone, since you can easily be influenced by the positive energy around you that Everybody is constantly emitting: Everybody wants a perfect body.

❹ last but not least 最后（但也很重要的一点是）

05 What sports are there?

真 题	题 型	年 份
Which of the following is the best way for a student to make new friends: joining a sports team, volunteering for a community activity, or traveling?	口语 第一题	2012/09/23
Playing sports teaches people more important lessons about life.	独立 写作题	2012/12/15
Which of the following activities do you think is the most beneficial for a child's growth? Doing team sports, talking with others, or traveling?	口语 第一题	2013/01/13
Some people prefer to do team sports; others prefer to do individual sports. Which do you prefer?	口语 第二题	2013/09/29
All students should attend social activities, such as joining a club or a sports team in school.	口语 第二题	2015/04/12

（续）

真 题	题 型	年 份
Playing sports teaches people important lessons about life.	独立写作题	2015/06/14
In their free time, young people (aged 14–18) spend time taking part in different activities such as music lessons or competitive sports. Some young people divide their time between different kinds of activities. But other young people will spend most of their time focusing on just one activity that is important for them. Which approach do you think is better?	口语第二题	2015/07/04
These days, children spend more time on doing homework or participating in organized activities related to school or sports. However, they should be given more time to do whatever they want.	独立写作题	2015/07/12
Nowadays, children rely too much on technology, like computers, smartphones, and video games for fun and entertainment. Playing with simpler toys or playing outside with friends would be better for children's development.	独立写作题	2016/02/28
It's a good idea for first year students to join a sports team or any other kind of campus organization.	口语第二题	2016/10/29

5.1　球类运动

soccer, basketball, tennis, badminton

5.2　常规运动

swimming, jogging, marathon, judo[1]

❶ judo ['dʒuːdəu] *n.* 柔道

5.3　极限运动

freestyle skiing, snowboarding, surfing, bungee jumping

5.4　电子竞技

electronic sports such as DOTA, LOL, Counter-Strike, and StarCraft II

常用运动动词搭配

动　词	项　目
do	gymnastics, judo, weight lifting, aerobics, yoga
play	badminton, golf, table tennis
go	fishing, skiing, bowling, climbing, jogging, swimming

06 How good are you at sports?

6.1　对运动非常在行

I know my way around: I've played it since I was 6, and still do it every week with my coworkers. I always win. I've participated in different competitions, in school, in the city, or in the neighborhood, and I've won prizes.

6.2　不太擅长运动

I suck at badminton. My body and mind just don't coordinate harmoniously. It sometimes feels like my brain doesn't control my hand. The ball just won't go where I want it to. Once I participated in a class competition, and I was horrible. and I was owned[1] by my opponent, in every game. Of course, I had just one game. I was cut as soon as possible.

❶ own [əun] *v.* 彻底击败 🔲 to so thoroughly beat someone, as to embarrass them

07 What's special about sports?

真　题	题　型	年　份
Some people prefer to do team sports; others prefer to do individual sports. Which do you prefer?	口语 第二题	2013/09/29

7.1 增强体力

It builds stamina. You have to run back and forth constantly. At first, you might feel out of breath. But weeks later, you'll feel more energetic. It's in fact, a very good cardio exercise, which helps with weight loss.

7.2 增强灵活性

It builds flexibility. You have to reach out, bend down, and switch positions all the time. Your reflexes[1] improve over time.

❶ reflex ['ri:fleks] *n.* 反应能力

7.3 增强手臂力量

It strengthens arm muscles. If you want your ball to beat the opponent, it must be powerful.

7.4 便宜

It is relatively affordable[2] because its location and equipment are relatively basic. You can play on a special court or you can just play outside.

❷ affordable [ə'fɔ:dəbl] *adj.* 便宜的
回 cheap

7.5 增进友谊

It is also a great way to bond with[3] friends. If you play doubles[4], winning together is surely a boost to the friendship.

❸ bond with 拉近感情
回 bring somebody closer

❹ doubles ['dʌbls] *n.* 双打

7.6 容易受伤

Sudden twists and turns can sometimes hurt your ankle if you don't warm up.

7.7 容易受重伤

It could lead to serious consequences, such as concussion[5]. My friend Jason experienced temporary[6] memory loss after hitting his head during a ski trip. He was then sent to the hospital, where he got a CT scan to check for internal bleeding. Luckily, nothing serious was found. He gradually recovered after a week.

❺ brain concussion 脑震荡
回 brain injury

❻ temporary ['tempəreri] *adj.* 暂时的
回 lasting for a limited time

08 How can I become good at sports?

真 题	题 型	年 份
Some think that natural talent and ability is more important for an athlete; others think that hard work is more important. What do you think?	口语 第二题	2013/12/14
To be successful in sports, which is more important? Talent, or hard work?	口语 第二题	2015/08/30

8.1 经常练习

I practice badminton frequently. In fact, to improve, I compete with better players twice every week. I got knocked out easily at first, but gradually, I became a qualified competitor. They say that people can master[1] any kind of sports or skill after 10,000 hours of practice, and I believe this very much. I have been playing badminton for two years now, at least 4 hours per week. That totals about 200 hours per year. So, if we apply the 10,000 hours rule, I will become a badminton master after 50 years. Hahahahhhaha. Most people lack perseverance. So, the key is to remember: it gets easier each day.

❶ master ['mɑːstə] *v.* 熟练掌握
📖 become skilled or proficient

8.2 分单项练习，各个击破

I worked to polish[2] my separate skills independently, like serving[3], smashing[4], and drop shot[5]. I hired a coach to train me, and each session we would focus on just one skill. Some of my friends just want to learn everything in a week. That's just impossible. Many would get frustrated when they felt they did not improve for a long time because they were only practicing the basics. But the thing that they do not realize is that they must let the basic skills improve gradually, and that you have to believe that one day, your skills will improve drastically[6] when you combine, and suddenly realize how to use all their skills in a real match.

❷ polish ['pɔliʃ] *v.* 磨练
📖 improve

❸ serving ['səːviŋ] *n.* 发球

❹ smashing ['smæʃiŋ] *n.* 扣杀

❺ drop shot 高远球

❻ drastically ['dræstikli] *adv.* 极大地

8.3 增强心理抗压能力

[7] mentality [men'tæləti]

n. 心理

🔲 mind

I also have to get used to losing and leading and not let the scores disturb my mentality[7]. I never play well when I count scores or when I play with strangers, because of my weak mentality. When I keep score, all my attention is focused on the scores. When I am losing, all I can think of is: the score gap is getting bigger; which further weakens my performance. On the other hand, when I am winning, I keep calculating the score gap, fearing that my opponent might catch up; I just can't relax and I get all tensed up.

09 Why do you like/hate watching sports?

真　题	题　型	年　份
Is watching sports programs a good use of time?	口语第一题	2012/09/22
Do you agree or disagree with the statement that watching sports programs on TV is not a good use of time?	口语第二题	2016/08/21
Many people spend a lot of time watching sports programs on TV or following their favorite sports teams, which can have negative effects on their lives.	口语第二题	2016/08/21

9.1 非常喜欢

[1] Champions League 冠军杯联赛

[2] replay [ri:'plei] n. 重播

[3] superstitiously

[,sju:pə'stiʃəsli] adv. 迷信地

I love watching sports. I am willing to stay up late until 3:00 a.m, just to watch my favorite team's game in the Championship League[1]. Some advise me to watch the replay[2] of the tournament, but I never do. They just don't understand. All fans superstitiously[3] believe that their mere act of watching the game has a decisive influence over the final results of the game. Watching it live makes me feel like I'm a part of the team.

9.2 喜欢运动但不看比赛

I rarely watch sports. Although I do like playing badminton myself, I just don't have time for TV, not to mention following the progress of major tournaments[4]. In extremely rare cases when I visit my friends, if they are all watching a tournament, say by Lin Dan, I join them. But I never watch games by myself.

❹ major tournaments 重大比赛

9.3 完全无感

I just don't get why people watch sports. If you really love it, just play it. You always see those nerdy guys[5] yelling about tactics[6] and strategies, as if they knew a thing. And you see fans attacking[7] each other after a game. Come on! It's just a game.

❺ nerdy guys 呆子
❻ tactic ['tæktik] *n.* 战术
❼ attack [ə'tæk] *v.* 言语攻击或物理攻击
⊠ bash

10 Who is your favorite athlete and why?

真　题	题　型	年　份
Is watching sports programs a good use of time?	口语 第一题	2012/09/22
Some think that natural talent and ability is more important for an athlete; others think that hard work is more important. What do you think?	口语 第二题	2013/12/14
To be successful in sports, which is more important? Talent, or hard work?	口语 第二题	2015/08/30
Do you agree or disagree with the statement that watching sports programs on TV is not a good use of time.	口语 第二题	2016/08/21
Many people spend a lot of time watching sports programs on TV or following their favorite sports teams, which can have negative effects on their lives.	口语 第二题	2016/08/21

10.1 林丹 Lin Dan

Well, there are tons of reasons. The first is, of course, his handsome appearance. I think he looks more attractive since entering his 30s, mainly because he looks more sophisticated[1]. He has admirable arm muscles. One of my colleagues started playing badminton merely because she was astonished by Lin Dan's enviable[2] muscle shape. Second, he is the best player in the world. He is steady, accurate, and ruthless[3]. He can dissolve[4] attacks from any angle or speed, and the way he handles the attacks always seems effortless[5]. When he finds opponents' weaknesses he always grasps the opportunity and executes[6] the winning shot perfectly.

10.2 罗纳尔多 Ronaldo

Although I don't play soccer often, I love to play the video game：Pro Evolution Soccer[7], created by Konami[8]. Ronaldo is definitely my favorite player since he has the highest body balance[9] in the game, which gives him the ability to break through any defense[10] with ease. Intrigued[11] by the game, I later went on YouTube to find matches by Ronaldo and surprisingly found out that he was even more beastlike[12] in the real world than in the video game. He seemed that he could never be stopped by backfields[13] and he could trick any goal keeper[14] with ease.

10.3 科比 Kobe

I think he is one of the best basketball players who have ever existed. He has been one of the most dominant forces in the league since he first played in the NBA. He is the reason why I fell in love with basketball. The way he plays with grace, talent, speed, and determination defines greatness. But what really speaks to me is his competitive spirit. Winning is all he cares about. When it comes to the final minutes, he is always the guy to step up and take over the game. Hunt or be hunted is always his mentality. His competitiveness drives him to still play at top level when he is 10 years older than most of the players in the league.

---

① sophisticated [sə'fistikeitid] *adj.* 老成的，久经世故的
  ≈ experienced

② enviable ['enviəbl] *adj.* 令人羡慕的
  ≈ admirable

③ ruthless ['ru:θləs] *adj.* 冷酷无情的

④ dissolve [di'zɔlv] *v.* 化解
  ≈ defend

⑤ effortless ['efətləs] *adj.* 不费吹灰之力的

⑥ execute ['eksikju:t] *v.* 击出
  ≈ hit

⑦ Pro Evolution Soccer 实况足球（电子游戏）

⑧ Konami 日本著名游戏公司

⑨ body balance 身体强度

⑩ break through any defense 突破任何防线

⑪ intrigue [in'tri:g] *v.* 激起……的好奇心
  ≈ to arouse interest in

⑫ beastlike ['bi:stlaik] *adj.* 像野兽一样的

⑬ backfield ['bækfi:ld] *n.* 后卫
  ≈ defenders

⑭ goal keeper 守门员

10.4　罗杰·费德勒 Roger Federer

One thing that strikes me most when comparing Federer with other players, is the natural ease and facility he has when executing even the most difficult shots. When other players seem to give everything to every shot, making a funny face each time, Roger remains stoic[15], calm, almost like he is playing with his mind. The result is beautifully effortless. Roger Federer is the complete package[16], whether he is as a tennis player or as a person. You never see him throw the racket, rant[17], get angry, or even complain. His only job is to get on the court, play good tennis and win as many matches as he can.

⑮ stoic ['stəuik] *adj.* 泰然自若的
🔲 not showing feelings
⑯ complete package 全能选手
⑰ rant [rænt] *v.* 咆哮
🔲 shout in a loud, uncontrolled and angry way

11　Is watching sports on TV a waste of time?

真　题	题　型	年　份
Is watching sports programs a good use of time?	口语第一题	2012/09/22
Do you agree or disagree with the statement that watching sports programs on TV is not a good use of time?	口语第二题	2016/08/21
Many people spend a lot of time watching sports programs on TV or following their favorite sports teams, which can have negative effects on their lives.	口语第二题	2016/08/21

11.1　浪费时间

Yes. Since most games, such as soccer and basketball, last for hours, it is extremely time-consuming to watch sports on TV. Once you start watching, you have to stay until the end of game to know the result. Otherwise, what's the whole point of watching the game? What makes matters worse is that sports fans usually watch a series of games such as the European Cup or the World Cup, which last for weeks or even months. Fans definitely stay up late in the night in order to watch the live games, which usually start at 3:00 a. m. For example, one of my friends, Jason, who is a fan of Real Madrid, often sacrifices his sleep in order to watch live games. He might just sleep for 2 hours and get up to watch a game that starts at 4: 00 a. m, After the game, he takes a shower and goes to work. He was diagnosed with an alcoholic fatty liver last month because of his irregular sleep pattern.

11.2 放松的最佳方式

① lying comfortably on my couch, **watching** a game together, **sharing** our passion, **predicting** the result of the game, and **making** bets：分词短语的平行结构

② weariness ['wirinəs] *n.* 疲劳

　▣ tiredness

Of course not. Watching sports on TV is a perfect way to relax. Whenever I feel tired from work or study, I buy some beers and invite some friends to my apartment, lying[1] comfortably on my couch, watching a game together, sharing our passion, predicting the result of the game, and making bets. After the game, the loser of the bet takes everybody out for a nice dinner. My weariness[2] all disappears after spending time with my friends watching a nice game together.

12 Should schools invest in a sports gym?

真　题	题　型	年　份
Your city is planning to spend more on one of the following three projects. Which do you think is the most important? Expanding tourism, building city parks, or improving the public transportation system?	口语第一题	2012/03/18
Your school used to offer three after-class activities：1）sports, 2）art, 3）volunteering, but this year, the school's extra money can only offer one activity. Which one do you choose and why?	口语第二题	2015/06/27
Your school used to offer three after-class activities：1）sports, 2）art, 3）volunteering, but this year, the school's extra money can only offer one activity. Which one do you choose and why?	口语第二题	2015/07/11
If the school received a barrel of money, what do you wish it would be spent on? A sports gym, a laboratory or a scientific research facility?	口语第一题	2016/01/24
If the school received a barrel of money, what do you wish it would be spent on? A sports gym or a laboratory?	口语第二题	2016/07/10
The university will spend money on the dormitory to improve the students' quality of life. Which of the following do you think is best? 1）providing a room for quiet study；2）building an exercise room；3）providing a movie room	独立写作题	2016/09/25

12.1 保证学生健康

Sure. It is a schools' mission to keep their students healthy and to help students cultivate[1] a healthy lifestyle. Also, a fancy gymnasium attracts top students from all over the country.

12.2 应该注重其他设施

No. Schools should spend their limited funds on more important domains[2] such as laboratories or the library. Even an investment in the dormitory[3] or the cafeteria is a wiser[4] choice, since a good night's sleep or an enjoyable meal would surely provide students with more energy to focus on their study than a few running machines.

❶ cultivate ['kʌltiveit] v. 培养
　 同 foster
❷ domain [dəu'mein] n. 领域
　 同 area
❸ dormitory ['dɔːmətri] n. 宿舍
　 同 dorm
❹ wiser [waizə] adj. 更明智的
　 原形：wise [waiz] adj. 明智的

13 Which one is more important for children's development? Sports or video games?

真 题	题 型	年 份
Which of the following is the best way for a student to make new friends: joining a sports team, volunteering for a community activity, or traveling?	口语第一题	2012/09/23
Playing sports teaches people more important lessons about life.	独立写作题	2012/12/15
Which of the following activities do you think is the most beneficial for a child's growth? Doing team sports, talking with others, or traveling?	口语第一题	2013/01/13
Some people prefer to do team sports; others prefer to do individual sports. Which do you prefer?	口语第二题	2013/09/29
Some people prefer to watch a sports game from the audience seat; others prefer to be in the sports field and compete with others. Which do you prefer?	口语第二题	2013/10/20
Some students prefer to join school clubs, such as sports teams, right after they enter college, while others wait until the second semester. What do you prefer?	口语第二题	2014/06/15
All students should attend social activities, such as joining a club or a sports team in school.	口语第二题	2015/04/12

（续）

真 题	题 型	年 份
Playing sports teaches people important lessons about life.	独立写作题	2015/06/14
In their free time, young people (aged 14 – 18) spend time taking part in different activities such as music lessons or competitive sports. Some young people divide their time between different kinds of activities. But other young people will spend most of their time focusing on just one activity that is important for them. Which approach do you think is better?	口语第二题	2015/07/04
These days, children spend more time on doing homework or participating in organized activities related to school or sports. However, they should be given more time to do whatever they want.	独立写作题	2015/07/12
Nowadays, children rely too much on technology, like computers, smartphones, and video games for fun and entertainment. Playing with simpler toys or playing outside with friends would be better for children's development.	独立写作题	2016/02/28
It's a good idea for first year students to join a sports team or any other kind of campus organization.	口语第二题	2016/10/29

13. 1　运动和电子游戏都重要

　　I think both are important, and therefore children should participate in both. Video games are good for children's intellectual development, whereas sports are beneficial to both children's physical and intellectual development.

13. 2　运动更重要

　　Research shows that children who constantly participate in sports tend to attain higher heights and better health than those who do not. Parents all wish their children to be at least 6 feet tall and be vigorous[1] and outgoing. Playing sports is a perfect way to achieve all the wishes of parents. For one thing, sports stimulate the growing of bone and muscle tissues. For another thing[2], playing team sports naturally teaches children how to cooperate and communicate with others. Both are vital skills for children's future success.

❶ vigorous ['vigərəs] *adj.*
精力充沛的
回 full of physical or mental strength
❷ for one thing, for another thing 的并列结构
（展开两个分论点的常用手法）

I think doing sports/exercising/working out frequently is very important, and most of us are not doing enough. Take my little cousin Andy for example. He is only 16, but he has problems with his body because he studies all the time and never goes to the gym. First, he wears very thick glasses. Without them, he runs into trees all the time. If, however, he had chosen to play fewer computer games and go out more, his eyesight could have been better. Also, he is overweight. He's only 6 feet tall, but he is over 200 pounds. If he runs a mile, he could almost have a heart attack. And there's more. He has high blood pressure. I think cases like him really warn us that when we are still young, we need to be more active.

14 Which sport are you interested in learning?

真 题	题 型	年 份
Which of the following qualities do you admire the most (or would you be most interested in having)? Art skills, language skills or sports skills? Use details and explanations in your response.	口语 第一题	2012/09/02
Which of the following activities would you like to do on a weekend afternoon? Doing exercise, watching TV, or spending some time with family?	口语 第一题	2012/10/28
Which new skill do you want to learn? Playing a musical instrument, flying a plane, or playing a new sport?	口语 第一题	2013/01/14

14.1 滑雪 Skiing & Snowboarding

Skiing and snowboarding are so popular in Beijing in recent years that if you are young and have never been to a ski resort, you are behind the times. I went to a ski resort with my college buddies during my sophomore[1] year, and became addicted. Sadly, I have been busy ever since I started working and have had almost no time to practice. However, if I ever have time to take a vacation, I will choose to purchase an airplane ticket and fly to Hokkaido[2] or Sweden[3], which have world-class ski resorts[4]. I will then hire a ski instructor and learn for a week

❶ sophomore ['sɔfəmɔ:]
  n. 大二
❷ Hokkaido [hɔ'kaidəu]
  n. 北海道
❸ Sweden ['swi:dn] n. 瑞典
❹ ski resorts 滑雪场

⑤ show off *v.* 炫耀

so that I can show off[5] my amazing skills to my friends on social media such as WeChat or WeiBo.

14. 2 骑马 Horse-riding

A few years ago, I went to BaShang Grassland with my friends and tried horse-riding for the first time. The actual experience was quite different from what I imagined, but it was still pretty fun. In my imagination, horse-riding was easy: all I needed to do was sit on the horse's back and control direction with the reins[6]. In reality, however, I had to use all my energy to keep myself from falling off, because it is extremely bumpy[7] on a horse's back when it runs fast. Nevertheless, I still found it fun. I watched the video that my friends took while I was riding. I looked like a nobleman[8], although it did look like I was struggling a little bit. So, if I have a chance, I would surely spend time mastering my horse-riding skills.

⑥ rein ［rein］ *n.* 缰绳
 回 rope

⑦ bumpy ［ˈbʌmpi］ *adj.*
 颠簸
 回 not smooth

⑧ nbleman ［ˈnəubəlmən］
 n. 贵族
 回 lord

14. 3 篮球 Basketball

I have watched the NBA ever since I was a little kid, and therefore I would like to improve my basketball skills, since it's my favorite sport. Also, I know that Americans love basketball. Because I'm likely to study abroad in the United States next year, I think basketball would be a great way for me to make some new friends. I'm not particularly confident in my oral communication skills, but basketball is the one thing that I'm good at. My plan is to communicate with my American fellows with sports.

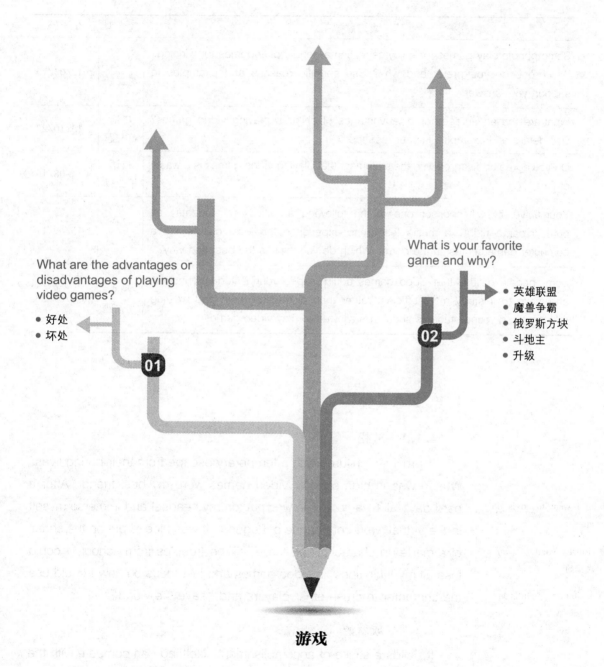

What are the advantages or disadvantages of playing video games?

- 好处
- 坏处

01

What is your favorite game and why?

- 英雄联盟
- 魔兽争霸
- 俄罗斯方块
- 斗地主
- 升级

02

游戏

01 What are the advantages or disadvantages of playing video games?

真　题	题　型	年　份
Some people play games for enjoyment; some people play games for winning. Which one do you prefer and why? Use specific reasons and examples to support your answer.	口语第二题	2012/03/10
What are the advantages or disadvantages of children playing video games? Use details and examples in your response.	口语第一题	2013/10/27
Do you agree or disagree with the statement that playing video games is a waste of time?	口语第二题	2014/08/16
Your university will sponsor one of the following activities for students: an outdoor camp night, a music festival to experience the local culture, or a computer game contest in the dorm. Which do you think is the best and why?	口语第一题	2015/09/17
Some people believe that video games could inspire young students' interest and make their study more efficient rather than distracting them and wasting their time, so young students should be allowed to play video games.	独立写作题	2016/01/23

1.1　好处

1.1.1　放松

It provides children with a temporary escape from their boring lives. When I was in high school, video games were my best friend. After a hard day, all I wanted to do was put[1] on my headset and immerse myself in the virtual[2] world of League of Legend. It was nice to put on the shoes of a made-up character and forget all the troubles from school. I could lose all my inhibitions[3] in video games and just focus on how I could use the character to crush other players and "save the world".

1.1.2　成就感

It builds a sense of accomplishment. Nothing can compete with the feeling when I succeed in some extremely challenging quest. I can feel the adrenaline[4] pumping inside my body. It gives gamers a feeling of importance, which many cannot obtain in real life. Most games contain

❶ all I want to do is do sth.

❷ virtual ［ˈvɜːtʃuəl］ *adj.* 虚拟的

❸ inhibition ［ˌinhiˈbiʃən］ *n.* 压抑　🔲 stress

❹ adrenaline ［əˈdrenəlin］ *n.* 肾上腺素　🔲 blood

certain puzzles that give people a self-esteem[5] boost when they solve them. I was struggling to play against the AI on the hard level for Warcraft III[6]. I spent tons of hours studying it and seeking advice from the online community. After a couple of weeks' practice, I finally beat the AI. I felt like I was not a C-minus student any more. I was the king of the game.

1.1.3 投入，不放弃

Most video games require your full concentration. They teach you to give all you've got on something you really want, which is a vital strength for young children. Sometimes the role you play in a game gives you the best version of yourself. You may stick with a problem as long as it takes and get up after a failure and try again. So, when children grow up, they will understand that good results need hard work. And when they face some real-life obstacles[7], they will not **stress out** or feel anxious, but give their best to come up with better ideas. And even when they fail, they will have enough courage to keep on trying until they make it.

1.1.4 团队协作

Multiplayer games teach children teamwork. Take the famous online game World of Warcraft[8] as an example. It is a game that sometimes requires players to **form** teams, as large as 40 people, in order to defeat a boss. Some specialize in attacking. Some are in charge of defending the whole team. Some are the healers[9]. Even minor mistakes from any of the three groups can cause all 40 people to die. So, a high degree of cooperation is expected from players. If children can cooperate seamlessly[10] in a 40-person-group, they will surely flourish[11] when they begin to work in real life, joining a work team that normally consists of only 10 members.

1.2 坏处

1.2.1 对身体不好

Children who still lack self-control may **get addicted** to video games easily, and addiction harms their health. I guess it is a common phenomenon[12] that all video game addicts love to sacrifice their sleep

⑤ self-esteem *n.* 自信
⑥ Warcraft III 魔兽争霸3

⑦ obstacle ['ɔbstəkl] *n.* 障碍

⑧ World of Warcraft 魔兽世界

⑨ healer ['hi:lə (r)] *n.* 治病术士

⑩ seamlessly ['si:mləsli] *adv.* 无缝地
  回 flawlessly
⑪ flourish ['flʌriʃ] *v.* 成功
  回 succeed

⑫ phenomenon [fi'nɔminən] *n.* 现象

time in exchange for more game time. Take myself as an example. I used to be addicted to StarCraft[13] , a very popular computer game at the time. I would sit in front of my laptop for hours, stare at the screen with my full attention, and hold the mouse tightly, without even changing my position once the whole night. I felt no discomfort when playing the game. But when the sun rose, when I shut down the game and went to the restroom, I felt the sourness[14] in my back, the stiffness[15] in my forearms, and the dryness in my throat[16] . It took me years to get my health back after I stopped playing video games.

1.2.2　影响学业

Most children will leave their study behind, when they are addicted to video games. Video games will give you a sense of fantasy, so you may get hooked on[17] it. You just want to keep playing to find out what happens next, wondering whether you will get stronger or not, if you will finish the next task or kill the next monster. So, you won't have time for your school work. The moment you come home, you switch on your game and start playing, because you really cannot think of anything else. You don't care about today's homework or your math test in a few weeks. The only thing on your mind is the game. Sooner or later, you realize that you are falling behind in your academic studies.

1.2.3　暴力倾向

Many of the most popular games emphasize negative themes[18] like sex, drugs and violence. To be more specific, criminal behavior, disrespect for authority and the law, killing of civilians or animals, abuse of drugs and alcohol[19] , sexual exploitation[20] , and violence toward women are common elements in today's games. For example, video games such as Grand Thief Auto[21] and Call of Duty[22] , for over 18 years, are training children to shoot and kill in a virtual world in which the values of life are lost. Playing these games for a long time can negatively affect the mental health of young people. Several peer-reviewed studies have shown that children who play violent video games are more likely to bully[23] and cyberbully[24] their peers, get into physical fights, be hostile[25] , argue with teachers, and show aggression towards their peers.

Glossary (margin notes):

⑬ StarCraft 星际争霸

⑭ sour ['sauənəs] n. 酸
⑮ stiffness ['stifnəs] n. 僵硬
⑯ forearm [fɔr'aːm] n. 前臂

⑰ get hooked onto 入迷的

⑱ theme [θiːm] n. 主题

⑲ abuse of drugs and alcohol 滥用药物和酗酒
⑳ sexual exploitation 性虐待
㉑ Grand Thief Auto 侠盗猎车手
㉒ Call of Duty 使命召唤
㉓ bully ['buli] v. 欺负
㉔ cyberbully ['saibə'buli] v. 网络欺凌
㉕ hostile ['hɔstail] adj. 敌意的

02 What is your favorite game and why?

2.1 英雄联盟 League of Legends（LOL）

Unlike most of the online games on the market, which normally have 6 or 8 characters you can choose from, LOL has more than 120 characters and, each character has its own, unique personality. You can pick one of them to match your style. If you are really brave and willing to put yourself on the front line[1] of the war zone[2], you can choose a character that specializes in attacking. If you find yourself a responsible person, you can be a healer[3], which will back up the whole team if they are in danger. When you have chosen your favorite character, all you have to do is fight against the enemy team. In order to win, you have to work together. That's why I always play the game with my friends, because we really know each other well and we have each other's backs. It's been five years since I first played the game. The feeling when I aced an enemy team[4] with my friends is still fresh.

❶ font line 前线
❷ war zone 战场
❸ healer ['hi:lə] n. 治疗术士

❹ ace an enemy team 团灭

2.2 魔兽争霸 Warcraft III

I love this game because it has most of my best childhood memories. I started to play this game when I was in 8th grade. The very first minute I played it, it became my biggest dream and obsession as a kid back then. It gives me the best sense of fantasy that I could ever have from a game. Ladies that ride dragons, dwarves that carry rifles[5], different kinds of heroes that have tons of magic arts[6], the list can go on and on. Every time I got back from school, the first thing I would do is play that game for an hour or two. Now, 15 years have passed and lots of people quit playing it since it's getting old. However, I still play it when I have some time off[7]. My love for that game will never fade away.

❺ dwarves that carry rifles 矮人火枪手
❻ magic art 法术

❼ time off 空闲时间

2.3 俄罗斯方块 Tetris

It is simple. Gamers and non-gamers can easily play this game. It doesn't require as much understanding as other games. It doesn't have difficult controls. It is about putting falling blocks in the proper place in order to clear a line or make a perfect clear. I am really good at this game since I love organizing. It feels great to clear up 4 or 5 lines at one time, especially when I am about to lose and a block that fits the blank perfectly shows up at the last second. Also, I feel free to change the blocks at the very last moment before they land. It makes me feel I have the power over them, thus making me play more, especially if my blocks are misplaced, causing me to lose.

2.4　斗地主 Doudizhu

It is one of the most popular card games in China. It is easy to learn but hard to master. The game is played with three people with one pack of cards. It starts with players bidding for the "landlord" position. Those who lose the bid or don't bid enter the game as the "peasants" team. Both the "peasants" have to work together against the "landlord" to win the game. The objective of the game is to be the first player to have no cards left. There is an element of luck involved, but what counts is not only luck but also skill of playing and strategy. Poor players with great hands may be defeated by skillful players with poor cards.

2.5　升级 Sheng ji

Sheng Ji is a traditionally Chinese poker game which involves two pairs of players, in which one pair compete with the other. The goal of this game is to get or prevent the other team from getting 80 points, depending on the position your team is on; defending or attacking. Good players all have the ability to memorize the cards that have been played, so that they can guess what cards are left, and then play accordingly and wisely. Besides good memory, tacit cooperation between players often increases the chance of winning. Sometimes, a brief eye-contact allows your partner to know your strategy and respond with full support. This game is just so much fun, and people get addicted to it easily.

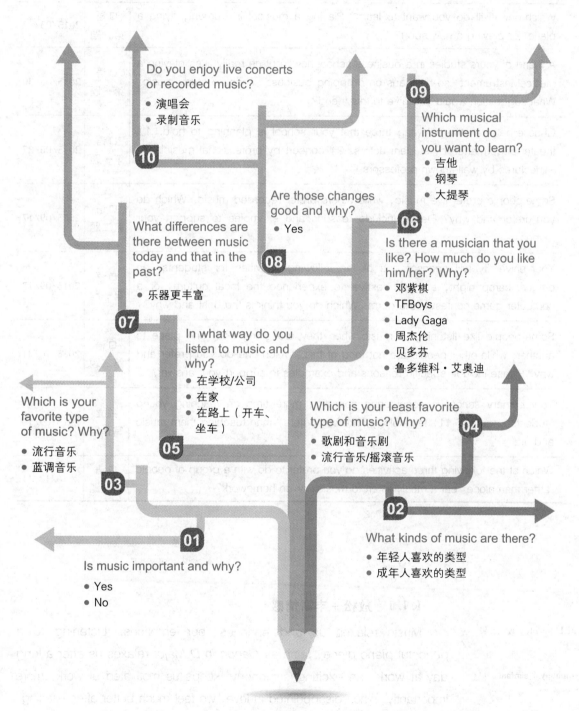

Do you enjoy live concerts or recorded music?
- 演唱会
- 录制音乐

10

Are those changes good and why?
- Yes

08

What differences are there between music today and that in the past?
- 乐器更丰富

07

09

Which musical instrument do you want to learn?
- 吉他
- 钢琴
- 大提琴

06

Is there a musician that you like? How much do you like him/her? Why?
- 邓紫棋
- TFBoys
- Lady Gaga
- 周杰伦
- 贝多芬
- 鲁多维科·艾奥迪

In what way do you listen to music and why?
- 在学校/公司
- 在家
- 在路上（开车、坐车）

05

Which is your favorite type of music? Why?
- 流行音乐
- 蓝调音乐

03

Which is your least favorite type of music? Why?
- 歌剧和音乐剧
- 流行音乐/摇滚音乐

04

02

What kinds of music are there?
- 年轻人喜欢的类型
- 成年人喜欢的类型

01

Is music important and why?
- Yes
- No

音乐

01 Is music important and why?

真 题	题 型	年 份
Which new skill do you want to learn? Playing a musical instrument, flying a plane, or playing a new sport?	口语 第一题	2015/03/07
A friend of yours studies in a business school now, but he really likes playing a musical instrument, so he plans on dropping business school to study music. What suggestion would you give to this friend?	口语 第一题	2015/05/30
Choose between the following three that your school is planning to hold. 1) theater performance by student actors; 2) concert by professional musicians; 3) lectures by well-known professors	口语 第一题	2015/06/27
Some people prefer live music, while others prefer recorded music. Which do you prefer and why? Please include reasons and examples to support your response.	口语 第二题	2015/09/17
Your university will sponsor one of the following activities for students: an outdoor camp night, a music festival to experience the local culture, or a computer game contest in the dorm. Which do you think is the best and why?	口语 第一题	2015/09/17
Some people like listening to music when they are going from one place to another, while other people are not fond of this. Which one do you prefer and why? Please include specific reasons and examples to support your answer.	口语 第二题	2015/10/31
Your primary school is considering spending more time on teaching young students (aged 5-11) technology (like computers) than teaching them music and art.	独立 写作题	2016/09/10
Which of the following three activities do you prefer to do with a group of people rather than alone: eat a meal, listen to music, or do homework?	口语 第一题	2016/12/11

1.1 Yes

1.1.1 放松 + 丰富情感

❶ enrich [in'ritʃ] v. 充实 丰富

❷ symphony ['simfəni] n. 交响乐

Music relaxes us and enriches[1] our emotions. Listening to a peaceful piano piece, such as *Canon in D Major* relaxes us after a long day at work; an exciting symphony[2] keeps us motivated at work; more importantly, when disappointed in love, we feel much better after listening to pop music, as if the singer was directly comforting and encouraging us.

1.1.2 表达用语言无法表达的内容

Music says things that cannot be said in words. Once a great musician performed his favorite piano piece to his friends. Everyone enjoyed it. One person in the audience asked what the song was about. The musician paused, smiled, shook his head and played the whole piece again, and said, "Well, it's about that."

1.1.3 听到音乐才能开始新的一天

Music gets my day started. On a cold winter morning, one just cannot resist the temptation to stay 5 more minutes in his bed, and 5 minutes usually ends up being an hour. Later I found a solution to solve the problem: music. As soon as I hear the arousing sound of a violin solo[3], singing like an exciting human voice, my body responds naturally. I feel pumped up[4] and ready to get up willingly.

❸ solo ['səuləu] *n.* 独奏曲
❹ pump up 振奋精神

1.1.4 留下记忆

Music gets under our skin. It creates strong feelings, and it creates strong memories. Try singing *Happy Birthday or Merry Christmas* and you'll understand. Are there images and memories rushing back to your mind? The tone and melody arouses[5] stronger feeling than mere words.

❺ arouse [ə'rauz] *v.* 激起

1.2　No

1.2.1 忙起来顾不上

Although I do enjoy music from time to time, I don't think it's indispensable[6]. When I get busy in work or study, I often forget about music for months. More importantly, I do not feel anything was missing in my life. Some would argue that music is an important way to relax, but I am able to find an outlet[7] for stress through other means, such as hanging out with my friends in a beer house, going on a ski trip, or playing computer games.

❻ indispensable [,indi'spensəbl] *adj.* 必不可少的

❼ outlet ['autlet] *n.* 出口，发泄的途径

02 What kinds of music are there?

2.1 年轻人喜欢的类型

Pop, Rock, Electro, R&B

2.2 成年人喜欢的类型

Jazz, Blues, Classics, Musical, Opera

03 Which is your favorite type of music? Why?

真 题	题 型	年 份
Talk about the kind of music you enjoy the least, and explain why you don't like it.	口语 第一题	2015/01/10
Which new skill do you want to learn? Playing a musical instrument, flying a plane, or playing a new sport?	口语 第一题	2015/03/07

3.1 流行音乐

I love pop music because everybody loves pop music. I expressed my eternal love for my first girlfriend with *Simple Love*, a pop song written by Jay Zhou. I guess that young people can relate more to pop music than any other kind, both because of its romantic lyrics[1] and the easy but catchy[2] melody. I can never truly wake up from sleep every morning before listening to some good pop music. I can easily spend more than an hour on music apps such as Wangyi Music, searching for inspiring songs, commenting and sharing my favorite ones on the Internet.

❶ lyrics ['liriks] *n.* 歌词

❷ catchy ['kætʃi] *adj.* 易记住的

3.2　蓝调音乐

I love R&B, especially David Tao's[3] songs. The genre is way more emotional than any other type, and that's because R&B music is filled with delicate transpositions[4] and variations[5] on end notes[6], which allows singers to express more subtle changes in emotions. My favorite piece is his *Regular Friends*. The song resonates[7] with me so much. It perfectly expresses the powerlessness and longing for unreachable love.

❸ David Tao 陶喆
❹ transposition [ˌtrænspəˈziʃ ən]
　　n. 变调
❺ variation [ˌvɛəriˈeiʃ ən]
　　n. 变奏
❻ end notes 尾音
❼ resonate [ˈrezəneit] *v.*
　　产生共鸣

04　Which is your least favorite type of music? Why?

真　题	题　型	年　份
Talk about the kind of music you enjoy the least, and explain why you don't like it.	口语 第一题	2015/01/10
Which new skill do you want to learn? Playing a musical instrument, flying a plane, or playing a new sport?	口语 第一题	2015/03/07

4.1　歌剧和音乐剧

I hate opera and musicals. I have no idea why anybody would enjoy such performances. It just seems crazy to have performers sing, dance, and have dialogues within the same setting. It appears to me that opera and musicals are simply chaos[1]. Why can we not just enjoy one simple type of performance at a time? The mingling[2] of these two forms sickens me, especially when actors' lines[2] are sung out dramatically. Also, operas are sung mostly in Italian, which I cannot understand. The key is often either too high or too low, which I cannot relate to. I like something I can sing along with.

❶ chaos [ˈkeiɔs] *n.* 混乱
❷ mingle [ˈmiŋgl] *v.* 混合
　　📖 mix
❸ line [lain] *n.* 台词

4.2 流行音乐/摇滚音乐

I hate pop/rock music, because everybody is so crazy about it. Some people just don't realize how loud they are playing the music at night. I almost got into a fight with my downstairs neighbor last year just because they were playing music too loudly and partying without inhibitions. The same issue applies to those who play loud music in the morning. A previous roommate of mine has this habit of setting his alarm clock using rock music, and the problem is that he usually gets up around 5:30 a.m.

05 In what way do you listen to music and why?

真 题	题 型	年 份
Some people prefer live music, while others prefer recorded music. Which do you prefer and why? Please include reasons and examples to support your response.	口语 第二题	2015/09/17
Some people like listening to music when they are going from one place to another, while other people are not fond of this. Which one do you prefer and why? Please include specific reasons and examples to support your answer.	口语 第二题	2015/10/31
Which of the following three activities do you prefer to do with a group of people rather than alone: eat a meal, listen to music, or do homework?	口语 第一题	2016/12/11

5.1 在学校/公司

❶ noise cancelling earphones 降噪耳机

❷ soothe [su:ð] v. 使放松，使宽心

❸ chatter ['tʃætə] n. 喋喋不休

I listen to music at work/school. My office/library is so noisy and can literally turn into chaos during the busiest hours. So, the best way to focus on my work is to put on my noise cancelling earphones[1] and listen to some soothing[2] music. All the constant chatter[3] from my colleagues/classmates instantly disappears, and the world soon turns into a better place.

5.2　在家

I listen to music at home. After a long day at work/school, I just need some time alone to peacefully enjoy some music that I love, to relax and feel alive. In order to maximize my listening experience, I spend thousands of dollars on BOSE's best loudspeakers. The steady and low pitch of the bass can take my mind off[4] stressful work immediately. Sometimes I get inspired by music and improvise[5] on my guitar or piano to blow off some steam[6] too.

5.3　在路上（开车、坐车）

I listen to music on the road. I have to ride a car/take a subway every day for 2 hours. Music kills time[7] and enriches my emotions. I love listening to FM radio stations such as 88.7（Hit FM）and 91.5（Easy FM）. The former plays pop music, mainly from top lists of US and UK. The latter has a session called *All that Jazz*. Sometimes I prefer jazz music without lyrics after a long day of work.

❹ take one's mind off 将注意力从……移开

❻ blow off some steam 发泄
❺ improvise ['imprəvaiz] v. 即兴创作

❼ kill time 消磨时光

06　Is there a musician that you like? How much do you like him/her? Why?

真　题	题　型	年　份
Talk about the kind of music you enjoy the least, and explain why you don't like it.	口语第一题	2015/01/10
Which new skill do you want to learn? Playing a musical instrument, flying a plane, or playing a new sport?	口语第一题	2015/03/07
Some people prefer live music, while others prefer recorded music. Which do you prefer and why? Please include reasons and examples to support your response.	口语第二题	2015/09/17

6.1 邓紫棋 G. E. M / Gloria Tang Tsz-Kei

I adore her as a goddess. I first saw her brilliant performance on *I am a Singer*[1], a famous Chinese reality show[2] that was aired on Hunan Satellite TV[3] in 2013. I was totally absorbed by her unbelievable voice register[4] and her ability to perfectly execute the high notes[5]. What's more, everyone is deeply touched by her powerful emotions, which are subtly[6] and ingeniously[7] embedded[8] in her charismatic[9] voice.

She is so successful yet so young that she instantly became my role model. She got second place on *I am a Singer*: *Season* 2 and was subsequently confirmed to take up one of the four posts of the mentor[10], on another popular music reality show — *The Voice of China*[11]: *Season* 4.

6.2 TFBoys

TFBoys is a famous Chinese young idol group who made their debut[12] in 2013. The three members are all cute, vigorous[13] boys with smiles that can dispel[14] all negative emotions. I love them mainly because of their most influential song, *the Guide Book of Youth*[15], whose lyrics goes: Follow me, left hand, right hand, a slow motion; right hand, left hand, the slow-motion repeats… The lyrics are extremely rhythmic[16] in Chinese, and the melody is just so catching that it sticks to your mind for weeks, no matter how hard you try to forget it. I bet that 99% of my peers love to sing this song in Karaoke.

6.3 Lady Gaga

My favorite singer is no doubt Lady Gaga. She has an incredible voice. Her singing talent sometimes goes unnoticed because everyone's too busy looking at what she's wearing. People should certainly start appreciating her phenomenal[17] voice more. Also, when she's on stage, she's on fire. There's never a dull moment when Gaga is on stage. Gaga loves getting dramatic and creative when it's her turn in the limelight[18]. Her songs are inspirational. She conveys positive messages like you should always be who you are, and you are born beautiful. She encourages many fans like me to stay strong and true to ourselves.

---

① *I am a Singer*《我是歌手》
② reality show 真人秀
③ Hunan Satellite TV 湖南卫视
④ voice register 音域
⑤ high notes 高音
⑥ subtle ['sʌtl] *adj.* 微妙的
⑦ ingenious [in'dʒi:niəs] *adj.* 高超技巧的
⑧ embed [im'bed] *v.* 嵌入
⑨ charismatic [ˌkæriz'mætik] *adj.* 有魅力的
⑩ mentor ['mentɔ:] *n.* 导师
⑪ *The Voice of China*《中国好声音》
⑫ debut ['debju] *n.* 演员首次演出
⑬ vigorous ['vigərəs] *adj.* 精力充沛的
⑭ dispel [di'spel] *v.* 驱散，赶跑
⑮ *the Guide Book of youth* 《青春修炼手册》（歌名）
⑯ rhythmic ['riðmik] *adj.* 有节奏的

⑰ phenomenal [fi'nɔminl] *adj.* 非凡的

⑱ limelight ['laimlait] *n.* 众人瞩目的中心

6.4 周杰伦 Jay Zhou

Most kids around my age grew up idolizing Jay Zhou, the most influential pop composer and singer in China. He created a unique and long-lasting pop music culture. It feels like a universal language that is spoken unimpededly[19] through young generations. It brings back precious memories of my youth.

He is the full package. He is and more than a musician. He is capable of editing, composing, and writing lyrics. He was the first one to bring fresh air to Chinese pop music. Many new generations of singers like G. E. M are his fans, and follow his style.

⑲ unimpededly
[ˌʌnimˈpiːdidli] *adv.* 无障碍地，无阻挡地

6.5 贝多芬 Beethoven

I love Beethoven. I have listened to all his compositions over and over again ever since I was little. I try to play all his pieces.

I admire Beethoven's talent. He was a musical prodigy[20] who displayed extraordinary talent when he was just 6. However, his life was a tragedy. He died young. His music conveyed this tragic life. Through his pieces, I can feel his despair, sorrow, fight against fate, and passion in life. I personally relate to his experiences and feel inspired by his masterpieces.

⑳ prodigy [ˈprɒdidʒi] *n.* 奇才

6.6 鲁多维科·艾奥迪 Ludovico Einaudi

If I'm in love with a musician, I must be in love with his/her songs. Among the many that I love, if I have to name one that I love the most, it has to be Ludovico Einaudi, a modern Italian composer. His famous piece *Nuvole Bianche* is my favorite of all songs. It translates as "White Cloud". I like him so much that I listened to all his pieces that I can find on the Internet. And I would also recommend his music to all my friends whenever possible.

His music expresses feelings that cannot be conveyed through words. Although I also love pop musicians, the mainstream theme of pop songs is always love, which can be well communicated through words. But his piece is different. I can clearly sense the sadness within the musical notes, yet at the same time I feel encouraged, soothed, and

㉑ inexplicable [ˌinikˈsplikəbl]
adj. 无法说明的

㉒ slumber [ˈslʌmbə] *n.* 睡眠

hopeful. It's really an inexplicable[21] experience that can only be understood by listening to the piece. Another quality which attracts me is that whenever I cannot fall asleep, his music can somehow relax me, and I always fall into a deep slumber[22] within 3 minutes.

07 What differences are there between music today and that in the past?

真 题	题 型	年 份
Talk about the kind of music you enjoy the least, and explain why you don't like it.	口语 第一题	2015/01/10
Which new skill do you want to learn? Playing a musical instrument, flying a plane, or playing a new sport?	口语 第一题	2015/03/07

乐器更丰富

❶ African percussions 非洲
打击乐器
❷ erhu *n.* 二胡
❸ banjo [ˈbændʒəu] *n.* 班
卓琴
❹ synthesizers [ˈsinθəsaizə]
n. 合成器

　　With advancement in technology, music evolves and diversifies. In the past, musical instruments were limited to the basics: piano, strings, flutes, saxophones, and drums. Now, with globalization, we have access to plentiful new instruments including African percussion[1], eastern string instruments such as erhu[2], as well as electric guitars, banjos[3], synthesizers[4], etc. Plus, everything is digitalized now. A modern composer can compose a piece without touching any real instruments. He can simply compose with virtual instruments provided in various kinds of music software and add all kinds of audio effects.

08 Are those changes good and why?

Yes

The changes are good for the most part. Although some would go nuts[1] with obsessively implementing the new elements provided by technology into songs, leading to a distorted or overemphasized style, most musicians know how to keep the balance and use these newly emerged instruments and special effects wisely.

❶ go nuts 发狂

09 Which musical instrument do you want to learn?

真　题	题　型	年　份
Talk about the kind of music you enjoy the least, and explain why you don't like it.	口语第一题	2015/01/10
Which new skill do you want to learn? Playing a musical instrument, flying a plane, or playing a new sport?	口语第一题	2015/03/07

9.1　吉他

I have always wanted to learn how to play the guitar, since you can easily get tons of fans after a simple performance at school. Another advantage of the guitar is that it is convenient to carry. You can bring your guitar to a party or to the yard of your dream girl/boy.

9.2　钢琴

Piano is definitely my favorite instrument, because it is so classy. Unlike the guitar, which often reminds me of buskers[1], the piano reminds me of an elegant concert in the Grand National Theater. I also like pianists more than guitarists. The former definitely knows more about the essence of music.

❶ busker [ˈbʌskə(r)] n. 街头艺人
🔲 street performers

9.3 大提琴

I have always wanted to learn how to play the cello ever since I saw a cello player at my favorite composer's concert. Of all the players on stage, the keyboardist, the violinist, the bass player, the drummer, the cellist undoubtedly grabbed my attention the most. Although both the violinist and the cellist are playing with almost identical actions with their arms, pulling the strings with a bow[2], the latter's pulling is definitely more graceful due to its greater force and wider range of both horizontal and vertical movement. The violin, in contrast, despite its engaging sound, simply just does not look as grand as that of the cello when played by great musicians.

❷ fiddlestick［'fidlstik］*n.*
小提琴或大提琴琴弓

10 Do you enjoy live concerts or recorded music?

真　题	题　型	年　份
Some people prefer live music, while others prefer recorded music. Which do you prefer and why? Please include reasons and examples to support your response.	口语第二题	2015/09/17

10.1 演唱会

Of course, live concerts are the better choice. I just went to my favorite composer's concert two weeks ago, at the Tianqiao Arts Performing Center[1], and it was just mind-blowing[2]. I mean, I know his pieces so well that I could sing along without any effort on any piece that he composed since the 1980s. But still, when I saw his real performance and listened to his music directly with my ears, I felt something quite different from the recorded music which I downloaded from the Internet; and this difference is hard to describe in words. You just feel that something more is attached to live music. So, I encourage everyone to go to a concert of your favorite singer or composer.

❶ Tianqiao Arts Performing Center 天桥艺术中心
❷ mind-blowing *adj.* 令人印象深刻的

10. 2　录制音乐

Well, I like recorded music better simply because it costs less. To begin with, concert tickets today often cost too much, from 200 Yuan to 1,000 Yuan. Last month I heard that my favorite singer was about to host a live concert in Beijing, so I went online to check the price of the ticket. I was shocked. All the good seats were already sold, and the ones left were all corners seats in the front rows. The cheapest would cost like 800 Yuan. So I gave up and went back to my iPhone app, Wangyiyun Music, which is basically free. New songs that just came out are sold at an extremely low price. For example, a song that I am recently crazy about is Taylor Swift and Zayn's *I Don't Wanna Live Forever*, and it only costs 2 Yuan.

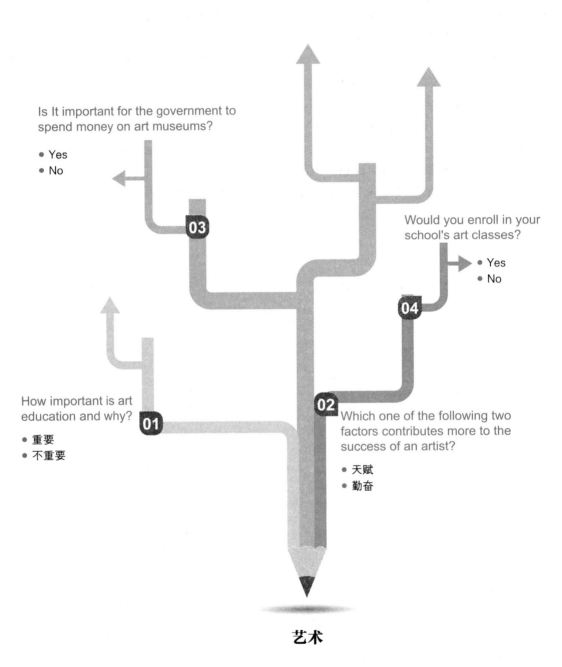

Is It important for the government to spend money on art museums?

- Yes
- No

03

Would you enroll in your school's art classes?

- Yes
- No

04

How important is art education and why?

- 重要
- 不重要

01

02

Which one of the following two factors contributes more to the success of an artist?

- 天赋
- 勤奋

艺术

01 How important is art education and why?

真　题	题　型	年　份
Do you agree or disagree with the statement that it's important for students to study art and music in school? Explain your answer in detail.	口语 第二题	2014/04/19
Your school used to offer three after-class activities：1）sports, 2）art, 3）volunteering, but this year, the school's extra money can only offer one activity. Which one do you choose and why?	独立 写作题	2015/11/08
Which of the following classes would you like to take? Math, painting or science?	口语 第一题	2016/12/03
Your primary school is considering spending more time on teaching young students（aged 5－11）technology（like computers）than teaching them music and art.	独立 写作题	2017/07/15

1.1　重要

1.1.1　增强创造力

Without art, students would never truly know how to express themselves by simply learning math and science. It will also boost their creativity[1]. For example, in a painting class, children are asked to create vivid[2] images of houses, people, and places. Sometimes, they are even asked to create abstract art, such as a painting that represents their memories or emotions. It obviously makes use of one's imagination. Furthermore, if children think creatively, it will become a habit and stay with them in the future.

❶ boost creativity 增加创造力

❷ vivid ['vivid] *adj.* 生动的

1.1.2　增强自信

Learning arts helps students to build up their self-esteem[3], since children would constantly gain a great sense of achievement from performing simple and light-hearted[4] activities such as drawing and singing. It just feels great when you sing a song perfectly or when you are done with a painting. I remember when I was little, when someone saw my artwork, I could gain immeasurable[5] joy from seeing his or her reactions. I felt so proud to be unique and express my artistic style.

❸ self-esteem [self-i'sti:m] *n.* 自信

❹ light-hearted *adj.* 轻松的

❺ immeasurable [i'meʒərəbl] *adj.* 无限的

1.2 不重要

1.2.1 其他学科教育更重要

Not important, because science education is more important. You can live your whole life without visiting the *Mona Lisa*⁶. Some argue that it has changed their lives. Imagine how much of change you'd feel if you suddenly didn't have electricity, or the plague⁷ was never deemed⁸ curable. Science has made a bigger difference than art. It has cured diseases, increased food production, made water purification⁹ possible, etc. If students spend too much time on art instead of science which has more practical values, they will realize how stupid they are when they become adults, If you can't explain to your kids why the sun rises in the east and sets in the west, I am pretty sure the *Mona Lisa* will be the last thing on your mind.

1.2.2 没时间

I don't have time to go to art classes. I have so much other schoolwork to do. For example, I study engineering and it is tough. I have to finish 20 credits per semester, all for compulsory¹⁰ courses. Everyday I study until midnight in the library. I am exhausted. It would drive me crazy if I had to learn courses outside my major field, and that would definitely affect my academic performance.

⑥ *Mona Lisa* 《蒙娜丽莎》

⑦ plague [pleig] *n.* 瘟疫

⑧ deem [di:m] *v.* 认为

⑨ purification [ˌpjuərifiˈkeiʃn] *n.* 净化

⑩ compulsory [kəmˈpʌlsəri] *adj.* 必修的

02 Which one of the following two factors contributes more to the success of an artist? (Natural talent or hard work)

真 题	题 型	年 份
Some people think that one needs to be talented to become an artist; others believe that anyone could be an artist with years of practice. Which do you agree with? Explain why.	口语 第二题	2012/02/24
Some people think that one needs to be talented to be an artist; others believe training and hard work are more crucial for someone to be an artist. Which do you think is more important? Give details and examples in your response.	口语 第二题	2013/06/15

（续）

真　题	题　型	年　份
Which one of the following two factors is more important to the success of an artist? Natural talent, or hard work?	口语 第二题	2016/02/27

2.1　天赋

画画

Talent is more important. Some people are just naturally more inclined[1] towards art. For example, I tried to learn to draw and paint for a year, but couldn't do it well even after a year of hard work. Give me a paint brush and a canvas[2] and I still don't know where to start. However, one day, I saw my little sister's water color painting. I was amazed by its wide range of colors. It seemed very skillful and creative to me. When I asked her about this, she told me she never had any training. She was just drawing pictures to loosen up[3] and have fun. From that point, I knew that hard work means something, but when it comes to success, talent is more of a vital[4] factor.

❶ inclined［inˈklaind］ *adj.* 有天赋的

❷ canvas［ˈkænvəs］ *n.* 油画布

❸ loosen up 放松

❹ vital［vaitl］ *adj.* 重要的

2.2　勤奋

2.2.1　雕刻

I was not very good at sculpting or drawing but I made a decision to spend the rest of my life learning it. I told myself that I could succeed without talent. I travelled all the way to Italy and went into the studios to learn from the finest artists of the day. It was not easy, but I found myself slowly improving. I spent years of daily practice working steadily. After three years, I realized I could sculpt[5] a figure, and after five years, I could sculpt movement. It wasn't until about the 7th year when I finally started developing a style of my own. The galleries started opening their doors and my work was being sold. If I believed art was a talent I would have given up long ago. The ability to create art is something that is earned through years of constant study and dedication[6]. It is not a gift given at birth.

❺ sculpt［skʌlpt］ *v.* 雕刻

❻ dedication［ˌdediˈkeiʃn］ *n.* 奉献

2.2.2　练习乐器

People have to work hard to get success. Even though some people don't have talent, hard work will get them to the point in the long run. For example, I have loved piano since I was a kid. I started playing in 4th grade, but I still couldn't complete a piece of simple music after 3 years. I didn't give up and kept doing 5 – 6 hours of practice every single day. The notes even played themselves in my dream. Knowing the truth, that I don't have talent, let me be more positive and open minded in the things that I was learning and experimenting. I didn't shy away when I made mistakes, instead I kept practicing until I could play a passage perfectly. Finally, my hard work paid off. I got the first prize in a piano contest and ended up winning a 4-year scholarship[7] to a music college.

❼ scholarship [ˈskɔləʃip]
 n. 奖学金

03 Is it important for the government to spend money on art museums?

真　题	题　型	年　份
It is more important for the government to spend money on art museums and concert halls than on recreational facilities such as swimming pools and playgrounds.	独立写作题	2010/12/15
Your city is going to build new places to attract more visitors. Among the following three options, which do you think is the best? 1）a local history museum；2）a modern art and film museum；3）a children's science museum	口语第一题	2016/09/10

3.1　Yes

3.1.1　让人们更好地了解城市

❶ evolve [iˈvɔlv] v. 进化

Museums show you the history of the city and how it evolved[1]. If I want to explore a city, a museum is always the first place to go. When I first visited Beijing, I went to the Palace museum. I was amazed by the architecture[2], art collections and photos. It showed me how the city

❷ architecture [ˈɑːkitektʃə]
 n. 建筑风格

served as the home of the Emperor and his household for almost five centuries, and how it eventually became the ceremonial[3] and political center of China. The museum has thousands of rooms with millions of artifacts[4] inside. It tells me everything I want to know about the city.

3.1.2 增加城市收入

One benefit of spending money on museums is that it generates a lot of revenue[5] for the government. When you open a travel magazine, art museums are always among the top-rated tourist attractions[6]. Good art museums attract even more tourists. For example, I live in Beijing, an historic city in China, where we have 50 million visitors a year. It's the museums that support the development of hotels, restaurants, car rental agencies, tour companies, souvenir[7] shops, and much more. All of these create jobs for people. If the government spends more money to build better museums, more tourists will come. The people in the city can earn more money to live a better life.

3.2 No

浪费时间

Travelling to the museum is time-consuming. Generally, museums are built in suburban[8] areas, which are extremely hard to travel to. For example, once I wanted to visit the military museum of China, which is located like 200 miles from downtown. I could not find any bus or subway that could get me there; neither could I afford to take a taxi, which was way too expensive for a student like me. In the end I had to call my friends and have them drive me there, which took like 2 hours.

③ ceremonial [ˌseriˈməuniəl] *adj.* 仪式的

④ artifact [ˈɑːtifækt] *n.* 人工制品

⑤ revenue [ˈrevənjuː] *n.* 税收

⑥ attraction [əˈtrækʃn] *n.* 景点

⑦ souvenir [ˈsuːvəniə] *n.* 纪念品

⑧ suburban [səˈbəːbən] *adj.* 郊区的

04 Would you enroll in your school's art classes?

真 题	题 型	年 份
Which one of the following history courses should be added? History of science, art history, or modern history of the 20th century?	口语 第一题	2016/01/23

Which one of the following classes would you choose? 1）science history；2）art history；3）European history	口语 第一题	2016/09/10

4.1　Yes

学会欣赏

I would. I can obviously understand the abstract masterpieces better after I took art classes at school. I couldn't appreciate arts before taking the class. Give me famous paintings from different eras, and I had no idea what the difference in technique was. And I couldn't relate to the pictures either. To me, a passionate piece with strong emotion underneath could look just like a mixture of mystical lines and dots. But then I applied to an art history class in college. I started to understand that lots of artists were working under a unique set of circumstances, which affected their works. There were personal, political, sociological[1] and religious factors behind creation. After I learned the stories behind these artworks, I could finally appreciate arts.

4.2　No

没意义

I never truly grasp the purpose of learning art history. Not everyone is an artist, so why bother to learn the history of a subject with which they will never get involved? I have always hated those people who constantly brag[2] about their "erudition[3]" of arts. For example, a friend of mine, Jason, can tell you the exact date when Mozart[4] composed his symphonies[5], but he cannot distinguish the most distinguishable music with his ears. To me, these people are just forcing themselves to remember the things they are not even interested in, for the mere[6] purpose of being "erudite".

❶ sociological [ˌsəuʃiəˈlɔdʒikəl]
adj. 社会学的

❷ brag [bræg] *v.* 吹牛
❸ erudition [ˌeruˈdiʃn] *v.* 博学
❹ Mozart [ˌməutsait] *n.* 莫扎特
❺ symphony [ˈsimfəni] *n.* 交响乐
❻ mere [miə] *adj.* 仅仅的

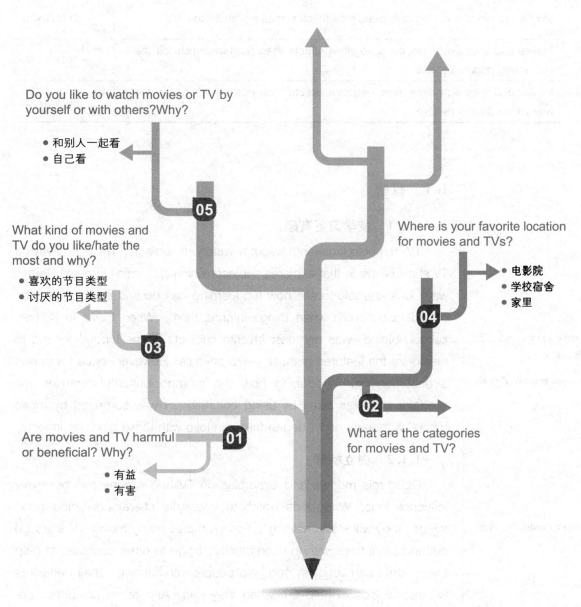

Do you like to watch movies or TV by yourself or with others?Why?
- 和别人一起看
- 自己看

What kind of movies and TV do you like/hate the most and why?
- 喜欢的节目类型
- 讨厌的节目类型

Where is your favorite location for movies and TVs?
- 电影院
- 学校宿舍
- 家里

Are movies and TV harmful or beneficial? Why?
- 有益
- 有害

What are the categories for movies and TV?

05

04

03

02

01

影视

01 Are movies and TV harmful or beneficial? Why?

真　题	题　型	年　份
Movies are worth watching only when they teach something about real life.	独立 写作题	2015/04/12
Movies and television have more negative effects than positive effects on the way young people behave.	口语 第一题	2016/05/28
Movies and television have more negative effects than positive effects on the way young people behave.	口语 第一题	2016/11/26

1.1　有益

1.1.1　使学习更有趣

TV can help kids learn about a variety of subjects. There is always a TV show or movie that explores subjects which kids enjoy in detail. In this way, kids are able to see how fun learning can be and establish a habit of finding out more when things interest them. When I was in primary school, biology was my least favorite subject. It was torture[1] for me to memorize the features of those weird animals. However, once I watched a documentary, introducing how the morpho butterfly[2] confuses the predator and gets away by using coloration. I was surprised by those natural wonders, and I began falling in love with those amazing insects.

1.1.2　树立榜样

Good role models and examples on TV and movies can positively influence kids. When kids watch their favorite characters doing good things, they will start imitating[3]. For example, many movie/TV stars go out and plant trees with the community, or go to other countries to help the children with schools, and help people with housing. Their behaviors will inspire kids to help out when they can. And some celebrities are good influences too. My favorite singer is Adele Adkins[4]. She is absolutely my idol. Her songs are inspirational[5]. She conveys positive messages like you should always be who you are, and you are born beautiful. She encourages many fans like me to stay strong and true to ourselves.

❶ torture ['tɔːtʃə] adj. 煎熬，折磨
❷ morpho butterfly 蓝蝴蝶
❸ imitate ['imiteit] v. 模仿
❹ Adele Adkins 阿黛尔
❺ inspirational [,inspə'reiʃənl] adj. 鼓舞人心的

1.2　有害

1.2.1　造成肥胖

Children are more likely to be overweight if they spend too much time watching TV. For example, I can sit on my couch watching TV for hours without moving. While I am watching, I always snack on[6] all kinds of junk food like popcorn, fries, or fried chicken. When the TV program is interesting, I eat. When it isn't, I eat even more as it is boring and I have nothing else to kill time[7]. Sometimes, I can't even remember how much I ate when I get hooked[8] on TV shows. Eventually, I put on a lot of weight without even realizing it.

1.2.2　暴力对孩子有消极影响

TV and movies expose children to negative influences, and cause negative behavior. TV shows and commercials often show violence, alcohol, drug use and sex in a positive light[9]. TV and movies form early impressions on what children see, and these early impressions determine how children see the world and, affect their grown-up behavior. For example, they are taught by TV that violence is the way to resolve conflict as they always see a TV or a movie hero beat up a bad guy to subdue[10] him. So, when they are facing conflict next time, they will start throwing punches without even thinking about it.

1.2.3　占用学习、社交时间

TV and movie viewing takes away the time that children need to develop important skills like language, creativity, motion, and social skills. These skills are developed in kids' early ages and are very critical. For example, when I was a kid, my language skills didn't improve by passively[11] listening to TV. They were developed by interacting with people, when talking and listening are used in the context of real life. School kids who watch too much TV and movies also tend to work less on their homework. When they keep watching TV till midnight, they become less alert during the day, which results in poor school performance.

6 snack on 用……代替点心

7 kill time 消磨时间

8 get hooked 被……迷住

9 positive light 正面角度

10 subdue [səb'dju:] v. 征服

11 passively ['pæsivli] adv. 被动地

02 What are the categories for movies and TV?

drama, comedy, sci-fi, thriller, horror, romance, sitcom, news, talk show, talent show, reality, documentary, war, disaster, sports

03 What kind of movies and TV do you like/hate the most and why?

真 题	题 型	年 份
Some people prefer to watch entertainment programs on television, while others prefer to watch educational programs. Which do you prefer and why?	口语第二题	2016/08/20
Many people spend a lot of time watching sports programs on TV or following their favorite sports teams, which can have negative effects on their lives.	口语第二题	2016/08/21

3.1 喜欢的节目类型

3.1.1 喜剧类节目

❶ *Friends*《老友记》

❷ Joey Tribbiani《老友记》中的一个角色

I still remember the last time I laughed my heart out while watching *Friends*[1]. My favorite character in this show is Joey Tribbiani[2]. He is so funny. Thanks to him, a classic chat-up line was born. "How you doing" is the best line to try when you aren't sure if someone fancies you, because if you get rejected you can always play it off as a solid Joey impression. And I believe everyone needs a little bit of laughter at some point in their lives. When things in my life wear me out and break me down, I always watch *Friends*. As soon as I start watching, I can forget all the uneasiness and troubles in real life.

3.1.2 运动类节目

It is unpredictable. With a movie or TV show, I generally have a pretty good idea what the ending is going to look like. With sports, I never know the outcome, which forces me to sit tightly and wait for the crucial moment of the game. For example, when Cleveland Cavaliers[3] were down by 1-3 in the NBA finals last year, everybody believed they would lose. However, LeBron James[4] delivered one of his mightiest[5] all-around performances and the Cleveland Cavaliers completed the greatest comeback in NBA Finals history and beat the Golden State[6] in game 7. It was the first time for a team to rally from[7] a 3-1 deficit[8] to win the best-of-seven-series. That's why I love watching sports. You never know what will happen next.

3.1.3　访谈节目

I love watching talk shows. It's a great way to learn English, to relax and to keep up with news. My favorite talk show currently is *Last Week Tonight* [9], hosted by John Oliver, a funny British man who lives and works in America. I love his accent and his brilliant mind. The boring news are made super funny through his smart remarks, and he loves making fun of Donald Trump, which is also a thing that I look forward to after a long day at school/work.

3.2　讨厌的节目类型

3.2.1　恐怖片

Horror movies are scary. I don't like the feeling of being scared. I am very sensitive to frightful[10] images. I have nightmares after I watch a horror movie. I still remember the first time I saw *Silent Hill* [11]. There are some creepy creatures in the movie and when the lights go off, it's pretty chilling. After I finished watching it, I imagined that someone else was standing beside my bed when I was trying to sleep. And because of this, I couldn't sleep well for a week. Besides, it is not interesting. Most of the horror movies lack story-telling[12]. I can not understand why everything was fine at the moment, and the next minute, bodies were suddenly being torn apart[13].

3.2.2　新闻

I hate watching news. I guess my hatred for it started when we were forced to watch CCTV news ever since we were in 5th grade. Everyday back then, at 7:00 p.m., our class teacher would march to the TV and turn it on, forcing us to sit up straight and watch it for a whole

③ Cleveland Cavaliers 克利夫兰骑士队

④ LeBron James 勒布朗詹姆斯

⑤ mighty ['maiti] *adj.* 强有力的

⑥ Golden State 金州勇士

⑦ rally from 开始好转

⑧ deficit ['defisit] *n.* 不足

⑨ *Last Week Tonight* 《上周今夜秀》

⑩ frightful ['fraitfl] *adj.* 可怕的

⑪ *Silent Hill* 《寂静岭》

⑫ story-telling 讲故事

⑬ tear… apart 撕碎

half hour, without the free movement. The broadcast of the hosts is just so boring that I always fall asleep after trying to listen to it for a minute.

3.2.3 爱情片

I hate romance movies. It's not that I don't have a boyfriend/girlfriend. I just cannot stand the slow pace of such movies. I prefer faster-paced movies such as *Transformers Series*. The actors and actresses are not only handsome, but the progression of their relationship is way faster than that in romance movies. I mean, in action movies, the hero can always kiss his love after saving her from the bad guy. But in romance movies, they have to break up like 4-5 times before he can really kiss her.

04 Where is your favorite location for movies and TVs?

真 题	题 型	年 份
The university will spend money on the dormitory to improve the students' quality of life. Which of the following do you think is best? 1) providing a room for quiet study 2) building an exercise room 3) providing a movie room	口语第一题	2013/10/05
Some schools prevent students from putting a TV in the dormitory. What are the advantages and disadvantages of this policy? Please include specific reasons and examples to support your answer.	口语第一题	2015/05/09

4.1 电影院

4.1.1 气氛好

❶ lights go out 灯光熄灭

❷ munch [mʌntʃ] v. 用力咀嚼

❸ loosen up 放松

I love the atmosphere in a theater when the lights go out[1] and everyone is quieting down. Nothing beats sitting in a theater with my friends munching[2] on popcorn and sipping my favorite smoothie while I watch my favorite actors battling with aliens on a huge screen. I feel I could transport to a world away from reality, and I enjoy every moment of it. After I walk out of the theater doors, I loosen up[3] and realize that I had, even for just a few hours, forgotten about the troubles of day-to-day life.

4.1.2　总被人打扰

I won't go to the theater if the audience is not respectful. Nothing ruins a movie other than people talking or kicking your seat. Some people just don't know how to behave themselves in public. In almost every movie theater that I have been to, there must be a guy using his cell phone to take photos while the flash is on or some other guy talking on the phone loudly like they are doing a-million-dollar business deal when the movie has already started. Some people might argue that many people would answer with a whisper, which would not cause too much trouble to those around him. However, no matter how softly he "thinks" he is whispering[4], it's not softly enough. You can hear every word he is saying even though it is supposed to be a private conversation. It really gets on my nerves and I feel like I could punch a punching bag at that time.

④ whisper ['wispə] *v.* 低语

4.2　学校宿舍

4.2.1　放松

It's the way that college life should be. When I am back from the library after doing assignments all day, nothing beats lying on the bed and watching TV with my roommates. It is a good way to loosen up. We talk about how we hate or love the character, predict the next scene, adore how handsome the actor is or admit the actress is our crush. When there is a major sports event like the *Super Bowl*[5] or *NBA finals*[6], students can gather and watch together. That's a feeling you will remember for your whole life.

⑤ Super Bowl 超级碗
⑥ NBA finals NBA 总决赛

4.2.2　因意见不同而争吵

Some students prefer to sit before the television set and enjoy their favorite programs. They do not care about the preference of the other students. Roommates might argue or even fight with each other when disagreement arises[7] about which programs to watch. I remember there was a time my roommate and I had a conflict about choosing the TV programs. I wanted to watch *Breaking Bad*[8], but he preferred to watch a BBC documentary. We ended up in a big fight and my friend was sent to the hospital. Both of us got suspended[9] from school. That was really awkward and stupid.

⑦ arise [ə'raiz] *v.* 出现

⑧ *Breaking Bad*《绝命毒师》

⑨ get suspended 被停学

4.3 家里

4.3.1 省钱

Watching movies at home can save money. We can pop our own popcorn[10] and bring our snacks. Being able to eat and drink whatever I want without paying more than it should be is nice. It is ridiculous that most of the drinks or candy bars for sale at movie theaters are so expensive. A soda or an ice cream may cost you 5 dollars in a movie theater, but, when bought from a vending machine[11], only costs 75 cents. And sometimes just watching a movie can cost you more than 10 dollars per ticket.

4.3.2 自在

I like being at home to lie around on the couch wearing pajamas and cuddling[12] with my boyfriend or my dog. I can pause when I need a break or pick up a call. If I lose interest in the movie that I am watching, I can just turn it off and go to sleep. However, if I watch a movie in the cinema, I have to sit there and keep watching even if the movie is boring, because I don't want to waste my money. Plus, I just hate the endless commercials before every movie, and a wait for the toilet after the movie ends.

4.3.3 不会被别人干扰

Sometimes the people you are watching a movie/TV shows with can be annoying. There's always someone who wants the back row, and another who is passionate about being as close to the middle as possible. Arguing about what TV channel or movie you should watch could also lead to a serious argument between friends. I remember there was a time my friend Jay and I had a conflict about choosing the TV programs. We ended up in a big fight, and we didn't talk to each other for a long time. That was really awkward and stupid.

4.3.4 上瘾

People may get hooked on TV. Sometimes I feel days pass way too fast if I watch movies or TV shows at home. Once you start watching, it never ends. I can sit there for hours and it will break my daily routine. I

---

⑩ pop our own popcorn 做爆米花

⑪ vendor machine 自动贩卖机

⑫ cuddle ['kʌdl] v. 拥抱

was preparing for my finals at home last Friday. I felt tired, so I decided to watch a movie to take a break. However, I just couldn't help myself and I kept watching it. One movie after another, and almost 4 hours had passed till I realized it. I didn't have enough time to go over all my notes for the final. I felt upset and failed my exam.

05 Do you like to watch movies or TV by yourself or with others?Why?

真　题	题　型	年　份
Which of the following activities would you like to do on a weekend afternoon? Doing exercise, watching TV, or spending some time with family?	口语 第一题	2015/01/31
Which do you prefer? Watching a movie silently or chatting with others?	口语 第二题	2015/08/22
One can learn about another person from the books and movies that person likes.	独立 写作题	2015/09/17

5.1　和别人一起看

I believe the whole point of watching a movie is to connect and to share ideas with others, especially when they can really hit it off with you. Popcorn does taste better when shared. Watching a fun movie with my friends doubles the fun. And it will make a scary movie less creepy if I watch it with other people. I still remember the first time I saw *Silent Hill*. There are some creepy creatures in the movie, and when the lights go off it's pretty chilling. I could barely watch 15 minutes into the movie by myself. However, with my friends sitting by my side, I could continue watching, and it turned out it was a pretty good movie.

Sometimes, sitting there quietly by myself when watching movie or TV programs can be boring, especially when the plot¹ is moving slow or nothing interesting is going on. However, if I watch movies with my best friends, we can talk to each other about how we hate or love the character,

❶ plot [plɒt] *n.* 情节

predict the next scene, adore how handsome the actor, is or admit the actress is our crush. At the end of the movie we could also discuss how the movie can end better. The list goes on. In this way, I can engage with people and know them better.

5.2 自己看

I can watch whatever I want and no one even has to know about it. I can sit wherever I want, while deciding where to sit with a group can be a pain. There's always someone who wants the back row, and another who is passionate about being as close to the middle as possible. Plus, I don't need to share food. I have all my snacks and popcorn. Also, I don't even need to worry about being a mess. I don't need to care about others staring at me for crying a lot during a movie or laughing out loud all over my face. I can let loose all my emotions.

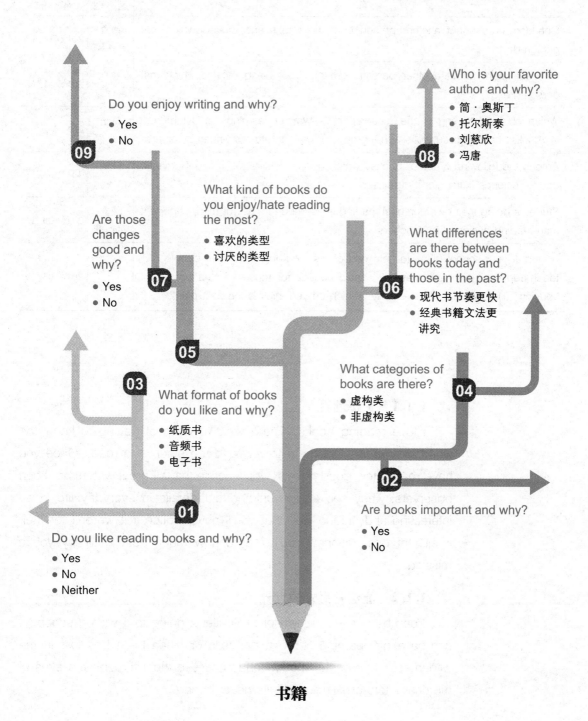

Do you enjoy writing and why?
- Yes
- No

09

Who is your favorite author and why?
- 简·奥斯丁
- 托尔斯泰
- 刘慈欣
- 冯唐

08

Are those changes good and why?
- Yes
- No

07

What kind of books do you enjoy/hate reading the most?
- 喜欢的类型
- 讨厌的类型

What differences are there between books today and those in the past?
- 现代书节奏更快
- 经典书籍文法更讲究

06

05

03

What format of books do you like and why?
- 纸质书
- 音频书
- 电子书

What categories of books are there?
- 虚构类
- 非虚构类

04

02

01

Do you like reading books and why?
- Yes
- No
- Neither

Are books important and why?
- Yes
- No

书籍

01 Do you like reading books and why?

真　题	题　型	年　份
One can learn about another person from the books and movies which that person likes.	独立写作题	2012/11/17
One can learn about another person from the books and movies which that person likes.	独立写作题	2013/11/17
Which of the following is the most effective way of learning: studying from textbooks, having discussions with a group, or reading articles written by others?	口语第一题	2015/02/01
Among the following types of books, which do you dislike the most? Romantic books, science fiction, or biography?	口语第一题	2015/04/18
Students doing their own personal reading is as important as, or more important than reading assigned by teachers.	独立写作题	2016/03/11
A club at your school plans to help one of the following groups of people: 1) teach pupils reading and math; 2) build houses for those who cannot afford housing; 3) take care of the elderly. Which do you think is the best plan?	独立写作题	2016/03/19

1.1　Yes

1.1.1　了解世界

I love reading books. There are two ways of getting to know the world around us. One is to travel, and the other is to read. Once you have read a few good novels, you'll notice that all great writers are keen observers. They see all the unimportant details in everyday life in an interesting and unique way that you'll never notice if it weren't for their intelligent descriptions. You'll realize how much detail and joy you're missing.

1.1.2　能够看另外的世界

I can be in Middle Earth or in Scotland going to a wizard school. I can be a girl learning to be a princess or I can be a boy lost in the wilderness. I can enter these worlds and see them through the eyes of the characters any time, and it's never boring.

1.2　No

1.2.1　看书无用，有网即可

I hate reading books. I just don't see the point of reading in modern society. We have so many ways to acquire information with TV or the Internet, not to mention the latest technologies such as Virtual Reality and Augmented Reality. I believe all books will be turned into either movies or these more advanced forms. Then, our younger generation can access them in a more interesting way. Books are destined to die out with the progress of science.

1.2.2　文人无病呻吟

To be frank, I hate reading. I have hated it ever since elementary school. I just don't get the point[1] of writing with those complex words and structures, which can easily be expressed in the vocabulary of a four-year-old. Furthermore, I have always had a few theories about why poets and writers do not speak plain English in their compositions[2]: they simply want to show off[3] their writing skills, or they are just crazy. So, why would I waste my precious time on the useless compositions of crazy people?

1.2.3　词汇和语法太难了

I have always wanted to like reading, but I've never succeed It's just that the complex words and sentences often make me want to sleep. I mean, who wouldn't when they read sentences with an average length of 50 words? Plus, the vocabulary in classics such as Jane Austen's works are just too hard for me. Although I am studying GRE recently and I have already begun to memorize GRE vocabulary, I still encounter many crazy words. Worse, sometimes I understand all the vocabulary in a sentence, but I just don't get what the author was trying to express. Both difficulty and frustration prevent me from reading.

1.3　Neither

I neither like nor hate reading books. I think it's a good way to kill time[4] on airplanes, since most electronic devices are banned during flights.

❶ don't get the point of
不懂

❷ composition [ˌkɔmpəˈziʃn]
n. 作品

❸ show off 炫耀，卖弄

❹ kill time 打发时间

⑤ carry-on luggage 随身携
带的行李
⑥ overhead bin 舱顶行李箱
⑦ alternative [ɔːˈltɜːnətiv]
n. 其他选择
🔲 choice

Some might argue that most airlines today allow the use of electronics after takeoff, but it's just way too troublesome to take your laptop out of the carry-on luggage[5] from the overhead bin[6], and to put it back soon after it runs out of battery. But still, I do not read if I have better alternatives[7].

02　Are books important and why?

真　题	题　型	年　份
One can learn about another person from the books and movies which that person likes.	独立写作题	2012/11/17
One can learn about another person from the books and movies which that person likes.	独立写作题	2013/11/17
Which of the following is the most effective way of learning：studying from textbooks，having discussions with a group or reading articles written by others?	口语第一题	2015/02/01
Among the following types of books, which do you dislike the most? Romantic books, science fiction, or biography?	口语第一题	2015/04/18
Students doing their own personal reading is as important as, or more important than reading assigned by teachers.	独立写作题	2016/03/11
A club at your school plans to help one of the following groups of people：1）teach pupils reading and math；2）build houses for those who cannot afford housing；3）take care of the elderly. Which do you think is the best plan?	独立写作题	2016/03/19

2.1　Yes

2.1.1　让我们更聪慧

❶ *The Girl on the Train* 英
国畅销小说:《火车上
的女孩》
❷ *Me Before You* 英国畅销
小说:《遇到你之前》
❸ 1984 英国左翼作家乔
治·奥威尔于 1949 年
出版的长篇政治小说

Books make us more intelligent. We can get in touch with new things that wouldn't be available otherwise. We can get to know modern cultures that are completely different from our own by reading bestsellers such as *The Girl on the Train*[1] or *Me Before You*[2]; we can get in touch with the past by reading George Orwell's famous novel *1984*[3]; we can dive into[4] an imaginary, magical world by reading *Harry Pottery*[5], *Game of Thrones*[6] and *Lord of the Rings*[7].

2.1.2 学习的手段和工具

Books are a valuable learning tool for individuals and academic institutions. Reading textbooks in school, for instance, allows students to develop a deeper understanding about knowledge. Reading books also enables students to sharpen and develop skills, such as critical thinking[8], communication, and phonetics[9]. Students can also use books as social tools to gain an understanding of and appreciation for people of other cultures, and may strengthen their skills in dealing with others, such as by listening and being sensitive to the unique perspectives and world views offered by others.

2.2 No

2.2.1 现在不再重要，因为有替代品

Books were important. There are just too many alternatives that we can use to replace the main functions of books. In the past, books gave us knowledge about the world around us, stimulated our imagination, told us our origin and history, and recorded precious knowledge by great men such as Aristotle, Plato and Confucius. But now all these things can be acquired by us in other forms such as documentaries, movies, simulations[10] on computers, and animation.

Well, my parents and teachers, especially my dad, have kept telling me the importance of reading. Whenever I encounter a problem[11], say, if I fail a writing test in Chinese, my father says, "Had you read more books in your spare time, you would have achieved a much higher score." Deep in my heart, I know that my father is right, but when it comes to the time for action, I always fail miserably[12]. One time he actually put a classic Chinese novel on my bedside table, *A Dream in the Red Mansions*[13], to lure[14] me to read. I actually did get curious at a time and started reading. I finished the first page, but never made it to the second. The words just make me want to sleep.

---

[4] dive into 投入
[5] *Harry Pottery*《哈利·波特》
[6] *Game of Thrones* 当红热播美剧:《权利的游戏》
[7] *Lord of the Rings*《指环王》
[8] critical thinking 批判性思维
[9] phonetics [fəu'netiks] n. 语音学
[10] simulation [ˌsimju'leiʃn] n. 模仿，模拟
[11] encounter a problem 遇到问题
[12] miserably ['mizərəbli] adv. 悲惨地
[13] *A Dream in the Red Mansions*《红楼梦》
[14] lure [luə] v. 引诱

03 What format of books do you like and why?

真　题	题　型	年　份
One can learn about another person from the books and movies which that person likes.	独立 写作题	2012/11/17
One can learn about another person from the books and movies which that person likes.	独立 写作题	2013/11/17
Among the following types of books, which do you dislike the most? Romantic books, science fiction, or biography?	口语 第一题	2015/04/18
Do you prefer to buy new books or used books?	口语 第二题	2016/11/13

3.1　纸质书

I like paper-based books best, simply because it feels great to hold a real book in my hands, and to read peacefully in bed with a lamp overhead, before going to sleep. Another reason which contributes to my preference for paper-based books is my OCD[1] for protecting my eyes.

❶ obsessive compulsive disorder 强迫症

3.2　音频书

I prefer to listen to audio books rather than to read paper-based books while driving because, well, although I'm an experienced driver, it's still too dangerous to read while driving. (smile)

3.3　电子书

The only time that I choose e-books is when I cannot find cheap paper-based books in bookstores. E-books tend to be cheaper than other formats.

I prefer e-books to other formats, since they are more convenient and cost much less. First, they are more convenient to purchase. Within a few clicks on the Kindle app, the purchase is completed without even the need to enter your credit card number, since it is already automatically recorded by the system. Second, e-books are more convenient to carry because all books can be stored in your mobile phone, kindle or computer. Last but not least, e-books save space. It saves us the trouble of purchasing a huge book shelf to store all our precious books.

04 What categories of books are there?

真 题	题 型	年 份
One can learn about another person from the books and movies which that person likes.	独立写作题	2012/11/17
One can learn about another person from the books and movies which that person likes.	独立写作题	2013/11/17
Among the following types of books, which do you dislike the most? Romantic books, science fiction, or biography?	口语第一题	2015/04/18

4.1 虚构类 Fiction

novel, short stories, thriller, psychological thriller, horror, fantasy, classics

4.2 非虚构类 Non-fiction

history, philosophy, psychology, biography, art, cookbooks, religion, self-help

05 What kind of books do you enjoy/hate reading the most?

真　题	题　型	年　份
One can learn about another person from the books and movies which that person likes.	独立写作题	2012/11/17
One can learn about another person from the books and movies which that person likes.	独立写作题	2013/11/17
Among the following types of books, which do you dislike the most? Romantic books, science fiction, or biography?	口语第一题	2015/04/18

5.1　喜欢的类型

5.1.1　科幻小说

My favorite is surely science fiction, mostly because it is the most intriguing[1]. I remember my first book was *The Martian*[2] by Andy Weir. It is famous and was nominated[3] as the best science fiction in 2013. It was later turned into a movie and was aired's[4] in 2015. The story depicts an astronaut[5] survival on Mars after an accident that has denied him the opportunity to return to Earth. The topic appeals to me, for my childhood dream was to become an astronomer.

5.1.2　惊悚小说

I enjoy reading thrillers[6], especially psychological thrillers[7], because they are extremely engaging. Kids today do not like to read for a reason, because there are way too many alternatives to relax, and to acquire information, such as television, the Internet, friends, and travel. So we need books that can firmly grab attention. Psychological thriller is exactly the genre[8] that we need. It has a nickname, which is "the page-turner", for the reason that people can not put the book down until they find out what happened to the protagonist[9]/leading character at last. Once, a friend of mine started reading *The Girl on the Train* during breakfast, which I recommended to her weeks ago. Because she was so engaged in the plot, she later called in to work sick, read the book straight for 10 hours and finished the whole book before going to sleep.

---

❶ intriguing [in'tri:giŋ]
　 adj. 有趣的
　 📖 interesting

❷ *The Martian* 《火星救援》

❸ nominate ['nɔmineit]
　 v. 提名

❹ air [ɛə] *v.* 播放，上映

❺ astronaut ['æstrənɔ:t]
　 n. 宇航员

❻ thriller ['θrilə] *n.* 惊悚小说

❼ psychological thriller
　 心理类惊悚小说

❽ genre [ʒɑ:ŋr] *n.* 体裁，类型

❾ protagonist
　 [prəu'tægənist] *n.* 主角

5.1.3　自传

I have a thing for reading biographies[10]. For me, reading biographies is the easiest way to figure out what to do with one's life. I used to be lost, vacillating[11] between college majors and later on career choices. Then, my father suggested that reading *Steve Jobs*[12] may help. So, I did. I learned from the book that Jobs was abandoned by his biological parents[13] at birth; that he was chosen and adopted by a great couple immediately after; and that his passion for making nicely designed products for the mass market came from his appreciation for the amazing design of his childhood house, which was "smart, cheap and good". During the process, I often paused and started thinking about my own past experiences, and how they had shaped my values. Later, midway through the book, I suddenly figured out that I want to become a _____. So later in life, whenever I become lost, I pick up a biography that I can relate to and start reading.

5.1.4　爱情小说

I prefer romance novels to all other genres[14]. I have never had a boyfriend/girlfriend before, because I am too shy to speak to the opposite sex. I know little about how they think and their opinions about matters. So I figured that reading romance novels might help, and it did. Many of my best friends are of the opposite sex now, as I have overcome my shyness by getting to know them through romance books. And I believe I will pretty soon have a boyfriend/girlfriend.

5.1.5　历史书

There will be a point when romance and thrillers can't satisfy our needs. That's when you move on to non-fiction, which typically has more depth. My favorite history book is *A Brief History of Humankind*[15] written by Yuval Noah Harari. He uses simple but colorful language to describe the entire history of mankind, all the way from the hunter-gatherer[16] period to modern society. The domains that are involved in the book include religion, empires, the origin of money, the scientific revolution, capitalism[17] and so on. This is a great book because it is both interesting and informative.

[10] biography [baiˈɔɡrəfi] *n.* 名人传记

[11] vacillate [ˈvæsileit] *v.* 摇摆

[12] *Steve Jobs*《乔布斯传》

[13] biological parents 亲生父母

[14] genre [ʒɑ:ŋr] *n.* 体裁，类别

[15] *A Brief History of Humankind*《人类简史》，以色列年轻作家尤瓦尔·赫拉利代表作

[16] hunter-gatherer 狩猎

[17] capitalism [ˈkæpitəlizəm] *n.* 资本主义

5.1.6 政治题材

My current favorite is George Orwell's *1984*, because it represents a landmark in my reading life. Unlike most bestsellers, *1984* involves intricate topics such as politics, class struggle between the top, middle, and bottom, as well as deep psychological issues such as brainwash and doublethink. It provoked my desire to read books with greater depth. Soon after I finished *1984*, I got interested in history and therefore purchased *A People's History of the United States*.

5.2 讨厌的类型

⑱ clichéd ['kliːˌfeid] *adj.* 俗套的

⑲ contrived [kən'traivd] *adj.* 很难相信的

I hate romance novels because they all use the same clichéd[18] plot. The heroine is always beautiful and sexy. The hero is always well-muscled, handsome and smart. There are always some weird contrived[19] reasons for the hero and heroine to meet. And when they meet, in 99% of the stories, the hero doesn't like the heroine for some reason, usually due to a misunderstanding. I also hate the contrived crisis, such as a hurricane, leaky boats, or broken-down cars that bring the hero and heroine together. And I hate how they always end happily ever after. Can't one of them just end in tragedy and separation? Today's romantic books are just boring and predictable.

06 What differences are there between books today and those in the past?

真 题	题 型	年 份
One can learn about another person from the books and movies which that person likes.	独立写作题	2012/11/17
One can learn about another person from the books and movies which that person likes.	独立写作题	2013/11/17
Among the following types of books, which do you dislike the most? Romantic books, science fiction, or biography?	口语第一题	2015/04/18

6.1　现代书节奏更快

Well, books today generally are fast-paced and more absorbing. The difference is obvious when you compare a classic such as *Wuthering Heights*[1] with a modern, psychological thriller such as *Gone Girl*[2]. It's not hard to notice that most classics are filled with exhaustive[3] depictions of scenery, weather or the appearance of buildings; whereas modern novels focus more on the progression of the plot, the portrayal of main characters' mental processes, subtle movements in facial expression, as well as the change of one's tone.

❶ *Wuthering Heights*《呼啸山庄》
❷ *Gone Girl*《消失的爱人》
❸ exhaustive [ɡ'zɔːstiv] *adj.* 全面的

6.2　经典书籍文法更讲究

Books written in the past tend to use more difficult vocabulary, and surely have better syntactic variety[4], whereas most modern books use slang[5] to grab attention and to satisfy the need for less "well-educated" modern people.

❹ syntactic variety 句法多样性
❺ slang [slæŋ] *n.* 俚语

07　Are those changes good and why?

7.1　Yes

7.1.1　省时间

Yes. I'm so pleased to see these changes because they save me the time to manually skip all the lengthy description of trivialities[1] such as the weather, the exterior of a wagon for a noble lady, or the costly furniture in an aristocrat's[2] house. Now I can quickly read through the book and find out what happened to the guy who cheated on his wife.

❶ triviality [ˌtrivi'æləti] *n.* 琐事

❷ aristocrat ['æristəkræt] *n.* 贵族

7.2 No

7.2.1 应该细细品味经典

No. We shouldn't turn everything into a fast-food model. Reading should be an enjoyment rather than a mission to be accomplished. A lot of people now read so that they can show off their "achievements": "I have read more than 50 books this year". But they never mention that 40 of them are gossip magazines or textbooks.

08 Who is your favorite author and why?

真 题	题 型	年 份
One can learn about another person from the books and movies which that person likes.	独立 写作题	2012/11/17
One can learn about another person from the books and movies which that person likes.	独立 写作题	2013/11/17
Which of the following is the most effective way of learning: studying from textbooks, having discussions with a group or reading articles written by others?	口语 第一题	2015/02/01
Among the following types of books, which do you dislike the most? Romantic books, science fiction, or biography?	口语 第一题	2015/04/18
Students doing their own personal reading is as important as, or more important than reading assigned by teachers.	独立 写作题	2016/03/11
A club at your school plans to help one of the following groups of people: 1) teach pupils reading and math; 2) build houses for those who cannot afford housing; 3) take care of the elderly. Which do you think is the best plan?	独立 写作题	2016/03/19
Do you prefer to buy new books or used books?	口语 第二题	2016/11/13

8.1 简·奥斯丁

My favorite author is of course Jane Austen, because I love her work *Pride and Prejudice*[1]. I usually prefer English writers to American writers. English writers use more complex vocabulary and syntax[2], which makes reading an absolute enjoyment. American writers, on the other hand, tend to grab attention with more interesting plots. But I digress, back to Austen. She is the best of the best. A single sentence in her novel can easily surpass[3] the length of half a page. Nevertheless, I never feel too tired to read these long and complex sentences, although sometimes I do have to stop to interpret the deeper meaning she tried to express. And the control she had over the progression of the story, the keen observations she made in life, and her unique interpretation of love all made her works perfect. She is definitely my favorite author.

8.2 托尔斯泰

My favorite author is Leo Tolstoy, because I love his work *War and Peace*[4]. I just started reading it recently and I am currently on Chapter 5, and I am totally absorbed by the amazing portrayal of scenes of domesticity[5] and the intriguing dialogues between members of the Great Houses. Tolstoy provides us with great opportunities to get to know the mental activities of others, which under normal circumstances, are completely invisible to us. We can also learn how to wittily[6] deal with tough[7] interpersonal matters. I'm sure I will improve my people skills after reading his great work.

8.3 刘慈欣

My favorite author is definitely Cixin Liu. His science fiction *The Three Body Problem* has been highly regarded since its publication in 2006. The book was later translated into English in 2014, and immediately after that, won the Hugo Award for Best Novel in 2015, and was nominated for the 2014 Nebula Award for Best Novel. I began to read his book recently because of President Obama's recommendation, and it surely did not disappoint me. Liu can write astrophysics[8] in a plain and simple way that also engages readers. The novel also touches many subjects, and the

[1] *Pride and Prejudice*《傲慢与偏见》

[2] syntax ['sintæks] *n.* 句法

[3] surpass [sə'pɑːs] *v.* 超过

[4] *War and Peace*《战争与和平》

[5] domesticity [,dəume'stisəti] *n.* 家庭生活

[6] wittily ['witəli] *adv.* 机智地

[7] interpersonal [,intə'pəːsənl] *adj.* 人际的

[8] astrophysics [æstrəu'fiziks] *n.* 天体物理学

one that impressed me the most is Liu's interpretation of creating characters in novels. According to him, the characters that authors create should have their own thoughts, rather than being controlled by the author like puppets. In other words, the characters should become alive at a certain point during the stage of composition. He also thinks that only a true master of art can create live characters like this. This perspective really astonished me. I guess this is the reason why Liu is my favorite author.

8.4　冯唐

⑨ *I liked a Girl at 18*
《十八岁给我一个
姑娘》

Feng Tang is my all-time favorite writer. What really speaks to me is his semi-autobiographical novel *I liked a Girl at 18* [9]. It talks about youth and growth. It talks about all my fantasies when I was that age. That's also the reason why it is popular with young adult readers. As a writer, his life is quite unique. He studied medicine at Peking University, with a degree in business, and was a former consultant for McKinsey & Co. He was also the strategic director of the biggest medical resources holding company in China. With so many titles and so many industries, he still had the talent, and most importantly, the time to write high quality books. That is also the reason why I favor him so much.

09 Do you enjoy writing and why?

真　题	题　型	年　份
One can learn about another person from the books and movies which that person likes.	独立写作题	2012/11/17
One can learn about another person from the books and movies which that person likes.	独立写作题	2013/11/17
Which of the following is the most effective way of learning: studying from textbooks, having discussion with a group or reading articles written by others?	口语第一题	2015/02/01

（续）

真　题	题　型	年　份
Among the following types of books, which do you dislike the most? Romantic books, science fiction, or biography?	口语 第一题	2015/04/18
Students doing their own personal reading is as important as, or more important than reading assigned by teachers.	独立 写作题	2016/03/11
A club at your school plans to help one of the following groups of people：1) teach pupils reading and math；2) build houses for those who cannot afford housing；3) take care of the elderly. Which do you think is the best plan?	独立 写作题	2016/03/19
Do you prefer to buy new books or used books?	口语 第二题	2016/11/13

9.1　Yes

9.1.1　阅读刺激写作欲望

Yes, I do. Ever since I began to read in large numbers, my interest in writing has increased proportionally[1]. When I see a graceful sentence, idiomatic[2] expressions, and unfamiliar syntax[3], I have this desire inside me that motivates me to study them, do research, and use them like the authors who had used them in their beautiful compositions.

❶ proportionally [prə'pɔːʃənli] *adv.* 成比例地

❷ idiomatic [,idiə'mætik] *adj.* 地道的

❸ syntax ['sintæks] *n.* 句法

9.1.2　天生就爱写

Yes. It's in my blood. My deep passion for writing began to blossom when I was a 4-year-old boy. My mom worked at the library and brought home books for me to read all the time. It wasn't long before I had stories of my own to tell. Now, at 28, stories run through my head like symphonies[4], all competing for the honor of being the next one to be put on paper or screen. Writing is such an integral part of who I am, that I can't ever imagine not writing. Writing infuses my life with so much joy. It's the one thing in life I know I can do well.

❹ symphony ['simfəni] *n.* 交响乐

9.2 No

怎么写都写不好

No, I hate writing. I have never been good at writing, neither in English nor in my mother tongue[5]: Chinese. I am good at math, though. It feels like I have a clear logic in my head, but when I try to turn it into words on a computer screen or paper, there are always just too many things that I want to express, and I have no idea what to say first. Another thing that always bothers me is that I don't know how much detail I should put into my writing. Although my writing teacher told us that we should put as much detail into our writing as possible, I'm often worried that too much detail would slow down the overall progression of my story. They say practice makes perfect, but I guess I just don't have enough motivation to get better at writing.

⑤ mother tongue *n.* 母语

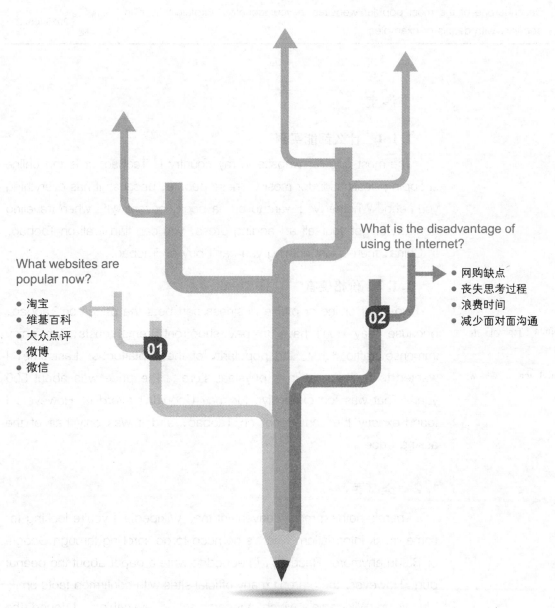

What websites are
popular now?

- 淘宝
- 维基百科
- 大众点评
- 微博
- 微信

01

What is the disadvantage of
using the Internet?

02

- 网购缺点
- 丧失思考过程
- 浪费时间
- 减少面对面沟通

网络

01 What websites are popular now?

真　题	题　型	年　份
Describe one of the most popular websites in your country. Explain why it is popular, with details or examples.	口语 第一题	2015/06/27

1.1　淘宝

1.1.1　什么都能买到

The most popular website in my country is Taobao. It is the online shopping destination for most Chinese people, because it has everything you need. Whether you want to buy a book, or rent WIFI when traveling abroad, or get yourself a wedding dress, you can find it all on Taobao. In China, there's just nothing you can't buy on Taobao.

1.1.2　价格便宜

No other online or offline business can beat the prices on Taobao, because they don't have to pay shopfront[1] rental costs, yet enjoy immense traffic due to the popularity of these platforms. Last time, I wanted to buy a coat in a physical store[2]. The price was about 500 yuan. That was too expensive for me. I couldn't afford it. However, I found exactly the same coat on Taobao, and it was only half of the asking price.

❶ shopfront ['ʃɒpfrʌnt] *n.* 店面

❷ physical store *n.* 实体店

1.2　维基百科

There's nothing more convenient than Wikipedia if you're looking for some quick information. There's no need to go scrolling through Google or Baidu anymore. Recently, I needed to write a paper about the peanut bug. However, there aren't many official sites with confirmed facts on it. Thanks to Wikipedia, which has articles on everything, I found the information I needed in a concise and easy way. The best thing is that there are references on the bottom of the page linked to Wikipedia, so I can have a deeper understanding of related issues and topics.

1.3 大众点评

Dazhongdianping is a very famous website in China. The site is like word-of-mouth[3] for the digital world. You can easily search for nearby restaurants, read plenty of reviews, and even view great local deals and photos of places. Last year, I moved to a new city, Chengdu. I knew nobody there, so Dazhongdianping became one of my most valuable resources. I remember, once I wanted to find a restaurant that makes the best cheesecake, so I used Dazhongdianping to help me narrow things down[4] according to distance, price and rating. And I found the best cheesecake ever! It was incredibly creamy[5] and rich! So, you see it's just so easy to find hot places to go by using the app.

Dazhongdianping is my best friend, because I never have an absolute idea about what to eat for lunch or dinner. That's when I pull out my cell phone, open the Dazhongdianping app, and let it recommend restaurants for me. It is also a great way for foodies[6] to find new delicious restaurants, since users can simply browse through the pictures of the ones that they are interested in. With the detailed reviews of other foodies, users can decide in seconds if that particular restaurant is worth going to. .

1.4 微博

1.4.1 了解时事

I love using Weibo very much, which is a Chinese microblogging website. For me, it's a great place to catch up on the latest news. For example, last winter, I followed @ Beijingnews as a snowstorm raged on. I saw pictures, read first-hand[7] information about conditions, and learned when it was safe to go out.

1.4.2 关注名人

I like Weibo, because I can use if to follow the people I like. presidential candidates[8], celebrities, artists, leaders and other prominent figures are very active on Weibo, and many of them engage with their followers on a regular basis. My favorite singer is Taylor Swift. I follow her on Weibo, and I very much enjoy reading her posts and seeing pictures of her daily life.

③ word-of-mouth [wə:d-əv-mauθ] adj. 口头传达的

④ narrow down 缩小，减少

⑤ creamy ['kri: mi] adj. 奶油般柔滑的

⑥ foodie [fu:di] n. 吃货，美食家

⑦ first-hand [fə:st-'hænd] adj. 第一手的

⑧ presidential candidates 总统候选人

1.5　微信

1.5.1　聊天

I think chatting on WeChat with friends has become an essential thing for of every youth in China. I chat with my family, friends, boyfriend/girlfriend on WeChat. When I feel bored, I scroll[9] through my contact list and see who I want to talk to. Sometimes I would ask my friends out through WeChat, and it's just so convenient. If you are a lazy person like me, you will love WeChat, since you can just press and hold the "talk" button and talk directly into your phone. You can just say bye-bye to typing. And your friends can listen to the audio message anytime they want. They can also replay the audio as many times as they like.

1.5.2　朋友圈

WeChat Moments is a great way to check the recent status' of friends. Most of my classmates are busy studying and preparing for tests, doing research and experiments, and thus have no time to catch up with old friends by telephone. Moments provides busy people with an easy way to connect with others. I have this habit of opening up WeChat Moments every night before sleep, and browsing through[10] the events that my friends posted. I can comment, give them a thumbs up, or just click their icon and start to chat with them individually. This is the perfect solution for busy people nowadays.

9 scroll [skrəʊl] *v.* 滚动

10 browse through 浏览，翻阅

02　What is the disadvantage of using the Internet?

真　题	题　型	年　份
Talk about the advantages of online shopping. Give examples and details in your response.	口语第一题	2013/11/23
Nowadays, students do many things like surfing the Internet and listening to music when they are learning. Do you agree or disagree that doing other things has a bad effect on learning?	独立写作题	2015/09/19

2.1　网购缺点

2.1.1　无法看到实物

I usually shop online, which saves me a lot of time, but the disadvantage is that I can't try items on to decide whether to buy them, and there is a chance that the clothes might not fit. Last time, I saw a model wearing a long coat on a magazine cover. She looked so cool in the coat that I bought the same one on the website. However, the coat turned out to be a disaster for me. I am just too short for it. Also, I don't have the opportunity to touch and feel items I am considering purchasing. However, with clothing, bedding[1], pillows, furniture, rugs[2] and other textile[3]-based merchandise[4], it can be hard to gauge[5] quality without hands-on contact.

2.1.2　运费增加成本

There are hidden costs[6] of online shopping, such as shipping charges. You'll get that product delivered to your home, but you might end up paying more for the shipping than the product's cost. Trust me. I hardly ever use my Coach Tote Bag, which I ordered online. The bag itself was about $100, but shipping and customs[7] costs I paid made the bag more than $200. Also, if you don't like the item you have purchased, returning it for a refund[8] can be costly too. Most online retailers[9] do not refund shipping costs. So, it often costs you more money than you planned to spend if you need to exchange an item.

2.2　丧失思考过程

The Internet is both a blessing and a curse[10]. It's certainly convenient to have the sum of all knowledge at our fingertips[11]. The problem is that when it comes to research, we seldom question the credibility[12] of the site or the information on the website. All we need to do is type a question[13] in the search bar[14], hit Enter and read the first link that appears. For today's students, doing research has shifted[15] from a relatively slow process of intellectual[16] curiosity and discovery to a fast-paced, short-term exercise aimed at locating just enough information to complete an assignment. For instance, many students use Wikipedia as

---

① bedding ['bediŋ] *n.* 床上用品

② rug [rʌg] *n.* 小块地毯

③ textile ['tekstail] *n.* 纺织品

④ merchandise ['mə:tʃəndaiz] *n.* 商品

⑤ gauge [geidʒ] *v.* 判定

⑥ hidden cost 隐藏成本

⑦ customs ['kʌstəms] *n.* 海关

⑧ refund [ri:'fʌnd] *n.* 退款

⑨ retailer [ri:'teilə] *n.* 零售商

⑩ a blessing and a curse 是福亦是祸

⑪ at our fingertips 唾手可得的

⑫ credibility [,kredi'biləti] *n.* 可靠性，可信性

⑬ all we need to do is do something

⑭ search bar 搜索栏

⑮ shift [ʃift] *v.* 转变，转换

⑯ intellectual [,intə'lektʃuəl] *adj.* 智力的

⑰ suspect [sə'spekt] *adj.*
不可信的，可疑的

⑱ biased ['baɪəst] *adj.* 有
偏见的，偏向性的

⑲ mindset ['maindset] *n.*
思维模式

⑳ critical thinking 批判性
思维

㉑ browse [brauz] *v.* 翻
阅，浏览

㉒ Mother Nature 大自然

a reference resource, and it can be a very good starting point for beginning a search on any given topic. Unfortunately, the fact that anyone can edit the encyclopedia leaves the data suspect[17]. Students may be reading information that is outdated or even incorrect, posted by someone who is not an expert in the field or by someone who is biased[18]. So, we need the mindset[19] of critical thinking[20] on identifying proper sources when we are using the Internet.

2.3 浪费时间

Social media can be a great tool for finding information and working together, but it can also be incredibly distracting. It's easy to lose hours browsing[21] through photos, tweets, and videos, which may reduce the amount of time spent on educational tasks. Last time, I was supposed to use the Internet to search for some resources for my midterm paper, but I somehow started checking my email and found out there would a big sale at Walmart next Monday. Then I began reading through Facebook posts and made some comments on my friends' newly posted pictures. I didn't realize how quickly hours went by. And due to the Internet, I wasted at least two hours without doing anything related to my paper. It's just so hard to resist those temptations, especially when they are only a click away on the desktop.

2.4 减少面对面沟通

People are social animals, and we need real communications with others. However, since the advent of the Internet, people have started to connect online, without the real interactions, such as the exchange of eye contact, and bodily contact like hugs, hand shake, or high-fives. My point is, there are things that can not be replaced by the pure text, audio, or video communication on the Internet. We have to go out more, and enjoy the real accompaniment of friends, families, and Mother Nature[22].

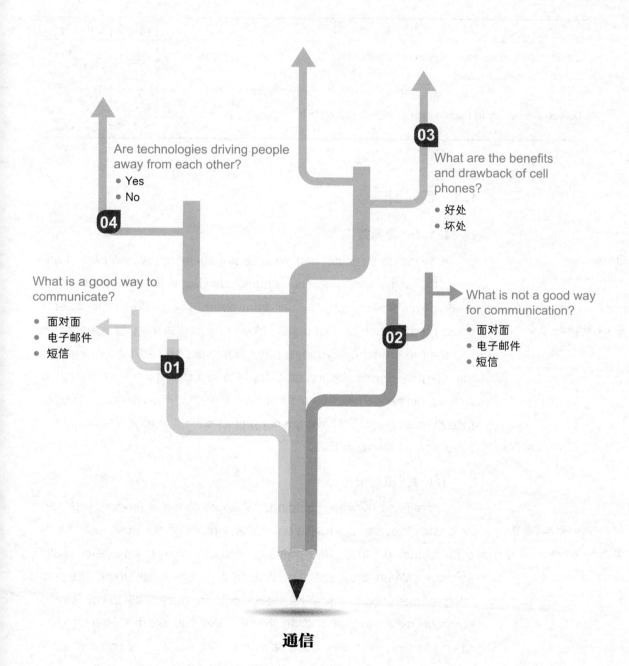

Are technologies driving people away from each other?
- Yes
- No

04

What are the benefits and drawback of cell phones?
- 好处
- 坏处

03

What is a good way to communicate?
- 面对面
- 电子邮件
- 短信

01

What is not a good way for communication?
- 面对面
- 电子邮件
- 短信

02

通信

01 What is a good way to communicate?
(face to face, emails, text messages)

真　题	题　型	年　份
Classmates and partners can work together face to face to finish projects better than by sending e-mails.	独立写作题	2015/01/25
Do you like talking to people face to face, sending text messages, or by emails?	口语第一题	2015/04/18

1.1　面对面

1.1.1　提高效率

It drives participation and ensures engagement[1]. When people are all in the same room, it encourages everybody to participate. Last week, I was waiting for an email from one of my group members so I could get our math project done[2]. You know, I was the group leader so I needed to collect everybody's part. However, he had totally forgotten that our project was due the next day. He told me he went out shopping with his girlfriend. I was so mad at him. If we had discussed our project face to face, we could have got our project done that day. We would not have wasted so much time.

1.1.2　没有误会

There is no misunderstanding. When someone is reading your text or emails, they can't perceive emotional expression like postures[3], facial expressions[4] or tone from those words. Some people are really sensitive. When they see the words, they are much more likely to interpret them negatively. By just texting "I am busy. Talk to you later", someone may interpret that incorrectly, like you are not interested in talking to him, and may become upset. But the truth is you are really busy with all the projects that are due tomorrow.

❶ engagement [in'geidʒmənt] n. 诺言

❷ get something done 把……完成

❸ body posture 肢体语言
❹ facial expression 面部表情

1.2　电子邮件

1.2.1　帮助回忆

You can go back and review. It is extremely frustrating when you just walk out the door and can't recall the conversation. Email, on the other hand, has the advantage of being permanent. It can be reviewed or used to refresh your memory. I attended a conference[5] last week. And I just couldn't concentrate on it, because my girlfriend had broken up with me that day. I was so sad. The worse thing was that I had to do a project my boss assigned to me during the conference. I had no clue what he mentioned in the conference. Luckily, he sent a meeting recap[10] to everybody via email later that day. So, I was able to pull it up and read it. After several minutes of reading, I knew everything about the project.

1.2.2　效率高

If I am the leader of a team project, I add my team members' email addresses ahead of time. So, when I have to set up a meeting or discussion, all I need to do is open my outlook, set up an invitation and send it out. It only takes a few seconds to keep everyone informed. However, if I call each member of my team by phone, there is always someone who doesn't pick it up. Even if I can use my cell phone to reach everyone, it will take too much time. Plus, it will be a nightmare if the meeting gets cancelled or the time changes. That means I have to call everyone again. But with email, all I have to do is send out another one and everybody will know it in a very short time.

1.3　短信

1.3.1　快速并且有时间考虑

I can't argue with the fact that emails get opened way less than text messages, because email is more likely to hit the spam[7] folder before anyone even sees it. If what you are communicating is time-sensitive[8], then you want to be sure your audience gets the message. It is awkward when you can't give an affirmative[9] response while someone else was waiting for you on the other end of the line. However, text messages give you enough attention to notice and still take your time to think and respond.

⑤ conference ['kɔnfərəns] *n.* 会议

⑥ recap ['ri:kæp] *n.* 扼要重述

⑦ spam [spæm] *n.* 垃圾邮件

⑧ time-sensitive 时效性

⑨ affirmative [ə'fə:mətiv] *adj.* 肯定的

1.3.2　记录

The same goes for situations in which you cannot get access to a pen or paper and you need to jot down[10] important information. You can enter the information into a text message, and then either send it to yourself or save it in the "draft folder"[11] on your phone. The information can be stored there forever and be pulled out at any moment you want in the future.

1.3.3　避免尴尬

It comes in handy when face to face communication or phone conversation is inappropriate[12]. Last time, my colleague was reporting to our boss at a meeting and he was missing some points. Of course, I couldn't say anything to interrupt the conversation or call him in the middle of the meeting. So, I sent him a text message. He felt the vibration[13] and he peeked at[14] his cell phone screen. Then he saw the message and he added these missing points later in the report. Thanks to these points, our boss said my colleague did a pretty good job.

⑩ jot down 草草记下

⑪ draft folder 草稿箱

⑫ inappropriate [ˌinəˈprəupriət] *adj.* 不适当的

⑬ vibration [vaiˈbreiʃn] *n.* 震动

⑭ peek at 偷看

02　What is not a good way for communication? (face to face, emails, text messages)

2.1　面对面

2.1.1　效率低

It will kill productivity[15] and work flow, because face to face conversations can often lead to many distractions. Last weekend, my team members and I had a discussion about a biology assignment. We were struggling with a team presentation and trying to figure out how to start. After three minutes discussing the solutions, one of the team members started to talk about a ball game, and everybody was excited and started to share their thoughts on that game. It took us 2 hours to finally realize the topic was off track[16]. Even though we tried to stick with the assignment, nobody could concentrate on it, because we were still

⑮ productivity [ˌprɔdʌkˈtivəti] *adj.* 生产力

⑯ off track 偏离轨道

thinking about that game. By the end of that day, we didn't finish the assignment, as we wasted too much time. It was really disappointing.

2.1.2　表情丰富，容易看穿

I actually like text messages and emails better, and the reason is quite simple: my facial expressions expose too much information, which could lead to serious problems. For example, once my girlfriend asked me, if she and my mom fell into the ocean at the same time, who would I rescue[17] first? I was surprised by the sudden interrogation[18]. I paused for a second, and told her that of course I would rescue her first. However, she didn't buy it at all. According to her, I did not look at her confidently and directly, and because my cheeks turned red. Had she asked me the same question through email, I would have answered perfectly.

⓱ rescue ['reskju:] v. 营救

⓲ interrogation
[in,terə'geiʃn] n. 审问，盘问

2.2　电子邮件

没效率

Sometimes, sending emails is not efficient. Last month, I sent an email to invite all my friends to come to my birthday party. But only three people showed up[19] that day. I was really disappointed, because I thought my friend were willing to come. A couple of days later, my friends called me and said, they just saw the email and asked me why I sent an email instead of calling them. They were really sorry for not coming to my birthday party. Then I realize people don't check their emails often. Since then I always use cell phone instead of emails to communicate with my friends. It's more direct and efficient.

⓳ show up 出现

2.3　短信

引起误解

There could be some misunderstandings when we communicate via text. When someone is reading your text, they can't receive emotional expressions like postures[20], facial expressions, [21]or tone from those words. Some people are really sensitive. When they see the words, they are much more likely to interpret them negatively. By just texting "I am busy. Talk to you later", someone may interpret it incorrectly, like you are not interested in talking to him, and become upset. But the truth is you are really busy with all the projects that are due tomorrow.

⓴ body posture 肢体语言

㉑ facial expression 面部表情

03 What are the benefits and drawback of cell phones?

真 题	题 型	年 份
Do you agree or disagree with the following statement: cell phones have improved our life?	口语 第二题	2015/03/07

3.1 好处

3.1.1 效率高

Cell phones allow you to reach out to others instantly. Sometimes, sending emails is not efficient. Last month, I sent an email to invite all my friends to come to my birthday party. But only three people showed up that day. I was really disappointed, because I thought my friends were willing to come. A couple of days later, my friends called me and said, they had just seen the email, and asked me why I sent an email instead of calling them. They were really sorry for not coming to my birthday party. Then I realized people don't check their emails as often. Since then I always use my cell phone instead of emails to communicate with my friends. It's more direct and efficient.

3.1.2 拉近距离

Cell phones have kept us wonderfully close together. We can talk to our friends and families anytime to find out how they are doing. We can share joy with our loved ones on special occasions, even from great distances via video chat, as if they are in the same room. We can make funny faces for our kids when we can't be there with them, so they will feel warm.

3.1.3 安全

Cell phones can keep us safe. Walking home alone at night seems less creepy if we have a cellphone in our hand. When you feel unsafe, you can pick up the phone and call for help. Emergency numbers can be preprogrammed into your phone to make it just one number away. Whenever you feel afraid walking alone at night, you can hold your cell phone up to your ear and talk as if there's someone listening on the other end. It really helps.

3.1.4　方便

With all these powerful apps with fancy features, everyone can use cell phones to better their lives. If you are tired of driving yourself to work in the early morning, you can use your cell phone to open Uber and let it find a driver to pick you up. If you are hungry and don't want to walk all the way to a restaurant, a takeout app[1] is a better option. Just order everything you want on your cell phone, and you can continue doing your work. The app will take care of the rest. After 10 minutes, you will be notified that your order is on the way. If you want to confirm some facts but can't find the references, all you need to do is pull out your cell phone and google it. The answer will appear in a second.

❶ takeout app 外卖网站

3.2　坏处

3.2.1　不安全

Everybody knows automobiles and cell phones don't mix[2]. Yet, still lots of people keep using their phones while driving, using the "It is an emergency; I need to take this call" excuse. It doesn't matter if it is hands-free or not. When you pick up a call while you are driving, you are distracted. It will slow or sometimes mislead your decision making, which is extremely dangerous on the road. When you are supposed to hit the brakes at the traffic light but you don't, because you are on your phone. You know what happens next.

❷ mix [miks] v. 相容

3.2.2　拉远距离

Most of us are no strangers to a scenario of a group of friends sitting down to a meal together, laughing, swapping[3] stories, and catching up on the news. However, they are busy with their "friends" on their Facebook or Instagram, not the real people in front of them. Sure, everybody has to use their cell phone once or twice at the table, like looking up movie times, checking e-mails, showing off photos, or taking a call or two. But when people do this all the time in front of others, especially their families, it really kills conversations and hurts people's feelings.

❸ swap [swɔp] v. 交换

04 Are technologies driving people away from each other?

真　题	题　型	年　份
Do you agree or disagree with the following statement: technological devices have brought distance between people? Please use details and examples in your response.	口语 第二题	2015/10/25

4.1　Yes

❶ scenario [siˈnɑːriəu] *n.* 情景

❷ swap [swɔp] *v.* 交换

Most of us are no strangers to a scenario[1] of a group of friends sitting down to a meal together, laughing, swapping[2] stories, and catching up on the news, but not necessarily with other people in front of them. Sure, everybody has to use their cell phone once or twice at the table, like looking up movie times, checking e-mails, showing off photos, or taking a call or two. But, when people do this all the time in front of others, especially families, it really kills conversations and hurts people's feelings. I am pretty sure these people will not get invited to their friend or family dinners in the future.

4.2　No

❸ obstacle [ˈɔbstəkl] *n.* 障碍

With the invention of mobile phones, laptops and tablets, people can communicate and keep in contact with each other without any obstacles[3]. When I was working in the U. S. , every time I got back from my long working shift, I would video chat with my Mum and Dad. I could see their lovely faces, hear my Mum's stories, like what an amazing deal she got in the shopping mall, and laugh at my Dad's cooking skills. With all the live images and emotions behind the sounds, even when I can't be at home, I still feel warm and less lonely. And I believe my families feel the same way.

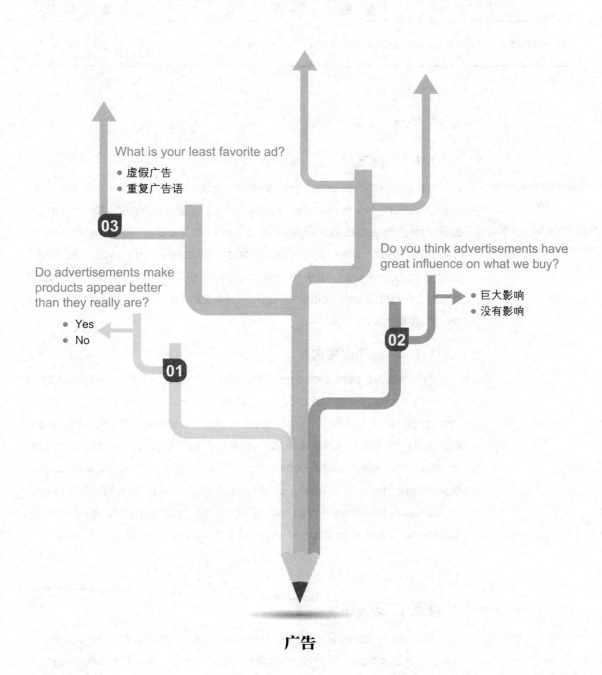

What is your least favorite ad?
- 虚假广告
- 重复广告语

03

Do you think advertisements have great influence on what we buy?
- 巨大影响
- 没有影响

02

Do advertisements make products appear better than they really are?
- Yes
- No

01

广告

01 Do advertisements make products appear better than they really are?

真 题	题 型	年 份
Advertisements make products appear better than they really are.	独立写作题	2015/03/28

1.1 Yes

1.1.1 海飞丝

❶ exaggerate [ig'zædʒəreit] v. 夸张，夸大

❷ Head & Shoulders 海飞丝

❸ dandruff ['dændrʌf] n. 头皮屑

It's perfectly natural for shampoo commercials to exaggerate[1] their effects. For example, the selling points and slogan for Head & Shoulders[2] is anti-dandruff and oil-control. In the ad, a man with tons of dandruff tried the shampoo, and somehow all the dandruff[3] disappeared. I was very troubled by dandruff in middle school, so I gladly bought a big bottle of Head & Shoulders, but it did not work at all. I felt like a fool.

1.1.2 康师傅牛肉面

❹ instant noodles 方便面

Ads always disappoint me. The real product is never as good as it appears on TV. For example, I once was naively excited by the amazing tasty videos of Master Kong's instant beef noddles[4]. In the ad, there was tons of beef, and like five different kinds of vegetables, not to mention the killer juicy seasoning. So I rushed to the small shop downstairs, bought a boxful of Master Kong's instant beef noddles, just to find out that there was no beef at all, no vegetables, no juicy seasoning[5], but only a small pack of salt and pepper.

❺ seasoning ['si:zəniŋ] n. 调味品

1.2 No

1.2.1 农夫山泉

❻ merit ['merit] n. 优点

❼ slogan ['sləʊgən] n. 广告语

Not every ad exaggerates the merits[6] of its products. For example, the famous slogan[7] for Nongfu Spring water is：A little sweetness in Nongfu Spring Water. Indeed, when I tried it for the first time, it was sweet. And it has been sweet all these years without any change. It has become my favorite brand of bottled water ever since. If you compare it with Wahaha[8] or Yibao[9], you will notice that the latter two brands all have this subtle bitter taste, which I do not enjoy at all. So this is one of the ads that do not attempt to beautify the product.

1.2.2 宝矿力

Most people wouldn't believe it, but there indeed are some ads that decrease the sales volume of their product. For example, I once saw an ad for POCARI Sweat[10] on a double-decker bus[11]. I was just about to cross the street on foot, and I saw the slogan, painted markedly on the body of the bus. It goes, "Different from the taste of sweat?" and I was like, "what the hell is it trying to express?" I was thinking, of course, the taste of my favorite sports beverage should taste different than that of real human sweat, and the next time when I was about to drink POCARI after a badminton match, I inevitably recalled this slogan, which made me feel that I was about to drink a whole bottle of human sweat. I had stopped drinking the brand for like two months, until I made myself forget about this horrible slogan.

1.2.3 脑白金

If there is a poll for Chinese to vote for their least favorite ad, I bet the ad for Melatonin would win. It's not that the ad sucked. It was OK. But the problem is, the company ran its ad too frequently, to the point that people started to feel sick. The ad was aired, if I remember correctly, about 10 years ago, when I was in middle school. We were asked to watch CCTV news every night at 7:00 p. m. , and the ad was placed right before the news started. So, in other words, we were forced to listen to the repetitive and invariable ad for years to come. Most adults have the habit of watching news to keep up with current events. In a way, they are forced to watch the ad as well. The result is, of course, aesthetic fatigue[12]. When people are overexposed to something, they will hate it eventually. I guess I will never buy Melatonin for the seniors in my family, just because of this terrible ad.

⑧ Wahaha 娃哈哈矿泉水
⑨ Yibao 怡宝矿泉水

⑩ POCARI Sweat 运动饮料品牌，宝矿力水特
⑪ double-decker bus 双层巴士

⑫ aesthetic fatigue 审美疲劳

第九类 广告

02 Do you think advertisements have great influence on what we buy?

真 题	题 型	年 份
Do you agree that advertisements have a great influence on what we buy?	口语 第一题	2016/07/10

2.1 巨大影响

2.1.1 激发情感

Advertisements have great influence on what people buy, because they somehow convince us that we can fulfill our desires if we merely buy a product. For example, Dior's commercials are not about the introduction of their products. They are more like dramas about handsome guys and beautiful women wearing those clothes and bags. They tell nothing about the bag being sold, which is not worth about $2,000 at all, but they tell everything about the fancies and dreams of those who might buy them. And every time I watch this commercial, I want to buy that bag the woman is carrying. And I wish to be as beautiful as the woman in the ad. I feel I would be so confident walking with a Dior bag.

2.1.2 名人效应

Usually, people are more likely to accept an advertising claim made by somebody famous, a person we admire and find appealing. We tend to think they are trustworthy. You might have a car commercial that features[1] a well-known race car driver. Now it may not be a very fast car. It could even be an inexpensive vehicle[2] with a low performance rating, but if a popular race car driver is shown driving it, and saying "I like my cars fast", then people will believe the car is impressive for its speed.

2.2 没有影响

I am totally immune to advertising, because it is deceptive[3]. I once watched a car commercial, which referred to its roomy cars over and over again. There was a guy who kept stopping and picking up different people.

---

① feature ['fiːtʃə] *v.* 以……为特点

② vehicle ['viːikl] *n.* 车辆

③ deceptive [di'septiv] *adj.* 导致误解的，欺骗性的

He picked up three or four people, and each time the narrator[4] said, "plenty of room for friends, plenty of room for families, plenty of room for everybody". The same message was repeated several times in the course of[5] the commercial. People get the sense that it's a spacious[6] car, but the reality is that it's a very small car. So, you see, most advertisements are not trying to help people make better decisions. They're usually trying to harvest their money more efficiently by engaging them emotionally. I don't watch advertisements at all.

④ narrator [nə'reitər] *n.* 叙述者

⑤ in the course of 在······期间

⑥ spacious ['speiʃəs] *adj.* 空间宽敞的

03　What is your least favorite ad?

3.1　虚假广告

I don't like any advertisement related to instant noodles[1] because it makes its products seem much better than they truly are. Usually, in an instant noodles commercial, there is a guy who is enjoying his delicious noodles, with lots of toppings, such as pork, shrimp, and lobster. It just seems so divine. What makes me feel angry is that, there is no meat at all in the instant noodles I buy in the supermarket. The "Chicken" flavor only includes chicken fat or powder[2], the "Beef" flavor includes beef fat and the "Shrimp" flavor includes shrimp powder. It just makes me feel indignant[3] as a consumer. Why can't the commercial just tell the truth?

❶ instant noodles 方便面

❷ powder ['paudə] *n.* 粉末

❸ indignant [in'dignənt] *adj.* 愤怒的

3.2　重复广告语

I hate advertisements that use repetition as a strategy. I once watched a car commercial, which referred to its roomy cars over and over again. There was a guy who kept stopping and picking up different people. He picked up three or four people, and each time the narrator said "plenty of room for friends, plenty of room for families, plenty of room for everybody". The same message was repeated several times in the course of the commercial. People get the sense that it's a spacious car, but the reality is that it's a very small car. And I got very bored when the statement "plenty of room" is repeated often enough.

第十类　交通

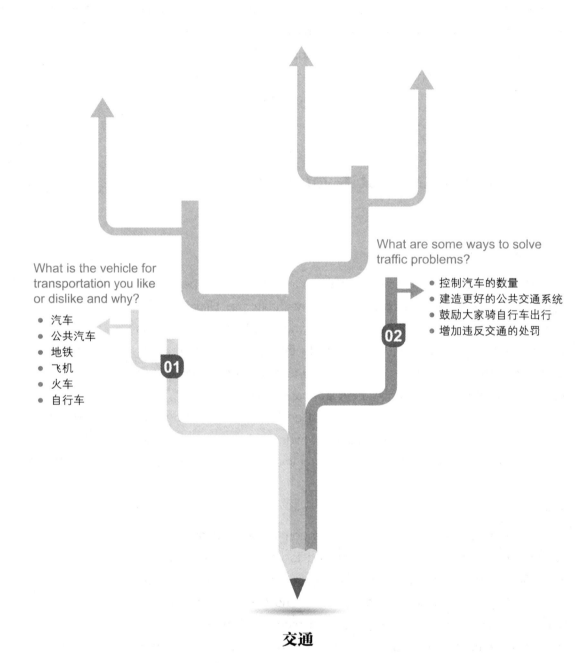

What is the vehicle for transportation you like or dislike and why?

- 汽车
- 公共汽车
- 地铁
- 飞机
- 火车
- 自行车

01

What are some ways to solve traffic problems?

- 控制汽车的数量
- 建造更好的公共交通系统
- 鼓励大家骑自行车出行
- 增加违反交通的处罚

02

交通

01 What is the vehicle for transportation you like or dislike and why? (cars, buses, subways, trains, airplanes, bicycles)

真　题	题　型	年　份
Some people prefer to own cars; others prefer to mainly use public transportation. Which one do you prefer?	口语 第二题	2013/03/30
Which transportation do you enjoy, bicycle, automobile or train?	口语 第一题	2014/02/22

1.1 汽车

1.1.1 舒适、自由

I feel comfortable when I am driving. When I am in the car, I don't need to worry about weather issues. If it is cold outside, I can turn my heater on. If it is hot, I can roll down[1] my window to enjoy the breeze[2]. I love the feeling of the fresh air on my face and the wind blowing through my hair. If I am bored, I can blast my hip-pop music[3] as loud as I want. Especially when it comes to road trips, belting out[4] the lyrics to my favorite tune[5] is the best experience. No matter what happens outside, once I am in my car, I am free.

❶ roll down 摇下车窗
❷ breeze [bri:z] n. 微风
❸ blast music 高音量放音乐
❹ belting out 高歌
❺ tune [tju: n] n. 曲调

1.1.2 危险

It is dangerous. Driving is the most dangerous thing most people do in a day. If I could avoid it, I would. When I'm in cities with convenient and fast public transit like subways, I don't drive. I can often see someone going 5 MPH on a 65 MPH highway, slamming on their gas pedals[6], and running into other cars' rear ends[7]. Things get worse when people are driving in some small cities because traffic rules mean nothing to them. If you follow the rules while driving, they think you are stupid.

❻ gas pedal 油门
❼ rear end 后部

1.1.3 堵车

I hate driving for one simple reason: traffic jams. I used to get up every day around 5:00 a. m. , just to avoid the morning rush hour, which could easily last for hours. Before that, I naively thought that I could still get to my company on time, even if I left home at 7:00 a. m, because I was extremely confident about my driving skills. But pretty soon I was proven wrong. There was this time that I encountered a serious traffic jam. I was on the eastern third-ring road and I thought I could make it to work just in time. Unfortunately, Beijing was holding a major international event — the Belt and Road Forum[8] for International Cooperation. The road was temporarily shut down as a result. So I was stuck on ShuangJing Bridge for like 40 minutes. I was 2 hours late in the end. My boss was really pissed off[9].

⑧ Belt and Road Forum 一带一路

⑨ pissed off 气疯了；怒冲冲的

1.2 公共汽车

1.2.1 省钱

Using the bus is an economical way of travelling. The cost varies according to the length of the trip, but on average, it costs around 4 dollars, which is way less than driving a car or taking a cab. The price is even cheaper if you buy a season pass[10]. I don't need to worry about insurance, gas, maintenance, parking fees etc. I used to spend around 25 dollars a week just for gas to get me to work. I also paid 60 – 75 dollars in monthly parking fees as well to park in downtown areas. By taking the bus for several months, I've saved well over 500 dollars.

⑩ season pass 季票

1.2.2 领略更多风景

I like taking buses. Sometimes on an airplane, I get to see spectacular views of the cities and countryside below. However, much of the flight probably involves staring at the endless sky. Traveling by bus through a new area gives me the unique opportunity to experience luxurious coastlines[11] and charming old towns. I can go for miles and miles across gorgeous, open farmland, or stare at the skyscrapers of whatever city I am passing through. This is no doubt the best way to travel through a new city or a new country.

⑪ coastline [ˈkəustlain] n. 海岸线

1.2.3 浪费时间

Sometimes the bus is so slow. It is normally required to be driven under a certain speed. So, travel by bus is way slower than travel by car or even by bike. Plus, I have to wait for the bus, and then I have to wait again, while the bus stops at every stop to let a herd of[12] people

⑫ a heard of 一群

out. Then the length of the journey feels 5 times longer than if I drive. One time, one bus did not show up until an hour had passed. It turned out the bus had broken down and had been replacing a flat tire[13] at the last stop. And when I got on for like five minutes, the bus was shut down again because of some engine failure. By the time I got home, it was 10:00 p. m and I was both starving and exhausted.

⑬ a flat tire 漏气的轮胎

1.3 地铁

1.3.1 可以干很多事

I think riding on the subway is much better than driving myself. It allows me to relax, read, or nap during the commute instead of feeling road rage. I can do pretty much anything I want on the subway. For example, I can listen to music on my iPhone or take out my laptop and work on some papers while sitting comfortably on a seat. Even better, I could eat breakfast or sleep the entire commute[14]. This is the perfect opportunity for me to catch up on sleep[15].

⑭ commute [kə'mju:t] v. 通勤

⑮ catch up some sleep 补充睡眠

1.3.2 快

The subway is fast. Driving in rush hour can be a nightmare in some big cities like Beijing. Taking a subway is the fastest way to travel in a big city. There's no traffic to contend with[16]. Instead of getting stuck in the street in a sea of cars[17], taking the subway is the best way for me to make sure to stay on schedule[18] or even arrive early at my destination. When you are going to an interview or taking an exam, the last thing you want is to be late.

⑯ contend with 与……做斗争

⑰ a sea of cars 大量
⑱ stay on schedule 按计划

1.3.3 不舒服

I don't like taking the subway, because it is not comfortable. I have no room to breathe especially during the morning and evening rush. Furthermore, with so many people being stuffed onto the subway, it smells awful. Sometimes it takes forever to get on because there are already too many people on the subway, standing there when the door opens. I once saw a station which was so jam-packed[19] that attendants[20] needed to drag riders out[21] of the subway so that the doors could close. When it is not rush hour, the beggars start to show up. Seeing people beg, ask for money, and sleep on the platforms is so disheartening[22].

⑲ jam-packed [dʒæm-pækt] adj. 塞得紧紧的
⑳ attendant [ə'tendənt] n. 乘务员
㉑ drag out 拖出来
㉒ dishearten [dis'ha:tn] v. 使人沮丧
▣ frustrate

1.3.4 不安全

I do not feel the subway is a safe environment for most women. Taking the subway at night can be quite dangerous even for men. Last week, I was harassed on the subway. I reported these instances to authorities like I'm supposed to, but the subway officers didn't do much about it. They ended up giving me some useless tips like, "This is what you should do to avoid harassment" instead of actually trying to bring the pervert[23] to justice[24].

1.3.5 拥挤

Once there was a breakdown in HUIXINXIJIENANKOU Station, so a crowd of people was accumulating on the platform. Trains were just passing by without stopping. After half an hour, one train finally stopped. When the door opened, because people were getting so impatient, nobody cared about politeness anymore. People started rushing into the train without letting passengers get off first. I literally saw a young girl, who already had her left foot on the platform, being pushed back into the train by the force of the crowd. She was yelling desperately, struggling with both her arms, "Let me out…!" But sadly, she disappeared the a blink of an eye[25].

1.4 飞机

1.4.1 快

It is the fastest way to get somewhere far away. If I only have a limited number of days to travel, and I truly want to spend quality time at my destination, then flying is still my best choice. If I am flying domestically, I can find a flight that will deliver me to the destination early in the day, allowing me to start my vacation as soon as I arrive. If it is for international travel, flying allows me to visit distant lands, experience exotic[26] cultures, and explore our planet in a shorter time than other types of transportation. A flight from Shanghai to Los Angeles only takes 12 hours. However, it takes a ship 2 weeks to cross the Pacific Ocean at full speed.

1.4.2 旅途有趣

I can have fun during the trip. Modern aircrafts are often equipped

[23] pervert [pəˈvəːt] *n.* 变态

[24] bring … to justice 绳之以法

[25] a blink of an eye 一转眼

[26] exotic [igˈzɔtik] *adj.* 异国情调的

with[27] fancy entertainment systems that put a selection of movies, television shows, music, and games right at our fingertips[28]. This can help pass the time more quickly while we are on a flight, and allow me to relax more in the process. I can enjoy great views as well. If I am lucky enough to get a window seat[29], I am often treated to some great views just outside the window. There is nothing quite like soaring over[30] the countryside, while lakes, rivers, mountains, and other beautiful landscapes pass beneath.

1.4.3 延迟

I hate taking airplanes, because flights always get delayed for different reasons like poor weather conditions, mechanical problems, or human mistakes. People have no choice but wait when delays happen. Things even get worse in some of the big airports. I don't trust their so-called "intelligent" system. I have heard so many times that the airport control system can't take a random screw-up[31]. And then everything will just shut down. I was planning to take a flight back to my hometown during the last spring festival. However, it took me five hours of just sitting and waiting at the airport before I could get aboard. It turned out the control system crashed, and nobody knew how to fix it.

1.4.4 害怕

I don't like to take airplanes. Flights give me lots of anxiety. It's because I'm scared of heights and I really hate falling. I don't like bungee jumps[32], being near ledges, or even looking down from a tall building. Last year, I took a flight from Denver to North Dakota[33]. There was suddenly a big drop followed by a couple of bumps[34]. It set my heart racing[35] and I thought I was going to die. I was almost screaming and gripping[36] the armrest as hard as I could during the rest of the flight. If I got to choose, I would rather spend more travel time to take a train or drive by myself. I feel safer that way.

1.4.5 花费的钱多

I barely take airplanes because the cost is a big problem. The flight ticket prices go up like a rocket, especially during the holiday seasons. Even if it is not holiday, if you travel to some small cities by airplane, the price is still very high. There is only one tiny airport in my hometown,

27 be equipped with 配备
28 fingertips ['fiŋgətip] adj. 指尖
29 window seat 靠窗的座位
30 soar over 翱翔
31 screw-up [skruː-ʌp] adj. 犯错误
32 bungee jump 蹦极
33 North Dakota 北达科他州（美国靠北部的一个州）
34 bump [bʌmp] n. 颠簸
35 set heart racing 心跳加快
36 grip [grip] v. 紧握

where only small planes can land . The price of just one single trip ticket is insane. Sometimes it is around 4,000 yuan for a 2-hour-flight from Beijing to my hometown. I can use that money to take 5 round trips by train at the same distance .

1.5 火车

更舒服

The seats on trains are more comfortable than airplanes', and they also offer more leg room . So even though many train rides are longer than an average plane ride, I don't have to be forced to sit there twisted into a pretzel[37]. I can walk around, stroll[38] to the café car , have a cup of real coffee and drink it at a real table. And the food is much better than the microwaved meals on a plane. There are real chefs that can cook delicious and healthy food on a train. If you're traveling in a sleeper car[39], the folding beds are spacious[40] and comfortable enough. And I find that the sound of the wheels can put me to sleep[41] very fast.

1.6 自行车

1.6.1 锻炼身体

Riding bikes helps me to keep fit[42] and brings fewer injuries. When I am cycling[43], it works my muscles from my ankles all the way up to my lower back. It is an efficient workout, as cycling gets my legs moving and my heart pumping without pounding my joints[44]. It is far lower impact and engages the muscles in the legs without much force coming down on the knees as running. So as long as I keep my legs pumping on my bike, it ends up being a smoother, lower-risk form of exercise than running.

1.6.2 保护环境

It is a great form of a green transportation. As we all know, cars consume too much gas and create much more carbon dioxide emissions[45], but riding a bike doesn't require fuel or batteries. It is indeed a pollution-free mode of transport. According to some recent research, cycling 10 km to work would save 1,500 kg of greenhouse gas emissions each year. Plus, bicycles reduce the need for clearing

---

㊲ pretzel ['pretsl] *n.* 双圈饼干

㊳ stroll [strəul] *v.* 闲逛 囧 walk

㊴ sleeper car 卧铺车

㊵ spacious ['speiʃəs] *adj.* 宽敞的 囧 roomy

㊶ put sb. into sleep 快速入眠

㊷ keep fit 保持（身体）健康

㊸ cyce ['saikl] *v.* 骑车

㊹ pound joints 重击关节部位

㊺ carbon dioxide emissions 二氧化碳排放

land for parking lots. In just one car parking space, 20 bikes can fit easily. So, if more people ride b-ikes, it means fewer cars on the road, which will lead to less clearing of beautiful land for parking lots.

1.6.3　自由

I love riding bikes a lot, because I can have complete freedom. The traffic in Beijing is like a nightmare. I am faster on my bike than most cars during rush hour. I can stop whenever I want. I can slow down and nobody honks[46]. I can explore new areas and revisit familiar places. I have been riding bikes since I was 6 and I am familiar with all the routes from my house to the school. Who doesn't like site-seeing and having people wave at you[47] as you pass by on your daily route?

[46] honk [hɔŋk] v. 汽车喇叭声

[47] wave at you 向你招手

1.6.4　方便（共享单车）

Bike sharing services like Mobike or OFO are going viral[48] now. When you use the service, you don't even have to own a bike. All you need to do is scan a QR code,[49] unlock a nearby bike, and ride it for however long you want at incredibly low prices. When you get to your destination, you can simply park and lock it. You are free to go and the sharing system will take care of the rest from there. Instead of worrying about where to park your own bike or about the bike thieves, the bike sharing service is extremely convenient.

[48] go viral 疯狂传播

[49] scan a QR code 扫二维码

1.6.5　路况差

I don't like to ride a bike anymore. Beijing is not as bike friendly a city as it used to be. There is not even a bike lane[50] in most areas, So, bikes have to use the same road as cars passing by. It is way too dangerous. My commute comprises[51] roads with parked cars lining the sides, drivers passing way too close and shouting abuse[52] when I take up the middle lane. Once, I almost got hit by a speeding car when I was riding my bike to school. I have quit cycling since then.

[50] bike lane 自行车道

[51] comprise [kəmˈpraɪz] v. 由……组成

[52] shout abuse 破口大骂

1.6.6　会被偷

There are too many bike thieves. Everybody has their bikes stolen once or twice. These thieves really have skills. It doesn't matter at all whether I use the biggest lock or lock it to a rack. They will leave me a wheel if they have mercy. My friend used to have a very fancy bicycle

① Brompton 折叠自行车
品牌

④ hop off 从……下来

called Brompton[53]. He treated it like a diamond, took it with him all the time. Last week, he told me he lost it while he was hopping off[54] and asking directions for just a few seconds. Since then, he never rides bikes anymore.

02 What are some ways to solve traffic problems?

真 题	题 型	年 份
Do you think that bicycles will be replaced by more modern vehicles such as cars or buses?	口语第一题	2012/07/15
What do you think we should do to decrease the usage of cars or other vehicles and solve the traffic problems?	口语第一题	2012/07/28
If you had to volunteer for a project, which one would you choose? Cleaning up the city, creating bicycle trails, or planting trees?	口语第一题	2013/07/14
Your city is planning to spend more on one of the following three projects. Which do you think is the most important? Expanding tourism, building city parks, or improving the public transportation system.	口语第一题	2014/11/08
What is the most useful action for people to help the environment in their local communities? 1) Plant trees and create parks； 2) Persuade local shops to stop providing plastic bags for consumers； 3) Increase access to public transportation (such as buses and trains) , and reduce the number of automobiles on roads.	独立写作题	2016/09/03

2.1　控制汽车的数量

① urbanization
[ˌəːbənaiˈzeiʃn] n. 城市化

The number of cars in big cities like Beijing has grown quickly as urbanization[1] and modernization progress. This has caused severe congestion in some downtown areas, especially at rush hour. If we don't limit the number of cars now, the congestion will only get worse.

Cars from provinces other than Beijing will be banned inside the 5th Ring Road on work days during the rush hours, from 7 to 9 a. m. and 5 to 8 p. m. The Chinese government recently launched an odd-even license plate[2] policy in Beijing. At major events or in severe weather conditions, personal vehicles will only be allowed on the road during alternating days.

❷ odd even license plate 单双号限行

2.2 建造更好的公共交通系统

Public transit is a powerful way to reduce traffic congestion. Without public transit, car drivers would have millions more hours of delays each year. We should create more reserved bus lanes that let more buses move more efficiently. Also, add more bus stations to shorten the time people have to wait, because some people prefer sitting in their cars suffering traffic jams to standing at a bus stop to wait for a bus. On top of that, experts should come up with more efficient bus routes to cover more area.

2.3 鼓励大家骑自行车出行

We should make more space for cycling. Mixing with traffic puts people off cycling. So, cycle lanes and tracks should be wide enough and separate from traffic. Also, a better job should be done of separating cycle lanes from pedestrians[3]. Shared-use pavement alongside roads benefits nobody. Still, we need to build more places to park our bikes. Good-quality cycle parking is essential for the start and end of a journey. This means providing secure stands near the entrance to buildings and on-street.

❸ pedestrian [pəˈdestriən] n. 行人

We should encourage more people to use bike sharing services like Mobike or OFO. When you use the service, you don't even have to own a bike. All you need to do is scan a QR code, unlock a nearby bike, and ride it for however long you want at incredibly low prices. When you get to your destination, you can simply park and lock it. You are free to go and the sharing system will take care of the rest from there. Instead of worrying about where to park your own bike or about the bike thieves, the bike sharing service is extremely convenient.

2.4　增加违反交通的处罚

The reason that some people don't follow the traffic rules is simple: they don't care about paying fines. That's why some people drive at 40mph on a 60mph road while someone else is doing 80mph passing by. How crazy is that? And that happens every single day in Beijing. I have seen people parking places where they shouldn't all the time. If we increase the penalty for traffic violations, people will realize they have to sacrifice way more to take risks. And that will ensure that more people follow the rules, which will solve traffic problems.

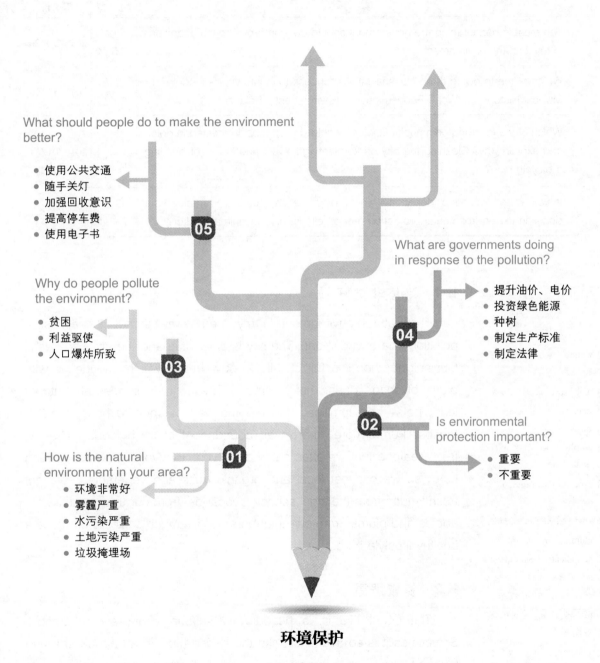

What should people do to make the environment better?

- 使用公共交通
- 随手关灯
- 加强回收意识
- 提高停车费
- 使用电子书

05

What are governments doing in response to the pollution?

- 提升油价、电价
- 投资绿色能源
- 种树
- 制定生产标准
- 制定法律

04

Why do people pollute the environment?

- 贫困
- 利益驱使
- 人口爆炸所致

03

02

Is environmental protection important?

- 重要
- 不重要

How is the natural environment in your area?

- 环境非常好
- 雾霾严重
- 水污染严重
- 土地污染严重
- 垃圾掩埋场

01

环境保护

01 How is the natural environment in your area?

真 题	题 型	年 份
The most important thing the government should do to improve health conditions is to clean the environment.	独立写作题	2013/10/20
Which of the following three classes will you choose to fit into your schedule? 1) Musical History；2) World Economics；3) Environmental Science	口语第一题	2015/11/14
Which of the following community services would you be most interested in doing and explain why? Cleaning the city park, planting flowers and trees, or building a bicycle lane?	口语第一题	2016/01/24
If you were making a donation, which organization would you make your donation to, environmental protection group, city library, or animal shelter?	口语第一题	2016/08/21

1.1 环境非常好

The natural environment in my area is awesome. It's almost a pollution-free environment. The sky is clear blue and the air is so fresh. Our neighborhood is full of tall, woody[1] trees, which provide us with plenty of shade during hot summers. These green spaces also attract kids, pets, and families, and are the perfect spot[2] to hang out with friends. Furthermore, there's an abundance[3] of fresh foods[4]. We eat fresh seafood that we often catch ourselves. Everyone grows something here, so we can eat local and organic fruits and vegetables. We get fresh lettuce from the kids' school, avocados[5] from our tree, and kiwis[6], apples and plums[7] from our neighbors. So it's much easier to embrace a healthy lifestyle here.

1.2 雾霾严重

The city I live in is periodically[8] suffering from severe smog[9]. Sometimes it is so thick, just like the dense fug[10] in an airport smoking lounge[11]. You can scarcely see across the street. And the air quality index can easily go above 500, rated "hazardous[12]" by United States standards. And if you blow one's nose[13] at the end of the day, it comes

① woody ['wudi] *adj.* 多树木的
② spot [spɔt] *n.* 地点场所
③ abundance [ə'bʌndəns] *n.* 丰富
④ whole food 天然健康食品
⑤ avocado [ævə'kɑ:dəu] *n.* 牛油果
⑥ kiwi ['ki:wi:] *n.* 猕猴桃
⑦ plum [plʌm] *n.* 李子
⑧ periodically [,piəri'ɔdikəli] *adv.* 周期性的
⑨ smog [smɔg] *n.* 雾霾
⑩ fug [fʌg] *n.* 室内的浑浊空气
⑪ lounge [laundʒ] *n.* 等候室，休息室
⑫ hazardous ['hæzədəs] *adj.* 有危害的
⑬ blow one's nose 擤鼻涕

out black. Sometimes you can even see the tiny particulates floating in the air, and most of them will inevitably[14] end up in people's lungs. I usually wear masks[15] outdoors and turn on air purifiers[16] at home, but I still worry about getting lung cancer.

1.3　水污染严重

In my area, clean drinking water is becoming a rare commodity. I can often see riverbanks filled with trash, such as cans of paint[17], plastic bags, and discarded furniture. It's just so disgusting. In addition, factories are filling rivers with toxic pollutants[18], some of which are colorless, but still pose a major threat to our health; some of which are quite colorful, turning the water jet black[19] in some area, then milky[20] white.

Cancer village has become a new Internet catchphrase, which describes the village where nearly all its inhabitants[21] got cancer because of pollutants from nearby rivers. Death rates are extremely high in these places. I just feel so sad that people are dying constantly, especially when such tragedies could be avoided if people were more concerned with protecting the environment.

1.4　土地污染严重

Compared to air pollution, soil pollution is more easily hidden and long-lasting. Unfortunately, the city I live in is facing intimidating[22] challenges in controlling soil pollution, which has contaminated[23] food crops[24] and jeopardized[25] public health. My mom always spends a lot of money on organic foods because she believes it is less exposed to pollution as compared to foods produced by conventional farming methods. Because of pollution, farmers have to plant their crops in polluted soil, and then water those crops with contaminated water. Naturally, the crops absorb the pollutants as they grow. As a result, the food supply is at risk. It's a shame that a lot of arable[26] land in my country has become too polluted to be farmed.

---

⑭ inevitably [in'evitəbli] *adv.* 不可避免地

⑮ mask [mɑːsk] *n.* 口罩

⑯ air purifier 空气净化器

⑰ cans of paint 油漆罐

⑱ toxic pollutant 有毒污染物

⑲ jet black 乌黑，漆黑

⑳ milky ['mɪlki] *adj.* 乳白色的，浑浊不清的

㉑ inhabitant [in'hæbitənt] *n.* 居民

㉒ intimidating [in,timi'deitiŋ] *adj.* 令人惊恐的

㉓ contaminate [kən'tæmineit] *v.* 污染

㉔ crop [krɔp] *n.* 农作物

㉕ jeopardize ['dʒepədaiz] *v.* 损害，危害

㉖ arable ['ærəbl] *adj.* 适于耕地的

1.5　垃圾掩埋场

27 one blemish in an otherwise perfect setting 美中不足

28 landfill ['lændfil] n. 垃圾掩埋场

29 inexpressible [ˌinik'spresəbl] adj. 无以言表的

30 rotten ['rɔtn] adj. 腐烂的

31 excrement ['ekskrimənt] n. 排泄物

Well, most of the time, I love my neighborhood. But there is just one blemish in an otherwise perfect setting[27] — a nearby landfill[28]. I love to sleep at night with my windows open, so that the air in my bedroom can be fresh for the whole night, and for most nights, the air indeed is fresh. However, there are some nights when the landfill is working, and the smell is just unbearable. The air is filled with an inexpressible[29] smell that is a mix of garbage, rotten[30] food, and excrement[31]. I would reluctantly close my window and turn on the air conditioning, which I never enjoy.

02　Is environmental protection important?

真　题	题　型	年　份
The most important thing the government should do to improve health conditions is to clean the environment.	独立写作题	2013/10/20

2.1　重要

2.1.1　影响生活质量

1 priority [prai'ɔrəti] n. 优先处理的事情

2 trap [træp] v. 困住

Yes. Environmental protection has to be our priority[1], since it is the only way to protect our, and especially our children's health. Many of them have missed the wonder of childhood because of serious pollution. When I was a kid, I climbed trees, fished in a nearby pond, and played outside with my friends from sun up to sun down. However, now in order to "escape" from smog, children are trapped[2] in their rooms next to air purifiers. They seldom have access to nature. Parents live in constant fear, worrying that their children might get sick. So I really want children to have the kinds of experiences I had as a child. But they would first need a healthy environment, with parks and gardens where they can play and explore without danger.

2.1.2　影响人们的身体健康

Yes. It is definitely our responsibility to protect the environment. The earth is our home. It is where we live, breathe, eat, and raise our children. Our health is dependent on the well-being[3] of Earth. When the air is polluted, we can get lung cancer; when drinking water is contaminated by excessive[4] lead[5], infant mortality rates[6] rise significantly; and when our crops absorb too many pollutants, we absorb deadly pollutants too. So, we should do whatever we can to prevent pollution. To protect ourselves we must first protect our planet.

③ well-being [wel-biŋ] n. 健康

④ excessive [ik'sesiv] adj. 过多的，过度的

⑤ lead [li:d] n. 铅

⑥ infant mortality rate 婴儿死亡率

2.1.3　危害自然资源

We need to protect the environment before it's too late. Our development in economics is largely gained at the cost of polluting natural resources such as clean water supply, arable land and the forest. Those are not unlimited resources. So when they run out[7], we will definitely be in big trouble. It will be too late to regret at that time. We should start acting now.

⑦ run out 用完

2.1.4　破坏食物链

Contamination from factories has already led to the extinction[8] of many animal and plant species. As more species disappear, our eco-systems become more vulnerable[9]. Eventually, the food chain[10] will be broken when too many species become extinct. In a forest, for example, frogs[11] eat grasshoppers[12], snakes eat frogs, and eagles[13] eat snakes. If all grasshoppers are killed by some deadly pollutant, the population of frogs will probably drop dramatically since their main source of food has vanished. Snakes and eagles will have a very difficult time then, and might also die out[14] soon.

⑧ extinction [ik'stiŋkʃn] n. （物种的）灭绝

⑨ vulnerable ['vʌlnərəbl] adj. 易受伤害的

⑩ food chain 食物链

⑪ frog [frɒg] n. 青蛙

⑫ grasshopper ['grɑːshɔpə(r)] n. 蚱蜢

⑬ eagle ['iːgl] n. 鹰

⑭ die out 消失，灭绝

2.1.5　导致人才流失

Environmental protection is very important, because it can help us stop the "brain drain[15]". Thousands of talented people are striving to escape from China just to breathe some cleaner air. Pollution is also dis-suading[16] foreign talents from coming to China. In my opinion, people are leaving because they are too disappointed. Cities are all too crowded with both people and automobiles. Contaminated crops are causing

⑮ brain drain 人才流失

⑯ dissuade [di'sweid] v. 劝阻

⑰ choke [tʃəuk] *v.* 使窒息

concerns about the food we eat. It is clear that pollution is choking[17] the future of China, making it a less attractive place for talents, both within and outside of China.

2.2 不重要

2.2.1 经济发展更重要

Economic development is of great importance, especially for developing countries such as China. You just can't have your cake and eat it too. Governments must choose between a good environment and a flourishing economy. Historically, most countries chose the latter, and tend to improve the environment after getting rich.

⑱ dynamite ['dainəmait] *n.* 炸药

⑲ stun [stʌn] *v.* 击晕

Economic development is of more importance because one cannot ask people to heal the environment, or even just mind it, if they can barely sustain themselves. For example, some poor people in tropical regions can earn good money by catching tropical fish. To catch the fish more easily, they use chemicals or dynamite[18] to stun[19] the fish. It is true that what they do will destroy the environment, but we cannot blame them because they need to earn money and feed themselves.

2.2.2 完全不在乎污染

⑳ triviality [ˌtrivi'æləti] *n.* 琐事

㉑ chronic disease 慢性病

㉒ optimistic [ˌɔpti'mistik] *adj.* 积极乐观的

No. I don't care about environmental protection at all. I don't mind about trivialities[20] such as the "possible" chronic diseases[21] caused by pollution. I am always optimistic[22] and prefer to seize the day. So I won't stay at home just because of air pollution. I love outdoor activities and I hate wearing masks, because masks are for losers. I just do whatever I want no matter if there is smog or not. I think I am doing just fine.

03 Why do people pollute the environment?

3.1 贫困

The environment tends to be jeopardized more in poorer areas, because when people can barely sustain themselves, nobody is in the mood to care for the environment. For example, some poor people in tropical regions can earn good money by catching tropical fish. To catch the fish more easily, they use chemicals or dynamite[1] to stun[2] the fish. It is true that what they do will destroy the environment, but we cannot blame them because they need to earn money and feed themselves.

3.2　利益驱使

Businesses and factories pollute the environment to maximize their profits. It happens a lot in the oil and gas industry, especially in developing countries. We all know what we are doing is harmful to the environment, but we keep doing it, because the profit for several wells[3] in a pad can be worth billions. I was a field engineer in an oil and gas company. One of the techniques we always used to increase the production is fracturing[4]. We pumped[5] various chemicals into the field. Ironically we knew some of them were toxic. These injections[6] were very close to the drinking water supply, which meant sooner or later they would enter into the nearby rivers and streams. And both the groundwater and the surface water will be contaminated as well. Developed countries are no better. In order to save costs, their companies outsource[7] their factories and export their waste to developing countries[8], which heavily pollute the environment.

3.3　人口爆炸所致

People do not pollute the environment on purpose. It's just that there are so many people. Human overpopulation silently aggravates[9] the environmental pollution, habitat loss and the overuse of natural resources. For example, freshwater is the most fundamental finite resource with no substitutes, yet we are consuming fresh water at least 10 times faster than it is being replenished[10]. Also, modern farming practices produce cheaper food, but they have grown to become the biggest threat to the global environment through the loss of ecosystems. Deforestation[11] is also the result of the need to find more arable land. So overpopulation has become one of the reasons that cause pollution.

❶ dynamite ['dainəmait] n. 炸药
❷ stun [stʌn] v. 击晕

❸ well [wel] n. 井

❹ fracture 水力压裂
❺ pump [pʌmp] v. 抽送
❻ injection [in'dʒekʃn] n. 注入

❼ outsource ['autsɔːs] v. 外包
❽ developing countries 发展中国家

❾ aggravate ['ægrəveit] v. 使恶化，使更严重

❿ replenish [ri'pleniʃ] v. 补充

⓫ deforestation [diˌfɔris'teiʃn] n. 森林开伐

04 What are governments doing in response to the pollution?

真　题	题　型	年　份
Describe some ways to reduce air pollution.	口语 第一题	2012/05/26
What is the most important action for the government to tackle environmental problems? 1）fund researches on new energy sources such as solar and wind power；2）protect forests and natural wildlife species；3）pass and enforce laws to reduce the pollution	口语 第一题	2013/08/17
The most effective way for governments to encourage energy conservation is by increasing the price of gasoline and electricity.	独立 写作题	2013/10/25
Nowadays, air pollution is a common problem in many places. What can people do to reduce air pollution? Include reasons and details to support your response.	口语 第一题	2015/05/09
Many companies sell products or services but at the same time cause environmental damage. Some people say it can be stopped by asking them to pay a penalty, such as a higher tax, when they cause environmental damage. Others say there are better ways to stop them from harming the environment. What do you think is the best way to prevent the environment from deteriorating?	独立 写作题	2015/12/12

4.1　提升油价、电价

❶ gasoline [ˈɡæsəliːn] n.
汽油

　　If governments are serious about energy conservation, they can start by increasing the price of gasoline[1] and electricity. Choices people make are largely driven by cost. In 2007 and 2008, when oil prices were hitting record highs, people were less willing to buy SUVs, since they consume more oil. But once prices had plunged[2] at the end of 2008, SUVs and trucks were once again the industry's biggest sellers. So, as for me, I will definitely choose to consume less, and the higher the price, the greater my incentive to make that choice.

❷ plunge [plʌndʒ] v. 突然
下降

❸ lessen car emissions 减
少汽车排放
❹ fluctuation [ˌflʌktjuˈeɪʃn]
n. 波动

　　I recently found out that increasing the price of gasoline is a great way to lessen car emissions[3], since I just got my driver's license and started driving. In the past, I never cared about the fluctuation[4] of oil prices. But now, I notice when oil prices surge, I often end up paying like 50 bucks more per month. That's a lot for a student like me. So I have switched to riding bikes when the price is too high.

4.2 投资绿色能源

Beijing recently issued its first pollution "red alert", closing schools, factories and construction sites, and ordering half of all private cars off the road, but these measures were only temporary. In a country where millions of people still look to industrialization[5] to save them selves from poverty, the government needs to introduce green energy. Fortunately, local governments are investing in wind energy and solar energy, as well as other renewable energies, to minimize the burning of fossil fuels[6]. Also, some governments encourage the use of green products by providing subsidies. For example, by buying an electric car, people can receive government subsidies[7], because electric cars are 100 percent eco-friendly. They do not emit[8] toxic gases or smoke in the environment as they on electrically powered engines.

⑤ industrialization
[in‚dʌstriəlaiˈzeiʃn] *n.*
工业化

⑥ fossil fuel 化石燃料

⑦ subsidy [ˈsʌbsədi] *n.* 补助金

⑧ emit [iˈmit] *v.* 排放

4.3 种树

I recently saw a video on Sina Weibo, which claims that the best way for governments to improve air quality is just to plant more trees. It is the cheapest among all methods, but at the same time the most effective. The video points out that several European countries are building huge purifiers next to residential areas, and some are using chemicals to remove smog; but none of the methods is cost-effective[9]. On the other hand, planting trees is the best way since PM 2.5 and other harmful chemicals in the air will stick to the leaves on trees. And when it rains, these harmful particles[10] will be washed away into the ground, which means there is no maintenance cost.

⑨ cost-effective
[kɔst-iˈfektiv] *adj.* 划算的

⑩ particle [ˈpɑːtikl] *n.* 颗粒

4.4 制定生产标准

In some countries, governments require that refrigerators, dishwashers and other appliances[11] meet certain efficiency targets, and electricity suppliers are required to label[12] their products. These disclosure[13] labels[14] for fuel sources and emissions would be analogous[15] to nutrition labels on food, so that consumers can determine whether the washing machine they want to buy is an energy saver.

⑪ appliance [əˈplaiəns] *n.* 家用电器

⑫ label [ˈleibl] *v.* 标注

⑬ disclosure [disˈkləuʒə] *n.* 公开，透露

⑭ label [ˈleibl] *n.* 标签

⑮ analogous [əˈnæləgəs] *adj.* 类似的

4.5 制定法律

In some countries, legislators have passed amendments[16] to the country's environmental protection laws, promising greater powers for environmental authorities and harsher punishments for polluters. However, there is a gap between legislation[17] and implementation[18]. In some countries, air pollution or water pollution control laws are pretty good compared to global standards, but no matter how good the laws look on paper, the true test will always be the willingness of local authorities to enforce[19] them.

⑯ amendment [əˈmendmənt] n. 修正案

⑰ legislation [ˌledʒisˈleiʃn] n. 立法

⑱ implementation [ˌimplimenˈteiʃn] n. 履行，执行

⑲ enforce [inˈfɔːs] v. 强制执行

05 What should people do to make the environment better?

真　题	题　型	年　份
Describe some ways to reduce air pollution.	口语 第一题	2012/05/26
Who has the biggest impact on reducing environmental contamination, government regulation or individual efforts?	口语 第二题	2015/03/14
Nowadays, air pollution is a common problem in many places. What can people do to reduce air pollution? Include reasons and details to support your response.	口语 第一题	2015/05/09
What is the most useful action for people to improve the environment in their local communities? 1) Plant trees and create parks; 2) Persuade local shops to stop providing plastic bags for consumers; 3) Increase access to public transportation (such as buses and trains), and reduce the automobiles on roads.	口语 第一题	2016/09/03

5.1 使用公共交通

Whether we're flying away on business trips or commuting to work on a daily basis, the way we travel is one of the biggest environmental polluters in our lives. It's hard to give up all these habits, but taking steps to reduce them will impact the environment. I got so excited when bike sharing systems started popping up across Beijing, because traveling by car across Beijing in rush hour[1] is often a nightmare. Even distances of a few kilometers can take up to an hour when traffic is bad. Now, thanks to the bike sharing system, I just grab a bike after I get off the metro. It's just so convenient. I can not only save time, but also get some exercise. And the most important thing is, that if we all do so, there will be fewer cars on the road and less fumes produced.

❶ rush hour 高峰时间

5.2 随手关灯

You've probably heard this a million times that you should turn the light off[2] when you leave the room, even if you're only off for a few minutes. It does make a difference[3] to the environment, since it saves energy. If you're forgetful, you can put stickers next to light switches to remind householders to save energy by turning lights off when leaving the room.

❷ turn off 关掉
❸ make a difference 起作用

5.3 加强回收意识

We should launch campaigns[4] to enhance people's awareness of environmental protection, such as recycling as many things as we can. Manufacturing industries[5] create a lot of pollution, so if we can reuse things like plastic shopping bags, clothing, paper and bottles, it definitely can help. For example, you have tons of clothes or things you want to get rid of. If they are still usable, you can give them to poor kids who live in the mountains. You may also choose to give them to the Red Cross. You get to kill three birds with one stone: protecting the environment, helping poor kids, and feeling good about yourself.

❹ launch campaigns 开展活动
❺ manufacturing industries 制造业

5.4 提高停车费

There are lots of things schools can do to protect the environment. They can raise the cost of campus parking to discourage students from driving to school. You know, I live in Beijing. There are just too many private cars, and the emissions from those cars causes very bad air pollution. A lot of people get diseases because of that. By raising the cost, it may encourage more students to take public transportation to school.

5.5　使用电子书

　　I just don't get why schools are still using paper-based books today, since all of which can be simply replaced by an iPad. I mean, everybody can afford an iPad now, right? So why are we still cutting down millions of trees each year and turn them into textbooks that we would only use for four months, and than throw away. If all schools around the world can switch[6] to electronic textbooks, it would surely be a great contribution to environmental protection.

⑥ switch［switʃ］v. 转向

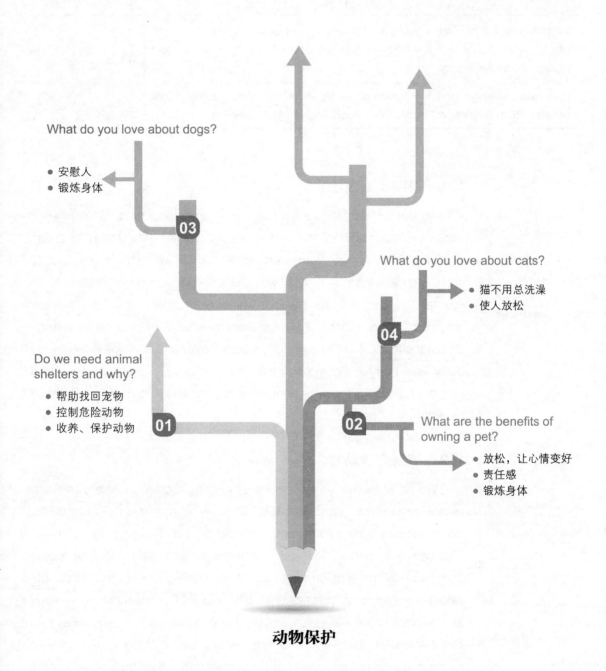

What do you love about dogs?

- 安慰人
- 锻炼身体

03

What do you love about cats?

- 猫不用总洗澡
- 使人放松

04

Do we need animal shelters and why?

- 帮助找回宠物
- 控制危险动物
- 收养、保护动物

01

02

What are the benefits of owning a pet?

- 放松，让心情变好
- 责任感
- 锻炼身体

动物保护

01　Do we need animal shelters, and why?

真　题	题　型	年　份
Which one of the following would you donate your money to? Choose one, and explain how you would use the money: community charity, environment protection, animal rescue.	口语 第一题	2013/09/13
If you were making a donation, which of the organizations would you make your donation to, environmental protection group, city library, or animal shelter?	口语 第一题	2015/03/28

1.1　帮助找回宠物

① stray [strei] *v.* 流浪

② reunite [ˌriːjuːˈnait] *v.* 重聚

③ shepherd [ˈʃepəd] *n.* 牧羊犬

Animal shelters are very helpful for returning lost pets. Sometimes it would be impossible to return pets without shelter assistance, because pets may stray[1] miles from their homes. Even when pets are found, those that find them may not have the patience, time, or resources to reunite[2] the pet with its owner. My grandmother once had a stray shepherd[3] living in her barn. However, he ran away and didn't return. When shelter workers examined his tags they found, he was three states away from home. When they contacted the owner, they discovered he had been missing for two years. Without shelters, he might never have found his way back.

1.2　控制危险动物

④ get rid of 摆脱，除去

⑤ raccoon [rəˈkuːn] *n.* 浣熊

We all know not all animals are friendly. Some animals can harm people or other animals. Because animal shelters exist, people of the community can call animal control to help get rid of[4] dangerous animals. This can help people feel safe. If there weren't any animal shelters, there wouldn't be a place for these dangerous animals to go and people would have no clue how to deal with them. For example, if a stray animal goes into someone's back yard and is hurting their pets, they can call the shelter to take the animal away. Or, if there is a snake or raccoon[5] that is not supposed to be in the house, then the animal control officer can remove them from the house.

Just as humans, pets such as dogs and cats also need to be loved. Sadly, many homeless pets are being abandoned, avoided, or even beaten by us. No wonder many lovely pets turn insecure and aggressive after wandering[6] too long on the streets. If, however, the government has more funds to allocate[7] to animal shelters, the staff there will surely provide the securities that these animals need. Moreover, they might even find these animals new homes.

6 wander ['wɔndə] *v.* 流浪
7 allocate ['æləukeit] *v.* 分配

1.3 收养，保护动物

If a pet is not wanted anymore, the shelter can take it in and give it a second chance at finding another home. If a family can no longer take care of the pet, they can drop it off[8] at the shelter instead of letting it go on the streets, where it has a greater chance of dying. The shelter can also make sure they find the right home for these pets. When animals arrive at a shelter they are checked for anything wrong. They make sure they get vaccinations[9]. Shelters provide food, water, protection, medical care, socialization and a simple feeling of security to these animals.

8 drop off 放下

9 vaccinations [,væksi'neiʃn] *n.* 接种疫苗

02 What are the benefits of owning a pet?

真　题	题　型	年　份
Your friend is considering getting a pet. What kind of pet, and what advice would you give him?	口语 第一题	2012/02/11
What do you think of having pets?	口语 第一题	2012/02/25
Which one of the following would you donate your money to? Choose one, and explain how you would use the money: community charity, environment protection, animal rescue.	口语 第一题	2013/09/13
If you were making a donation, which of the organizations would you make your donation to, environmental protection group, city library, or animal shelter?	口语 第一题	2015/03/28

（续）

真　题	题　型	年　份
Children can benefit in important ways from taking care of a pet.	独立 写作题	2015/07/04
What kind of activity do you think children do can cultivate a sense of responsi-bility? 1）Keep a pet；2）do house chores；3）help take care of their younger sisters or brothers. Use specific details and examples in your response.	口语 第一题	2015/10/31

2.1　放松，让心情变好

For those who love animals, it is almost impossible to stay in a bad mood[1] when you look into the soft eyes of a dog or have a soft furry cat rub up against your leg. Further, I find it even easier to snap out of[2] a dark mood when I engage in conversations with my dogs. They always seem to agree with me, and listen quite assuredly[3] with no judgment attached. After a long day at school, when you return home, having a pet all excited by your side, licking and compelling[4] you really helps you to loosen up[5]. They are always happy to see me, and don't mind listening to any complaints I might make about the day.

2.2　责任感

Caring for pets is a great way to teach children responsibility. It gives them a taste of what it feels like to be relied on. It is more effective than any other way I know. For example, feeding a pet is something concrete that all children can understand. They know what it feels like to get hungry and they understand that food is the cure for hunger. When their pet "attacks" the food and gets satisfied they will know what they have done is really important. They will come to see that their parents are doing the same for them as what they are doing for their pets. They will be more willing to get involved in family activities like helping parents with chores[5]. They will be more responsible for their own tasks.

2.3　锻炼身体

Having a pet encourages you to exercise more. For example, if you

❶ stay in a bad mood 心情
不好
❷ snap out of 从……中摆
脱出来
❸ assuredly [əˈʃuəridli]
adv. 确定地
🔲 surely
❹ loosen up 放松

❺ chore [tʃɔː] n. 家务

have a dog, you have to walk your dog on a daily basis. Also, you need to spend maybe an hour a day to play with your dog to make it happy. It doesn't matter if you throw balls around or play hide-and-seek[6]. it helps you to get some exercise. As long as you have your dog, all this keeps you in kind of a daily routine and helps you keep healthy and fit.

❻ hide-and-seek 捉迷藏

03 What do you love about dogs?

3.1 安慰人

Dogs are really good at comforting people. When I feel blue, they cuddle up agaist me and give me a moment of comfort. They keep me warm and always make me feel safe. After·a bad day, when I come home, all I want to do is see my dog's cute face and let him lick my hands. I feel better and forget all the troubles in a very short time. When I feel angry and want to complain, my dogs will always be there to listen to me. They never judge me, and stay by my side, supporting me.

3.2 锻炼身体

Having a dog encourages you to exercise more. For example, if you have a dog, you have to walk it on a daily basis. Also, you need to spend maybe an hour a day to play with your dog to make it happy. It doesn't matter if you throw balls around or play hide-and-seek. It helps you to get some exercise. As long as you have your dog, all this keeps you in kind of a daily routine and helps you keep healthy and fit.

04 What do you love about cats?

4.1 猫不用总洗澡

Unlike dogs, kitties don't usually need to be bathed. Instead, they self-clean. That helps a lot for a lazy person like me. I don't need to spend too much time cleaning them. I used to have a dog. He was always messing around in the neighborhood. So he was always dirty. I had to bathe him like 2 times a week. It was a very hard time to clean him as he always refused to take bath. However, when I got my cats, I found out they could take care of themselves very well. They would use their tongues to lick their bodies and use teeth to dig out[1] tougher debris. So I can save much time for doing other things.

❶ dig out 挖出

4.2 使人放松

Cats are just so cute. They are lazy creatures who lie on your floor, beds, desks, lap or bathtub. When you come home, they approach you quietly and ask you for a back massage. Occasionally, they might be in a bad mood and knock over[2] the food you put in their plate. You might get mad. But when you do want to yell at them, they somehow can sense it and start to pretend to be innocent by flipping their stomach upward toward you. Then your anger instantly disappears and you feel light-hearted[3] again.

❷ knock over 打翻

❸ light-hearted 轻松愉快的

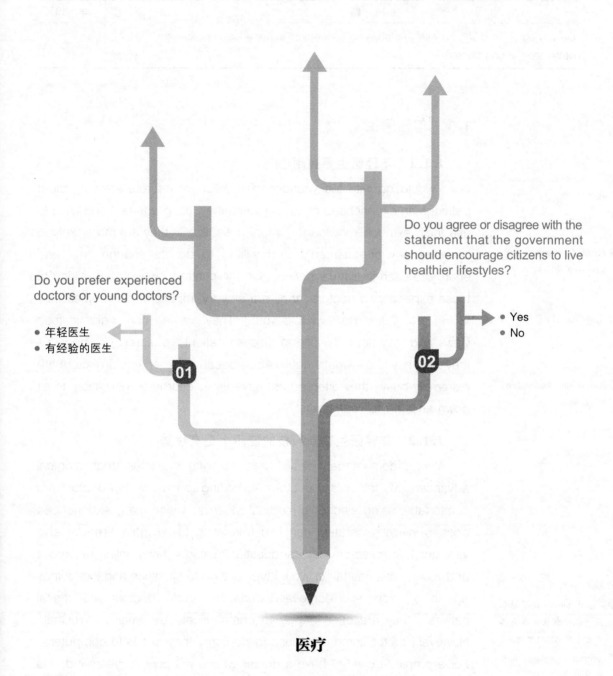

Do you prefer experienced doctors or young doctors?

- 年轻医生
- 有经验的医生

01

Do you agree or disagree with the statement that the government should encourage citizens to live healthier lifestyles?

02

- Yes
- No

医疗

第十三类 医疗

01 Do you prefer experienced doctors or young doctors?

真　题	题　型	年　份
Do you agree or disagree with the following statement: experienced doctors are better than young doctors?	独立写作题	2016/09/25

1.1 年轻医生

1.1.1 年轻医生更有耐心

I would go with the younger one. Younger doctors are way more patient than experienced ones, because they just graduated and want to use their textbook knowledge on real patients. So they are more likely to be more service oriented[1], and willing to devote enough time and energy to each individual patient. On the contrary, when I am talking to those experienced doctors, they are all very impatient. Sometimes they yell at me: "Just do as I told you!" They are far more rigid[2] in their views and may not be willing to discuss patients' preferences, because they feel they know what's right. Also, because experienced doctors are extremely busy, they often do not have time, energy or inclination[3] to sit down and talk to you patiently.

1.1.2 年轻医生在新科技的使用上更有优势

Young doctors can easily keep up with the latest technological advances. My father is a doctor. According to him, young doctors are comfortable using electronic medical records, which many experienced doctors in his generation can find frustrating to navigate. They're also very quick to research medical questions using various online resources and tools, while my father would typically go to his office and look things up[4] in a textbook. Moreover, because young doctors are digital natives[5], they are often happy to communicate by email or WeChat. However, as for some experienced doctors, they just hate computers. For example, I used to have a doctor who was about 70 years old. He was a hesitant[6] typist[7] who preferred paper prescriptions[8]. The problem was I could never understand his handwriting. Thank God, now, my doctor is a guy who is probably the same age as me. I can always get

---

① oriented [ˈɔːrientid] *adj.* 以……为方向的

② rigid [ˈridʒid] *adj.* 死板的

③ inclination [ˌinkliˈneiʃən] *n.* 意向

④ look up 查阅
⑤ digital natives 数字原住民（从小就生长在有各式数字产品环境里的人）
⑥ hesitant [ˈhezitənt] *adj.* 犹豫的
⑦ typist [ˈtaipist] *n.* 打字员
⑧ prescription [priˈskripʃn] *n.* 处方

his prompt[9] replies by email. Also, I can take home freshly printed data analyses to study by myself.

1.1.3　年轻医生在科学前沿

"Experience" may consist of doing the same thing over and over without changes. They tend to simply ignore medical breakthroughs and prefer to hold on to their old ways. And this might not best serve patients. We need new doctors who have the latest knowledge, because medicine is constantly evolving[10] and few things remain static. In addition, although young doctors may not have much clinical experience[11] because they haven't seen many patients, I think that any shortcomings in years will be offset[12] by their willingness to go the extra mile for patients.

1.2　有经验的医生

1.2.1　有经验的医生检查更有针对性

I prefer more experienced doctors, because young doctors usually spend less time listening to the patient's story. Instead, they routinely order different kinds of tests, which literally cost thousands of dollars. However, experienced doctors often trust their clinical skills more and are able to use tests more selectively. Though some patients prefer doctors who order lots of tests, believing that they're getting cutting-edge[13] care, I still think it's unnecessary. I just don't want to spend a lot of money doing different kinds of tests just because I am getting a very bad cold.

1.2.2　有经验的医生手术成功率更高

I prefer a doctor who has white hair, or at least a tinge[14] of gray, especially when it comes to surgery! I just have more confidence and trust in elderly doctors, who have far more clinical experience, not just textbook knowledge. Studies have shown that the surgeon's experience is the most important factor in having a safe and successful operation. The more experience surgeons have, the better their patients' outcomes. Of course, quantity alone is not necessarily a guarantee of quality, but it is an indication of competency. My friend Deepa is a top student in medical school. He told me that younger doctors have more

⑨ prompt［prɔmpt］*adj.* 迅速的

⑩ evolve［i'vɔlv］*v.* 逐步发展

⑪ clinical experience 临床经验

⑫ offset［'ɔːfset］*v.* 抵消，补偿

⑬ cutting-edge［'kʌtiŋ-edʒ］*adj.* 先进的，尖端的

⑭ tinge［tindʒ］*n.* 些许

⑮ panic ［'pænik］ *adj.* 恐
慌的

⑯ tricky ［'triki］ *adj.* 棘
手的

knowledge of new technology, but they easily start to panic[15] when it comes to complicated or tricky[16] situations. However, experienced doctors can maintain perfect calm to think about what they should do because they have faced it a hundred times. So, at this point, I wouldn't want to depend on my friend for a heart surgery. It's just too risky.

02 Do you agree or disagree with the statement that the government should encourage citizens to live healthier lifestyles?

真　题	题　型	年　份
Do you agree or disagree with the statement that the government should encourage citizens to live healthier lifestyles?	独立 写作题	2016/03/13

2.1　Yes

2.1.1　省钱

Governments should encourage citizens to live healthier because it can save money in the long term. Currently, governments spend trillions of dollars every year on healthcare, and about half of that budget is spent treating so-called lifestyle diseases like diabetes and heart disease, which are largely preventable. For example, one city has eliminated fees for residents in city gyms. It cut expenditures[1] for the city, but in the long run, it saves costs for treating chronic[2] diseases that are associated with obesity[3]. Some cities are also developing bike sharing systems, like Beijing. I got so excited when bike sharing services started popping up across Beijing. When you use the service, you don't even have to own a bike. All you need to do is scan a QR code and unlock a nearby bike, ride it for however long you want at incredibly low prices. Also, when I am cycling, it works my muscles from my ankles all the way up to my lower back. It is an efficient workout, as

① expenditure ［ik'spenditʃə］
n. 花费

② chronic ［'krɔnik］ *adj.* 慢
性的，长期的

③ obesity ［əu'bi:səti］ *n.*
肥胖症

cycling gets my legs moving and my heart pumping without pounding my joints. All these are great examples of how governments can fulfill their responsibility.

2.1.2　这是政府职责，私人企业只想赚钱

It's governments' responsibility to encourage people to live a healthy lifestyle, because some people do not have self-control and some private entities make profits by taking advantage of this irrational pattern in humans. For example, every year, the average Chinese person eats 50 pounds of sugar, which is about 15 teaspoons a day. We ingest 8,500 milligrams of salt a day, double the recommended amount, and all that comes from processed food. It's no wonder that many adults and kids are obese[4] and have diabetes[5]. However, companies today still actively market products that contain high levels of salt, sugar and fat. They profit from the natural human tendency to seek out highly caloric food. And this is where the government needs to step in, to set standards for the food we eat. For example, taxes on junk food may alter consumption[6] patterns. And they can set standards on how many ounces[7] of soda a business can sell. Changing individual behavior is only possible when it is supported by an environment that helps make healthy choices.

2.2　No

2.2.1　所有人应该一起努力

The govern ment alone isn't the solution. We all have to do our part to make ourselves healthier. For example, parents can put more fruits and vegetables on the table and teach children healthy habits. Schools can give more importance to a well-balanced and diversified diet, reducing the supply of junk food. Doctors can help parents and kids understand the importance of early prevention. Only when all of us engage in the effort can we live a healthier life.

2.2.2　健康靠自己

Living a healthy lifestyle is a matter of personal choice. In reality, the public is flooded with marketing messages regarding health and well-being[8]. Restaurants respond to consumers' demand for nutritional[9]

❹ obese [əʊ'biːs] *adj.* 极为肥胖的

❺ diabetes [ˌdaɪə'biːtiːz] *n.* 糖尿病

❻ consumption [kən'sʌmpʃn] *n.* 消费

❼ ounce [aʊns] *n.* 盎司

❽ well being [wel-biŋ] *adj.* 健康

❾ nutritional [njuˈtrɪʃənl] *adj.* 营养的

⑩ intervention
　[ˌɪntə'venʃn] *n.* 干预

⑪ workout ['wɔːkaut] *n.*
　锻炼

information. Entire industries are built around the public's demand for diet and healthy living, from diet sodas to weight-loss programs. When people do not buy the "right" foods, this is not evidence of inadequate government intervention[10]; it is evidence of choices based on complex personal preferences. If an individual has the determination to lead a healthy life, he needs very little help from the state. For example, I often have days that start early and end late, so, I try my best to find time to do exercise. I usually fit in a workout[11] in the morning or at night. However, if a person does not have the intention to quit drinking even though he knows it's bad for his health, and then I think the government should spend more time and money reducing the air pollution and improving the transportation system, rather than persuading this alcoholic to stop drinking.

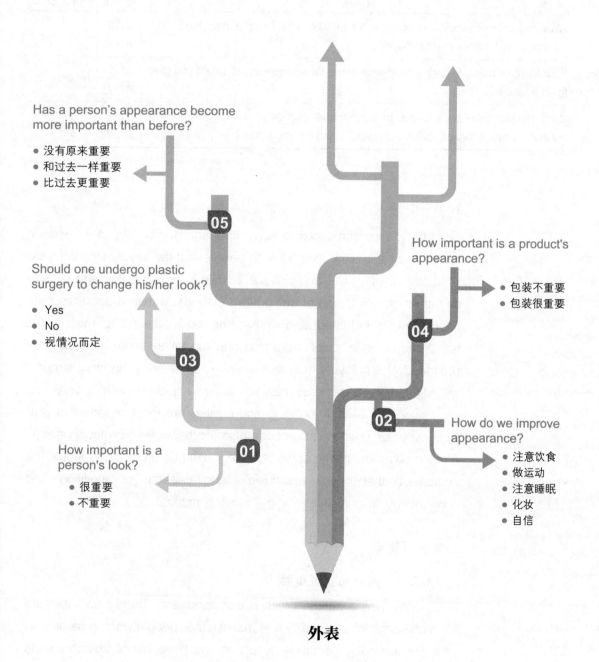

Has a person's appearance become more important than before?

- 没有原来重要
- 和过去一样重要
- 比过去更重要

05

Should one undergo plastic surgery to change his/her look?

- Yes
- No
- 视情况而定

03

How important is a person's look?

- 很重要
- 不重要

01

How important is a product's appearance?

- 包装不重要
- 包装很重要

04

02

How do we improve appearance?

- 注意饮食
- 做运动
- 注意睡眠
- 化妆
- 自信

外表

01 How important is a person's look?

真　题	题　型	年　份
What suggestions would you give a friend who is starting a new job? Give examples and details in your response.	口语 第一题	2013/4/20
Your friend is going to an important interview. What suggestions would you give to your friend?	口语 第一题	2015/03/07
Some people believe it's better to wear formal clothes at work, while others believe it's better to wear casual clothes. Which do you prefer?	口语 第二题	2016/03/26

1.1　很重要

　　I think a person's look is very important. It can help a lot when it comes to finding a job. We'd like to believe that the key to securing a job is strictly talent, drive[1] and skill set[2], while it turns out that appearance can affect the likelihood of being hired even more than a good resume. A person in a well-fitted[3] and wrinkle-free[4] outfit, clean fingernails, neat hair, and a little color from makeup is taken more seriously by prospective[5] employers. On the contrary, a person who is unkempt[6], with dirty nails and messy hair will leave employers with a very bad impression. While your job skills and abilities are most important to your work, your grooming[7] and attitude also represent your professionalism. Also, a tidy person who cares about appearance gives other people the impression that he is responsible and capable of surviving and confronting[8] difficult situations in a positive manner.

1.2　不重要

1.2.1　内心品质更重要

　　I don't think a person's look is that important. There's no substitute for a charismatic[9] personality that makes other people want to be around you. For example, generous people always have lots of lifelong friends because they are willing to offer their time, energy, or efforts without the expectation of something in return. People who are optimistic are usually able to interpret situations in a promising light. Also, people who are

❶ drive [draiv] *n.* 干劲儿
❷ skill set 技能组合
❸ well-fitted [wel-'fitid] *adj.* 适合的，合身的
❹ wrinkle-free ['riŋkl-fri:] *adj.* 免烫的，不起皱的
❺ prospective [prə'spektiv] *adj.* 可能的
　　🔲 expected
❻ unkempt [ˌʌn'kempt] *adj.* 不整洁的
　　🔲 messy
❼ grooming ['gru:miŋ] *n.* 打扮
❽ confront [kən'frʌnt] *v.* 正视（困难局面）
❾ charismatic [ˌkæriz'mætik] *adj.* 有魅力的

reliable are more likely to win other people's trust, because they can be consistently depended upon. So good looks may help you get into a conversation with somebody quickly, but if you have a boring personality the conversation will soon be over.

1.2.2 视情况而定

I think it depends. Looks matter a lot in some industries. For example, the film industry has gotten very tough to get into. Directors prefer someone who has good looks because good looks do boost a film's reputation and increase box office[10] sales. Movies are audiences' fantasies and people go to movies to break their daily routine in life. Thus, people are inclined to[11] imagine their heroes are good-looking guys. The same is true for the modeling industry. Victoria's Secret models are all beautiful, tall and slender,[12] with perfect proportions[13], because designers want them to show off their designs in the best way. Also, models who have the look, style and body can make companies go mad for them, because models can help them sell their products and earn more money. So, we can see that some people are more willing to hire attractive people for those public service jobs. But in the IT industry, where employee's work is primarily with computers, no one cares whether he/she is a stunner[14] or just an ordinary-looking person, as long as they're good at their work. Appearance will never replace talent, skill or intelligence.

⑩ box office *n.* 票房

⑪ be inclined to 倾向于

⑫ slender ['slendə] *adj.* 苗条的，细长的

⑬ proportion [prə'pɔːʃn] *n.* 比例

⑭ stunner ['stʌnə] *n.* 大美女

02 How do we improve appearance?

真　题	题　型	年　份
Your friend has bad eating habits. What suggestions would you like to give the friend?	口语第一题	2012/03/18
Which of the following activities would you like to do on a weekend afternoon? Doing exercise, watching TV, or spending some time with family?	口语第一题	2012/10/28
The university dining hall is changing its food service to include more healthy food with lower calories. What do you think are the advantages and disadvantages of this change?	口语第一题	2013/10/12

（续）

真 题	题 型	年 份
Talk about the things you do that keep you healthy. Give examples and details in your explanation.	口语 第一题	2013/11/22
Which of the following do you prefer? Doing exercise everyday, or only when you are free? Explain your choice in detail.	口语 第一题	2016/09/24

2.1 注意饮食

❶ adage ['ædidʒ] n. 格言

❷ substitute ['sʌbstitjuːt] n. 替代者

❸ frozen pizza 速冻比萨

❹ break out 出（疹子、痘痘、汗）

❺ acne ['ækni] n. 痤疮

We've all heard the old adage[1], "You are what you eat." And that is so true. There is no substitute[2] for eating healthy if you want to look your best in the long run. Whether it's your heart, brain, bones, eyes, skin, or hair you seek to nurture, there are foods up to the task. I used to have very bad eating habits. I ate bagels and cream cheese in the morning, chicken burgers at lunch, and frozen pizza[3] in the evening. Those foods contain too many calories. So, I weighed something like 160 pounds at that time. And I found myself suddenly breaking out[4] in acne[5]. So I began to give more importance to a well-balanced and diversified diet. I started buying more fruits, vegetables, meats and fishes. Within 5 months, I lost like 20 pounds, and my skin is much clearer than before.

2.2 做运动

❻ ritual ['ritʃuəl] n. 惯例，习俗

❼ rosy ['rəuzi] adj. 红润的

The No. 1 way to improve your appearance is to consider exercise as a non-negotiable ritual[6]. Exercising regularly slows down the aging process, gives you smooth skin and makes your muscles look leaner, and thus more attractive. I usually do yoga to keep fit. It's very convenient because I can learn all moves from YouTube. For me, the obvious benefit of working out is to lose weight. I lost about 30 pounds after I picked up yoga! It also greatly improves my circulation. After about a week of working out, I noticed that my cheeks have become naturally rosier[7]!

2.3 注意睡眠

One of the best things that you can do to improve your appearance is getting more rest. Prioritizing[8] sleep will guarantee people appear attractive and refreshed. If people don't get adequate sleep, they will begin to show signs of aging, because sleep is a restorative[9] process in which your body repairs itself. When I don't get enough sleep, I get dark circles[10] and bags under my eyes. I look like a haggard[11] zombie[12]. That definitely scares the boldest man/children. So now I usually sleep from 11:00 p.m. to 7:00 a.m., and try to be consistent in my bedtime. Even though the exact amount of sleep a person needs may vary according to age and lifestyle, usually seven to eight hours of uninterrupted sleep at night are recommended.

2.4 化妆

My best tip is to start wearing a little bit makeup. Wearing makeup can make you prettier and even confident, and putting it on can be fun too! Also, it is the easiest way to enhance your appearance. There are tons of great YouTube tutorials on makeup application. I can't even tell you how much my appearance has changed since I started exploring those makeup videos. I feel like a new person. I used to put a dark line around my eyes and call it a day. Now I use BB cream, blush, mascara[13], highlighters[14], eyebrow pencils[15] and lipsticks. I have a complete, professional "look" now, and it feels great.

2.5 自信

People always focus too much on physical appearance, but ignore the impact of inner spirit — confidence. Confidence changes the expression in one's eyes, which I think, is the most important part of anybody's appearance. It determines a person's spirit. Those who are too self-conscious[16] about their drawbacks, such as small eyes, single-fold eyelid[17], flat nose, thick lips, will never show a firm and steady eye. But those who embrace their features, both the good and the bad, are definitely more attractive. Your sprit is more important than your appearance.

---

⑧ prioritize [prai'ɔrətaiz] v. 优先考虑

⑨ restorative [ri'stɔ:rətiv] adj. 恢复健康的，促进复元的

⑩ dark circle under the eye 黑眼圈

⑪ haggard ['hægəd] adj. 憔悴的

⑫ zombie ['zɔmbi] n. 僵尸

⑬ mascara [mæ'skɑ:rə] n. 睫毛膏

⑭ highlighter ['hailaitər] n. 化妆用的光影粉

⑮ eyebrow pencil 眉笔

⑯ self-conscious [self-'kɔnʃəs] adj. 局促不安的，腼腆的

⑰ single-fold eyelid 单眼皮

03 Should one undergo plastic surgery to change their look?

真　题	题　型	年　份
Do you agree or disagree with the following statement：it is okay for people to use surgery to change their appearance?	口语 第一题	2016/07/16

3.1　Yes

❶ plastic surgery 整形手术

❷ lines [laɪns] n. 皱纹

❸ facelift ['feɪslɪft] n. 面部拉皮手术

❹ rejuvenate [rɪ'dʒuːvɪneɪt] v. 使年轻 使恢复活力

Of course！People can choose to get plastic surgery[1] if they have the need. My aunt Sarah got surgery 2 years ago，because she felt sad and insecure about her aging face. The lines[2] on her face just bothered her a lot. She told me she didn't want to look old and tired. So she got a facelift[3]. And that was really a self-confidence booster for her. Now she is so happy. She is 57 years old now，but she looks like a young lady. She told me that feeling beautiful，healthy，and rejuvenated[4] inside and out was absolutely priceless.

3.2　No

❺ vicious cycle 恶性循环

❻ Botox injection 肉毒杆菌注射

❼ nerve damage 神经损伤

❽ complication [kɔmpli'keiʃn] n. 并发症

I think it's a bad idea to improve one's appearance through plastic surgery. You only have one body, and once you change it through surgery, things will never really be the same again. And it can become a vicious cycle[5]. I have a friend who got plastic surgery last year, because she was obsessed with looking like her favorite actress Fan Bingbing. However，she thought that the result was disappointing. She has had Botox injections[6]，which left her with a fixed duck face. So she got more surgery to "fix" it. She told me she experienced a lot of depression and pain during this process. In addition to that，there are multiple risks，as with any surgery. Scars and nerve damage[7] are all possible complications[8]. So love yourself，and leave your pretty face alone.

3.3　视情况而定

❾ hooked nose 鹰钩鼻

I think it depends. If people are getting surgery for themselves, such as fixing scars from a childhood accident or a hooked nose[9]，then， it would be a good thing to do because it changes their whole life for the better. On the contrary, if people are getting surgery for someone else, that would be a totally different situation. Sometimes people get surgery because of pressure from a boyfriend, a gift from parents, or social recognition. But none of these are good reasons to get surgery. Getting your breasts done won't make an unfaithful boyfriend stop cheating. Getting a brow lift won't make a husband with a wandering eye stop looking at younger women. Getting liposuction[10] won't get you that job promotion you've been denied. Surgery can absolutely enhance your life, but in the end, it's just fixing something on the outside. It can't fix your whole life.

⑩ liposuction ['lipə'trɔpik]
n. 抽脂手术

04 How important is a product's appearance?

真　题	题　型	年　份
Do you agree or disagree with the statement that advertisements make products seem better than they really are?	独立写作题	TPO17

4.1　包装不重要

　　I think we have put too much emphasis on[1] packaging[2]. I'm not saying that packaging isn't important — it certainly is. My point is that when companies put more emphasis on their packaging than their products, it results in the disappointment we've all experienced. I once bought mooncakes in a large fancy metal box, which was decorated with exquisite[3] patterns. And it was very expensive. However, it turned out there were only 2 mooncakes in the box and they tasted like feet! I felt so disappointed. How could they cheat me like this? Nowadays, it is just so common to see that some products are over-packaged which serves no real purpose other than to make something look pretty. It's just not necessary for everyday products.

❶ put emphasis on 重视
❷ packaging ['pækidʒiŋ]
n. 包装

❸ exquisite ['ekskwizit]
adj. 精美的

4.2　包装很重要

4.2.1　可以吸引顾客

④ container [kən'teinə] *n.*
容器

I think giving the container[4] a pleasing appearance is very important, so that consumers will feel comfortable displaying it in their home. For example, in the past, a lot of companies sold cookies in a plain cardboard[5] box. But now they might sell them in a nice metal box, and they might decorate that box with beautiful pictures. That way, when customers present the cookies to guests, they look nice and classy. Attractive containers like that can make a product much more appealing.

⑤ cardboard ['ka:dbɔ:d] *n.*
硬纸板

4.2.2　市场竞争过于激烈

It is very important to make the package appealing, because there are thousands of products on the market competing for customers' attention. Most customers don't have the time or energy to weigh[6] the advantages and disadvantages of the products in their shopping carts, so they use a shortcut[7] to make their decision. That shortcut is products' packaging. Think about it: A new product on a shelf, a consumer seeing it for the first time, not having any association with it. If the packaging is weak, plain and boring, no one would want it. But if it is exciting, informative, creative and alluring[8], it can make a great first impression. Packaging is how a product introduces itself. To succeed, your brand packaging has to stand out and look different from your competitors. For example, as a shopper walks through the coffee aisle[9] of the local grocery store, the bright orange, pink and white packaging of the Dunkin' Donuts coffee brand may be easily recognizable for the consumer to grab on his way by the coffee shelf. It's just so eye-catching!

⑥ weigh [wei] *v.* 权衡考虑

⑦ shortcut ['ʃɔ:tkʌt] *n.* 捷径

⑧ alluring [ə'luəriŋ] *adj.*
迷人的

⑨ aisle [ail] *n.* 走道，过道

4.2.3　有助于品牌形象的建立

Packaging is powerful because it tells consumers why your product and brand are different. In other words, it is a helpful marketing tool through in-store advertising. A uniquely designed package helps consumers remember your products next time they are shopping. Take a moment to think about some of your favorite brands. They all have one thing in common：they are memorable. Over the decades, brands like Coke have made minor changes to their packaging and stayed true to their original look. Also, Apple is known for its clean, white, minimalist[10] packaging. And think of Tiffany & Co. For most people, the iconic[11] blue box is more recognizable than the jewelry itself.

⑩ minimalist ['miniməlist] *adj.* 极简的

⑪ iconic [ai'kɔnik] *adj.* 象征性的

4.2.4　有人为拆包装而活

I think many manufacturers realized the importance of good packaging in the early 80s. Steve Jobs was one of them. Just look at the gorgeous packaging of Apple products；just search on YouTube for the keyword "unboxing[12]". Millions of results come up within a second. People just love the feeling of getting a present, a gift, or a high-tech item that they have been saving money for months for. I totally get these people who love posting videos about unboxing. I was just thrilled when I received my GoPro Hero 5 camera last summer, and when I was opening the package. I will never forget that feeling.

⑫ unbox [ˌʌn'bɔks] *v.* 拆箱，从箱子中取出

5　Has a person's appearance become more important than before?

真　题	题　型	年　份
What suggestions would you give a friend who is starting a new job? Give examples and details in your response.	口语第一题	2013/4/20
Your friend is going to an important interview. What suggestions would you give to your friend?	口语第一题	2015/03/07

5.1　没有原来重要

I disagree with this statement. For example, we used to judge teachers based on their appearance. I had a science teacher who always wore a white lab coat over his suit. It did seem to make him look more qualified and generally like a better educated teacher. So, what a

❶ perception [pə'sepʃn]
n. 看法

teacher wears affects students' perceptions[1] of them. However, now, thanks to the Internet, we have online classes. Even though I live in Beijing, I can study with a teacher from America to practice my English by using Skype. And I have no idea what he looks like or how he is dressed, but it doesn't matter at all. To me, he is the best English teacher ever! So I think appearance is less important than before because of the Internet.

5.2 和过去一样重要

I don't agree with the statement. Our habit of "judging a book by its cover[2]" stays exactly the same as before. It is human nature to judge by physical experience. Those who are fortunate enough to be born beautiful or handsome have an edge[3] over others, either now or in the past. This happens because beauty is an indicator[4] of other characteristics, such as good health. Our minds are still looking at factors, such as great-looking hair, teeth and skin, as indicators of survival and success. And that's why employers use them when they choose people who they think will make the most money or do the best job for their organization.

❷ judge a book by its cover
以貌取人

❸ edge [edʒ] n. 优势

❹ indicator ['indikeitə] n.
指示物

5.3 比过去更重要

I think a person's appearance is more important than before. Imagine you have two candidates for a job. They are both of the same sex. They both graduated from world elite[5] universities. Their CVs are equally good, and they both give good interviews. You cannot help noticing, though, that one is ugly and the other is handsome. Are you swayed by their appearance? Perhaps not. But most people might be. Thanks to the spread of education, nowadays, most people meet the requirements in terms of[6] skill set. However, beauty has become a necessary qualification, especially in public service jobs.

❺ elite [ei'li:t] adj. 精英的

❻ in terms of 就……而言

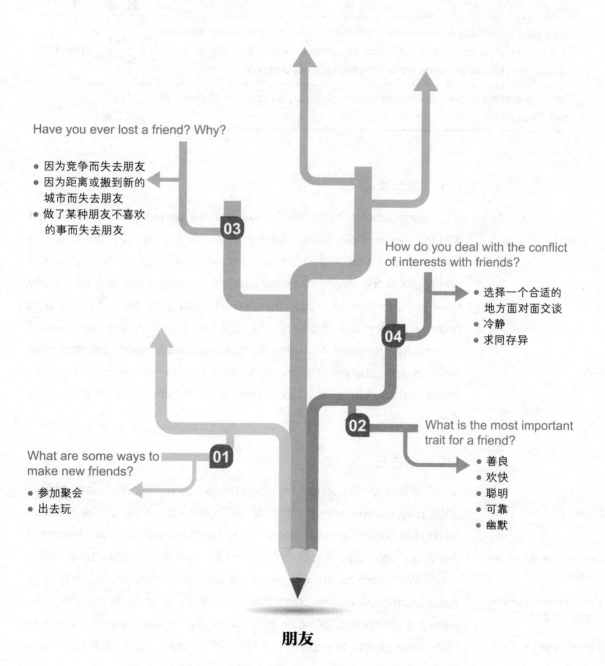

Have you ever lost a friend? Why?

- 因为竞争而失去朋友
- 因为距离或搬到新的城市而失去朋友
- 做了某种朋友不喜欢的事而失去朋友

03

How do you deal with the conflict of interests with friends?

- 选择一个合适的地方面对面交谈
- 冷静
- 求同存异

04

What is the most important trait for a friend?

- 善良
- 欢快
- 聪明
- 可靠
- 幽默

02

What are some ways to make new friends?

- 参加聚会
- 出去玩

01

朋友

第十五类　朋友

01　What are some ways to make new friends?

真　题	题　型	年　份
Nowadays, children rely too much on technology, like computers, smartphones, and video games for fun and entertainment; playing with simpler toys or playing outside with friends would be better for children's development.	口语 第一题	2015/06/14
Which one of the following invitations would you go to, a family dinner party, or a friend's party?	口语 第二题	2016/11/16

1.1　参加聚会

I come across many colorful experiences when I fill my Friday night with trips to multiple clubs, bars and house parties. By going out to parties on the weekend, I am exposed to new sorts of music, people and experiences. Many students who are normally busy with their study have opportunities to better their social skills and make friends at a party. My friend Jay and I first met at a friend's party. We were playing a game that required 4 people to compete. Pretty soon, we started to team up and crushed other players. After the game, we started to talk, found out we had a lot in common, and became good friends since then.

1.2　出去玩

❶ loosen up 放松

❷ pick-up [pik-ʌk] *adj.* 组队的

❸ give someone a look 给某人一个眼色

❹ arsenal [ˈɑːsinl] *n.* 武器库

The day-to-day school workload can sometimes seem unbearable. I often play outside with my friends to loosen up[1]. One of the greatest feelings in playing outside is getting to hang out with friends. My friend Jay and I often play a pick-up[2] (5 on 5) basketball game at an open court. We communicate with our eyes and body movements. When he gives me a look[3] on the court, I know exactly what he is planning. As there are always lots of other players there, we can take many moves from these people to expand our arsenal[4] of tricks. No matter how awful we feel before the game, we feel refreshed after.

Joining an outdoor activity is a great way to connect with people. Many of our first friendships were formed through sports activities. That's how I met my friend Jay. We were on the same basketball team. One time, he was supposed to take the shot, as he is a much better shooter, but he passed the ball to me because I had an open look⁵. His trust really boosted my confidence and I made the shot. In that game, we had each other's back and we worked together to win the game. After the game, we found out we had other common interests besides basketball. Since then, we have become really good friends.

❺ open look 空位

02 What are the most important trait for a friend?

真　题	题　型	年　份
Which of your traits do your friends like the best? Kindness, cheerfulness, or intelligence?	口语第一题	2015/07/11
Getting advice from friends who are older than you is more valuable than getting that from your peers.	口语第二题	2016/02/28
It is better to make friends with people who are intelligent than with those who have a good sense of humor.	口语第二题	2016/12/10

2.1 善良

A kind person can always make you feel better. When he or she senses you are in a bad mood, he or she will give you a sincere¹ smile, a hug, or a pat on the shoulder, which all can immediately cheer you up. My friend Alice always goes out of her way to cheer up those who are in need. When I see the smile on these people's faces, my heart melts. One time, she saw an old man struggling with a heavy bag at the airport. Most people just walk by and make snide² remarks about how people who are too old to carry their luggage should stay home. But my friend carried the bag to the cart for him. I was so touched by her action and that also encouraged me to be a kind person just like her.

❶ sincere [sin'siə] *adj.* 真诚的

❷ snide [snaid] *adj.* 讽刺的

第十五类 朋友

2.2 欢快

It is a powerful emotion. A person in a good mood can often complete tasks and overcome obstacles[3] in life much easier than a person who is depressed or sad. For example, we had a basketball game the other day, and I was the point guard[4]. It was a championship game, and I was supposed to play well. But I was really in a bad mood, so I wasn't as sharp as I usually am. By the end of the first half, our team was 20 points behind. My best friend Jay came to me at halftime with his big smile. When I saw his smile, my stress started to release. He told me the shot I made a couple of minutes ago was really impressive. His smile and words really cheered me up. In the second half, I was able to bring my A-game and helped the team win in the end.

2.3 聪明

An intelligent friend is the best teacher. They give us good advice. As the saying goes, a friend in need is a friend indeed. For example, my best friend Jay is extremely intelligent, sociable, and resourceful. He always tells me what to do when I mess things up[5]. There was this time when I got into trouble with my girlfriend. He encouraged me to apologize to my girlfriend and to put myself in her shoes[6]. We got back together finally. This has turned me into a person with a whole different life perspective. Obviously, having an intelligent friend is helpful for one's self-improvement.

2.4 可靠

A friend who is truly reliable can be a friend for life. If you cannot trust a friend, the relationship won't last long. Lack of trust is a harmful attack to any relationship. I once shared one of my deepest secrets with my best friend. Unfortunately, this so called "best friend" quickly told another friend. Pretty soon, everybody in my school knew it. Years have passed, but the anger and shame I felt when my friend broke his promise of secrecy is still very real.

③ obstacle ['ɒbstəkl] *n.* 困难

④ point guard 得分后卫

⑤ mess up 搞砸

⑥ put oneself in one's shoes 站在某人的角度

2.5 幽默

Humorous friends are our greatest assets[7]. They make our life full of happiness and joy. They help me to release stress and to keep an optimistic attitude. My best friend Jay is a very funny guy. He is the kind of person who always makes me laugh. Sometimes he likes funny dances. I wasn't feeling great last summer. I was living in an awful apartment and struggling with school work. Then, Jay sent me a video of himself dancing to *Gangnam Style*[8]. It was very hilarious[9] seeing his weird moves. And at that moment, I forgot all the troubles in my real life.

Humorous communication boosts the emotional connection that will bring people closer together, and increase happiness, especially when my friends and I have disagreements. During difficult times in our relationship, sharing heartfelt laughter will be enough to bridge the gap[10] and fill the crack[11]. When my best friend Jay and I have had arguments, he has been the one who always cracks some silly jokes[12]. Then we would have a good laugh and enjoy the rest of the day. Humor is really the most powerful tool for managing conflicts and reducing tension.

❼ asset ['æset] *n.* 优点

❽ *Gangnam Style* 《江南style》

❾ hilarious [hi'lɛəriəs] *adj.* 滑稽的

❿ bridge the gap 缩小差距

⓫ fill the crack 填补裂缝

⓬ crack jokes 讲笑话

03 Have you ever lost a friend? Why?

真 题	题 型	年 份
When you have been friends with someone for a long time, it is important to continue your friendship with that person even if he or she does something you do not like.	口语 第二题	2013/03/30
Some believe that we should spend more time far away from the people we care about, because it is necessary for people to understand the importance of relationships, while others think being away from people we care about can damage our relationships with them.	口语 第二题	2015/11/15
It is often not a good thing to move to a new city or a new country because you will lose touch with old friends.	口语 第二题	2016/01/23
Competition between friends often negatively impacts friendships. Use specific details and examples to support your opinion.	独立 写作题	2016/07/01

3.1　因为竞争而失去朋友

3.1.1　失去信任

Friends lose trust in each other when they have are exposed to situations of competition. For example, I experienced betrayal[1] from one of my co-workers when I first started working in a company. Before we worked in the same position, we were good friends. Since my boss announced that whoever between us completed the project within a month, he would be promoted to a higher-level position. Of course, it was a competition between us. Naturally, both of us wanted to capture such a golden opportunity. As a result, he betrayed me and stepped on me for achieving a better position. From that experience, I always tell myself that I will not try to compete with my friends in the work place, because I have no desire to lose friendships with anybody again.

3.1.2　不愿分享

Competition leads people to have more self-attention, and to disregard[2] giving and sharing. For instance, when I was in high school, my classmates and I had exams frequently. Because the teachers evaluated[3] performance of students based on score percentage systems, everyone had to compete with others to get good grades. In fact, nobody wanted to share study materials with others. They even paid no attention to their friends who needed help with school work. So tension was accumulating[4] in the class, and all of my classmates were drifting apart because of this terrible system.

3.1.3　竞争帮助走出舒适区域

It forces us to step out of our comfort zone[5]. The great thing about having friends as your competitors is that you have to be more innovative[6]. You have to think outside the box and go after new options in order to get ahead. When I was in high school, I was pretty good at Math. So was my friend Jay. We both wanted to prove that we were better than the other. So we would approach the question from other angles and come up with smarter ideas. Eventually, we both improved our math skills enormously. And we got much higher grades in school. If we gave up our competitive spirit, we wouldn't be as good as we are right now.

① betrayal [bi'treiəl] n.
背叛

② disregard [,disri'gɑ:d] v.
忽视

③ evaluate [i'væljueit] v.
评价

④ accumulate [ə'kju:mjuleit]
v. 累积

⑤ comfort zone 舒适区域

⑥ innovative ['inəuveitiv]
adj. 革新的

3.2　因为距离或搬到新城市并失去朋友

It's common knowledge that long-distance relationships are difficult and most likely doomed[7]. Jay and I were best friends back in college in my hometown. We would go play basketball after school all the time. If we had time off during weekends, we would go to see a movie together or just grab a beer in a local bar. We hung out almost every day. Then, after graduation, we moved to different cities for work. We started getting busy, there was always an event to attend, and making time for each other was a constant battle of highly conflicting schedules. We realized long distance friendships are really hard to maintain under the crushing pace of life[8]. Later, I found him on Facebook. Seeing his pictures posted with his new friends makes me realize that we are completely different people now.

People often move to different cities to go to their dream schools or pursue new careers. That doesn't mean the friendship has to end. Jay and I were best friends back in college in my hometown. Then I moved to a big city for work but he decided to stay. We were really busy with our work and life. However, we always squeezed in time to schedule video chats online. We used video chat to see each other's faces, show each other's apartments, and introduce each other's new friends into our life. I always sent him old-school letters and he sent me back gift cards. These all made me feel special and served as mementos[9] of our friendship.

3.3　做了某件朋友不喜欢的事而失去朋友

That hurts my feelings. If my friend did something wrong and if it really hurt, I would choose to end the friendship. Back in high school, my most trusted friend lied to me. Everybody at school knew the truth except me. I still hung out with him. Then I found out his lies and I simply shut him out of my life. This was the first time I have ever chosen to stick to my guns[10] because I realized how terrible I felt around him. I never turned back after that, because even if I could forgive him, I would never forget. Life is too short to worry about the people who don't matter.

❼ doomed［doomd］*adj.* 注定的

❽ crushing pace of life 快节奏

❾ memento［mə'mentəu］*n.* 纪念品

❿ stick to one's guns 坚持自己的意见

04 How do you deal with conflicts of interests with friends?

真 题	题 型	年 份
Do you agree or disagree with the following statement? It is possible for friends to maintain their friendship even when they have disagreements over certain issues.	口语 第二题	2015/09/05

4.1 选择一个合适的地方面对面交谈

I will choose face-to-face contact instead of having a conversation about the issue over text, messenger, email, or phone. It is the best approach to solving conflicts because it reduces the likelihood of miscommunication. You can't tell a person's tone or facial expression[1] from a text message. Also, I will pick a private place like a small coffee shop where other people I know are not around. This way, my friend will feel comfortable and respected. Having a cup of coffee with my friend in a quiet and nice place really helps to resolve a conflict.

❶ facial expression 面部表情

4.2 冷静

In a heated situation, it's easy to lash out[2] at the person who offended me, which would cause me to say or do things I later regret. I would nicely remind my friend that maybe we should take some time to clear our heads. I would go for a walk and put on a headset with some light music to loosen up[3]. Or take a warm bath with some candles to refresh me. Or maybe engage in an activity like running that provides an outlet for me to vent my frustrations. When I finally calmed down, I would be able to think the conflict through. So I can come up with better ways to solve it with my friend.

❷ lash out 猛击

❸ loosen up 放松

4.3 求同存异

Resolving a conflict should not be seen as a contest to see who was right or wrong. It is okay to agree to disagree, because no disagreement is worth losing a friend. When I see a conversation turning into a disagreement, I stop and remind myself that our friendship means more to me than the issue at hand. Jay and I have been friends for years. There was a time when we had a big argument about a sports game. I could feel the tension between us as we were arguing. So I stopped and held my breath for several seconds to make myself calm down. Then I realized he is way more important to me than the stupid sports game. So I agreed with his opinion. Over the years, we've disagreed on lots of topics, but we are still good friends.

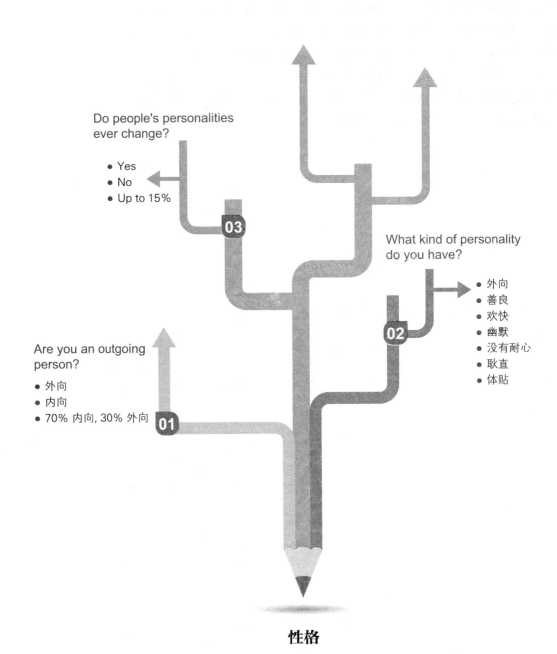

Do people's personalities ever change?

- Yes
- No
- Up to 15%

03

What kind of personality do you have?

- 外向
- 善良
- 欢快
- 幽默
- 没有耐心
- 耿直
- 体贴

02

Are you an outgoing person?

- 外向
- 内向
- 70% 内向, 30% 外向

01

性格

01 Are you an outgoing person?

真 题	题 型	年 份
Some students prefer to live alone or live with their friends when they study abroad. Other students prefer to live with a local family when they study abroad. Which way do you prefer and why?	口语 第二题	2012/07/22
Which of the following three activities do you prefer to do with a group of people rather than alone? Eat a meal, listen to music, or do homework?	口语 第一题	2012/08/19
Which of the following three activities do you prefer to do with a group of people rather than alone? Eat a meal, listen to music, or do homework?	口语 第一题	2012/08/25
Which of the following activities would you do with friends rather than alone? Taking a walk, watching a movie or traveling?	口语 第一题	2012/10/28
When there's a challenge, would you prefer to face it alone, or would you rather seek help from others?	口语 第二题	2013/04/20
Some people prefer to celebrate special occasions like birthdays with their friends; others prefer to be alone at such occasions. Which do you prefer? Use examples and details to support your response.	口语 第二题	2013/08/17
Which of the following activities would you do with friends rather than alone? Taking a walk, watching a movie or traveling?	口语 第一题	2013/11/16
Some people like to spend their spare time with family members and friends; some people like to spend it alone. Which do you prefer?	口语 第二题	2014/03/02
Some students prefer to live alone or live with their friends when they study abroad. Other students prefer to live with a local family when they study abroad. Which way do you prefer and why?	口语 第二题	2014/05/25
Some people prefer to celebrate special occasions like birthdays with their friends; others prefer to be alone at such occasions. Which do you prefer? Use examples and details to support your response.	口语 第二题	2014/11/29
Which of the following activities do you think is more beneficial for a child's growth? Doing team sports, talking with others or traveling?	口语 第一题	2014/12/13
Some people like to share their thoughts through publications like newspapers and blogs. Others prefer to only share them with friends. Which one do you prefer?	口语 第二题	2014/12/27
Some people like to spend their spare time with family members and friends; some people like to spend it alone. Which do you prefer?	口语 第二题	2014/12/27

（续）

真　题	题　型	年　份
When there's a challenge, would you prefer to face it alone, or would you rather seek help from others?	口语 第二题	2015/05/30
Nowadays, children rely too much on technology, like computers, smartphones, and video games for fun and entertainment; playing with simpler toys or playing outside with friends would be better for the children's development.	口语 第一题	2015/06/14
Which do you prefer? Watching a movie silently or chatting with others?	口语 第二题	2015/08/22
When parents cannot afford time to accompany their children, they could choose to send their children to child-care centers, where many children are cared for together; or they could send their children to an individual caregiver. Which one is better?	口语 第二题	2015/11/08
Do you agree or disagree with the following statement? If you want to be successful in running a business, being outgoing and friendly is very important.	口语 第二题	2016/08/21
Which of the following three activities do you prefer to do with a group of people rather than alone? Eat a meal, listen to music or do homework?	口语 第一题	2016/12/11

1.1　外向

1.1.1　和朋友一起玩

❶ extrovert ['ekstrəvə:t]
　 n. 性格外向者

❷ time off 空闲时间

I am an extrovert[1]. I have a very big social circle. I just simply like to hang out with a bunch of people rather than being alone. If I have some time off[2], I call my friends and we can watch a movie while talking about our favorite actors, go to the mall to buy some fancy new electronics or have dinner at a new restaurant together. As long as I am with my friends, it doubles the fun. When you see me in a photo, I am never alone; I'm always with a bunch of people.

1.1.2　向朋友学到很多东西

I like to be with people, because I can always learn something from them. For example, a friend might recommend me a movie that I have not heard of, tell me about a fascinating book he/she has read, or have a different view about a political issue. I learn tons of new and interesting things by sharing with my friends. I feel the same when it comes to study. I couldn't bear studying alone. I would have a hard time concentrating if I have questions and have no one to ask. If I study with my friends, I can always have their perspectives and get things done efficiently.

1.2　内向

1.2.1　自己更舒服

I rather like being alone. It makes me feel uneasy when I hang out with lots of people, because I have to cope with[3] others all the time. Working with friends and people at school every day makes me tired. I really need some quality time just by myself. Staying alone, I can listen to my favorite music and do my other favorite things without being disturbed by others or listening to their opinions. Being alone allows me to look at myself.

❸ cope with 处理，应付

1.3　70% 内向，30% 外向

I remember once reading in a magazine that everybody is somewhere between an extrovert[4] and an introvert[5]. I guess I am exactly the case. The magazine continued to claim that an extrovert gains energy through interaction with others. If left alone for a long time, they might become agitated[6] and depressed. On the other hand, introverts consume their energy while being with other people, and regain their energy when they are spending time alone. I feel like I'm more like the latter. However, occasionally, I feel the need to talk to others too. I mean, I also need companionship sometimes, but it cannot be too much. For instance, it feels nice to chat with others after I spend two days alone in my apartment. But if the chat lasts for more than 2 hours, I will feel exhausted. So, I guess the important thing here is to find the balance.

❹ extrovert ['ekstrəvə: t] *n.* 性格外向者
❺ introvert ['intrəvə:t] *n.* 性格内向者
❻ agitated ['ædʒiteitid] *adj.* 激动的

02 What kind of personality do you have?

真　题	题　型	年　份
Which of your traits do your friends like the best? Kindness, cheerfulness, or intelligence?	口语 第一题	2012/05/20
It is better to make friends with intelligent people than with people who have a good sense of humor.	独立 写作题	2015/06/27
Some people prefer to buy a product as soon as it is on the market. Other people prefer to purchase a product when it has been on the market for some time. Which do you prefer and why?	口语 第二题	2016/09/03
Which of your traits do your friends like the best? Kindness, cheerfulness, or intelligence?	口语 第一题	2016/09/25
Some people prefer to finish assignments a long time before the due date, while others prefer to finish the assignment right before the deadline. Which one do you prefer and why?	口语 第二题	2016/09/25

2.1　外向

❶ extrovert ['ekstrəvə: t]
n. 性格外向者

An outgoing person has a very big social circle. He or she can introduce you to people you might have otherwise not known. They're great at networking and seem to always know someone who can help you out. For example, my friend Jay is an extrovert[1]. He knows everyone in my school. There was a time I was stuck with a math project and couldn't work it out. When I brought this up, Jay already had a ton of people in mind to put me in touch with. Thanks to Jay, I got help from some helpful professors and a couple of students who are really good at math, and I completed a really good project.

2.2　善良

❷ sincere [sin'siə] *adj.* 真
诚的

A kind person can always make you feel better. When he or she senses you are in a bad mood, he or she will give you a sincere[2] smile, a hug, or a pat on the shoulder, all of which can immediately cheer you up. My friend Alice always goes out of her way to cheer up those who are in need. When I see the smiles on these people's faces, my heart melts. One time, she saw an old man struggling with a heavy bag at the airport. Most people would just walk by and make a snide[3] remark about that people too old to carry their luggage should stay home. But my friend carried the bag to the cart for him. I was so touched by her action and that it also encouraged me to be a kind person, just like her.

③ snide [snaid] *adj.* 讽刺的

2.3　欢快

It is a powerful emotion. A person in a good mood usually can complete tasks and overcome obstacles[4] in life much easier than a person who is depressed or sad. For example, we had a basketball game the other day. And I was the point guard[5]. It was a championship game and I was supposed to play well. But I was really in a bad mood, so I wasn't as sharp as I usually am. By the end of the first half, our team was 20 points behind. My best friend Jay came to me at halftime with his big smile. When I saw his smile, my stress started to release. He told me the shot I made a couple of minutes ago was really impressive. His smile and words really cheered me up. At the second half, I was able to bring my A-game[6], and I helped the team win in the end.

④ obstacle ['ɔbstəkl] *n.* 困难

⑤ point guard 得分后卫

⑥ bring my A-game 状态好

2.4　幽默

Humorous friends are our greatest assets[7]. They make our life full of happiness and joy. They help me to release stress and to keep an optimistic attitude. My best friend Jay is a very funny guy. He is the kind of person who always makes me laugh. Sometimes, he likes funny dances. I wasn't feeling great last summer. I was living in an awful apartment and struggling with school work. Then, Jay sent me a video of himself dancing to *Gangnam Style*[8]. It was very hilarious[9] seeing his weird moves. At that moment, I forgot all my troubles in real life.

Humorous communication boosts the emotional connection that will bring people closer together, and increases happiness, especially when my friends and I have disagreements. During the difficult time in my relationship, sharing heartfelt laughter will be enough to bridge the gap[10] and fill the crack[11]. When my best friend Jay and I have arguments, he is the one who always crack some silly jokes[12]. Then we would have a good

⑦ asset ['æset] *n.* 优点

⑧ *Gangnam Style* 《江南style》

⑨ hilarious [hi'lɛəriəs] *adj.* 滑稽的

⑩ bridge the gap 缩小差距

⑪ fill the crack 填补裂缝

⑫ crack some silly jokes 讲愚蠢的笑话

laugh and enjoy the rest of the day. Humor is really the most powerful tool for managing conflict and reducing tension when they are running high.

2.5 没有耐心

I am an extremely impatient person. When it comes to shopping, I like to buy my favorite product as soon as it is in the market. You can always spot me in a waiting line outside the store at 3 a. m. Getting the product a couple of hours earlier than others is a big deal to me. That's also the reason why I always finish my schoolwork a long time before the due date. I start working on it as soon as I get the assignment. I can't wait till the last minute, because I am always busy with something else. Life is too short for putting things off[13] and wasting time.

⑬ put off 拖延

2.6 耿直

I am a straightforward person. If I don't like someone, I will show my dislike for him all over my face. If I am unhappy, I will say it out aloud. If I want to eat the last chicken nuggets[14] left on the table, I will call for it and grab it without asking permission from others. If I am tired during a card game, I will drop my cards and tell everyone that I am tired and have to get rest. I guess there are pros and cons[15] for my way of dealing with people. On the bright side, at least everyone knows what I am thinking and I, for most of the time, am happy. On the negative side, some people might find it unpleasant to be friends or coworkers with me, since I do not care so much about others' feelings.

⑭ chicken nuggets 鸡块

⑮ pros and cons 好处和坏处

2.7 体贴

I would like to always think before I speak to others. In other words, I often sugar-coat[16] what I say. For example, my friend Sen just asked me yesterday if his new hairstyle looks cute. To be honest, it looks as if he just came out of prison. But instead of telling him the truth, I told him that it looks dangerous, in a good way. In this way, he will not be offended and even might feel happy for his new hair. At the same time, if he is smart enough, he might get my hint from the word "dangerous" and might consequently try for a longer hairstyle the next time.

⑯ sugar-coat 粉饰

03 Do people's personalities ever change?

真　题	题　型	年　份
Do you agree or disagree with the statement that people's personalities never change?	口语 第二题	2014/03/16
Do you think you can learn a lot about a stranger from the first observation, or you have to know his personality for a long time?	口语 第二题	2016/03/13
Do you think you can learn a lot about a stranger from the first observation, or you have to know his personality for a long time?	口语 第二题	2016/05/07

3.1　Yes

I think environment can shape people's personalities over time. For instance, I was an introvert[1] when I was in college. I preferred to do everything alone. I would eat my lunch by myself and then go back to my dorm to finish my school assignments alone. I never joined study groups or went to parties with lots of people. However, everything changed after I graduated. I was working in a big company and I had to cope with many co-workers, because we had to finish tons of team projects. So, I started to learn how to work with people, how to connect and build relationships. After work, I would go to bars or grab a cup of coffee with my colleagues. I felt great to fit in with the group. Everybody liked me as an outgoing person.

❶ introvert ['intrəvə:t] *n.*
内向性格者

3.2　No

People's personalities never change. I am a naturally casual and spontaneous[2] guy. When I was in college, I played video games all night long and didn't get up till the afternoon. But then I graduated and started to work for a big company. My work schedule was very structured, and my manager was obsessive[3] about schedules. Even though I forced myself to start getting up early every morning and going to bed regularly. I still couldn't stick to it. My boss fired me when I was late for the third time in a week. After that, I started to realize that it is really hard for me to change my personality.

❷ spontaneous [spɒn'teiniəs] *adj.* 自然的

❸ obsessive [əb'sesiv] *adj.* 着迷的

3.3　Up to 15%

④ vividly ['vividli] *adv.* 生
动地
⑤ *Modern Family*《摩登
家庭》
⑥ Philip Dumpy《摩登家
庭》中的一个主角

⑦ perseverance [ˌpəːsiˈviərəns]
n. 坚持不懈

I remember vividly[4] that in one episode of my favorite TV series *Modern Family*[5] , my favorite character Philip Dumpy[6] said that people's personality cannot change much. The maximum amount is approximately 15% , if they really make an effort. But his philosophy is that people's characteristics are pretty much fixed and cannot change much. I totally agree with him. But I guess there might be exceptions for people with truly exceptional perseverance[7] .

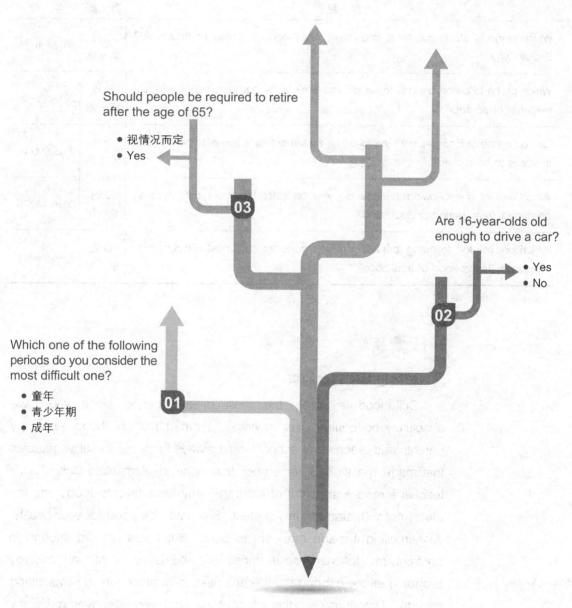

Should people be required to retire after the age of 65?

- 视情况而定
- Yes

Are 16-year-olds old enough to drive a car?

- Yes
- No

Which one of the following periods do you consider the most difficult one?

- 童年
- 青少年期
- 成年

03

02

01

年龄

01 Which one of the following periods do you consider the most difficult one? (childhood, teens or adulthood)

真　题	题　型	年　份
Which stage of life is the most important, childhood, juvenile, or adulthood? Explain why.	口语 第一题	2012/06/15
Which of the following periods in life do you think is the hardest, being a kid, a teenager or an adult?	口语 第一题	2014/06/29
Do you agree or disagree with the following statement: it is easier to be an adult than it is to be a child?	口语 第二题	2015/11/14
Which one of the following periods do you consider the most difficult one, childhood, teen period or adulthood?	口语 第一题	2016/08/20
Which one of the following periods do you consider the most difficult one, childhood, teen period or adulthood?	口语 第一题	2016/08/21

1.1　童年

被强迫做不喜欢的事

Childhood is surely the most difficult period since you have absolutely no control over anything. I hated my childhood since my parents and teachers at school would always force me to eat vegetables that made me sick. I remember that once in elementary school, my teacher forced a spoonful of cabbage, my least favorite food, into my plate, not with standing my protest. She said, it's good for your health. Just smelling it made me want to puke. But I was not old enough to confront my teacher, so I chose an alternative: I started secretly dropping all the cabbage[1] under the heating radiator[2] which I was sitting next to. Unfortunately, this clandestine [3]act was discovered by my teacher, who later pulled me up to the front of our class, and made me eat all the cabbage that was left in my plate. Eventually, I threw up[4] in front of my whole class.

❶ cabbage ['kæbidʒ] n. 卷心菜
❷ heating radiator 暖气片
❸ clandestine [klæn'destin] adj. 秘密的　secret
❹ puke [pju:k] v. 呕吐

1.2　青少年期

1.2.1　高考

The teen period is definitely the most difficult one.

Well, teenagers have to deal with pressure from school. In China for example, students have to face the infamous[5] College Entrance Examination[6], which requires students to dedicate[7] almost three full years of their lives completely to preparation for this test. Without a decent test score, students will never have a chance to enter a decent[8] college. Without a decent college degree, students will never have a chance to get a decent job. As a result, many students who feel nervous about the test suffer from anxiety and insomnia. Those who do not perform well on the real test day might end up being depressed, and some might even commit[9] suicide.

1.2.2　与父母的冲突

Teenagers are going through a transitional phase in their life, which is hard. Teenagers want independence, but in the eyes of their parents, they are still kids. Thus, conflict between parents and children occurs frequently. With the rise of hormones, teenagers have trouble controlling their temper, which also escalates[10] the conflict with their parents. My mom used to say that I was in my rebellious period[11] during my teenage years, as I was likely to defy[12] everything they told me to do. For example, I wanted to become a professional musician during high school. So, I asked my parents if I could postpone my entrance into college so that I could have a gap year[13] to try out in a band. They replied, "Not over our dead bodies." I was furious. I thought they were unreasonable and I knew that I had the strong urge and believed that I could become a top-class player in the music industry. Sadly, I was not able to form a sound[14] argument and convince them that I was right. At last, I reluctantly[15] went to study accounting in a regular university.

1.2.3　社交压力——男女朋友

People start to date in their teens, and an issue soon appears for a lot of teenagers: how to get a boyfriend or girlfriend. We are social animals, so we compare ourselves to others constantly. When our

❺ infamous ['infəməs]
adj. 臭名昭著的
同 notorious

❻ College Entrance
Examination 高考

❼ dedicate ['dedikeit] *v.*
把……奉献给

❽ decent ['di:sənt] *adj.* 相
当好的

❾ commit [kə'mit] *v.* 做
错事

❿ escalate ['eskəleit] *v.* 使
升级

⓫ rebellious period *n.* 叛
逆期

⓬ defy [di'fai] *v.* 挑战，
蔑视
同 challenge

⓭ gap year *n.* 空档期（高
中与大学之间，或大学
与工作之间）

⓮ sound [saund] *adj.* 健
全的

⓯ reluctantly [ri'lʌktəntli]
adv. 不情愿地

classmates get handsome boyfriend or girlfriends, we would subconsciously feel the need to also get a boyfriend or girlfriend. The pressure is intense for teens since they are not mature[16] enough to adjust their inner feelings. In other words, they feel they could lose face without a girlfriend/boyfriend.

⑯ mature [mə'tʃuə] *adj.* 成熟

1.3 成年

1.3.1 经济独立

All of a sudden, you have to take care of yourself financially. I did not realize that there are so much expenses that you have to pay for, before I actually have to deal with them myself. For example, after graduation, I rented a two-bedroom apartment with my best college buddy Max. During the first winter, we thought the heating fee was cheap so we turned the temperature gauge all the way to up. Our apartment was so hot that we had to open windows in the living room to let the hot air out. Then came the bill: $400 total for January and February. We were astounded[17]. As a result, during the following winter, we turn the gauge[18] to the minimum that we could stand, and chose to wear sweaters and cotton-padded[19] jackets in order to save money.

⑰ astounded [əs'taundid] *adj.* 被震惊的

⑱ gauge [geidʒ] *n.* 阀门 （温度控制器）

⑲ cotton-padded ['kɔtn-pædid] *adj.* 棉花填充的

1.3.2 搬出父母家

Moving out from my parents' house was really a pain in the ass. I remember that I spent months locating the perfect apartment to rent. In the first month, I asked the real estate agents to help me look for high-end[20] apartments; most of them were good but not good enough, and some of which lacked sufficient[21] sunlight because of orientation of the windows. Some of which had terrible interior design, some of which were just too old and dirty to live in. Then I lowered my expectations and started looking for apartments in the middle range. The rent became cheaper, but the room size was decreasing too. I felt wearisome after two months into the journey of locating my perfect dwelling[22]. It just took me too much energy and time, since I was extremely busy at work at the time. At last, I gave up and choose a not-so-good apartment near my company.

⑳ high-end [hai-end] *adj.* 高端的

㉑ sufficient [sə'fiʃənt] *adj.* 充足的

㉒ dwelling ['dweliŋ] *n.* 住宅
◉ house, residence

1.3.3　结婚生子

Soon after I reached adulthood, my parents got worried that I couldn't find my other half, and would spend the rest of my life being single. As a result, they started to introduce all kinds of girls to me, and would force me to date them, regardless of my own will. My mom would often say, "We have seen thousands of people, so we know what suits you best." So, not only do I have to face pressure from work, now I also have to face pressure that comes from my parents.

02 Are 16-year-olds old enough to drive a car?

真　题	题　型	年　份
Do you agree or disagree with this statement: a 16-year old is not mature enough to drive.	口语第二题	2013/03/24
16-year-olds are old enough to drive a car.	口语第二题	2013/06/08

1.4　Yes

Sure. 16-year-olds are definitely both intellectually and responsibly mature enough to drive a car. Driving a car is not that hard technically. The only issue we should consider is whether teenagers are able to drive safely and responsibly. We all have gone through the adolescent[1] phase where we would pursue the pleasant sensation of fast speed, without considering the danger we might bring to others while driving. But I'm sure with enough warning from parents and the government, most teenagers can drive with care for others.

❶ adolescent [ˌædəˈlesnt]
adj. 不成熟的

1.5　No

No. Teenagers are surely not ready to take full responsibility for driving a car. I was in a serious rear-end[2] accident back when I was 19,

❷ rear-end [riə-end] *n.*
后部

which I was mainly responsible for. I was having a really bad day. My girlfriend had just broken up with me and I was depressed. So, I turned the music volume to the maximum while driving and was singing along with the radio. I was so immersed in one song that I didn't notice that the car in front of me was stopping because of road congestion[3]. When I noticed it, it was already too late. I realized that at the speed at the time, there was no way that I could stop my car from crashing into the car in front. It was fortunate that nobody got hurt. But still, if I were driving faster or I panicked and steered my car into other lanes, worse things could have happened. My point is that even 19-year-olds might not be mature enough to drive a car, let alone a 16-year-old.

❸ road congestion 堵车

03 Should people be required to retire after the age of 65?

真 题	题 型	年 份
Do you agree or disagree with the following statement: people should be required to retire after the age of 65?	口语第二题	2016/05/28

3.1 视情况而定

Policies should vary according to individual circumstances. With the improvement of medical science, there are tons of people who are still robust and have strong will to continue their work; some even consider their undertaking as their own child or even purpose of life. Forcing these people to retire is just unreasonable, when they are utterly competent to continue creating wealth for the whole society. Not employing these amazingly experienced experts is a complete waste of resources. For example, my grandpa is almost 80 years old, but he is still working as a professor at a university in Beijing and he is definitely the expert in his field. And the most important thing is that he loves his work and his students love him.

3.2　Yes

People should be forced to retire after 65. Many elderly citizens consider themselves to be competent enough to continue their work, but in reality, they are not. So, a mandatory policy is required to force those who are not in good shape to step down. For those who are truly competent[1], we could allow exceptions if these people can pass certain medical examinations to prove that they are competent both physically and mentally.

❶ competent ['kɔmpitənt] *adj.* 有能力的

第十八类　父母

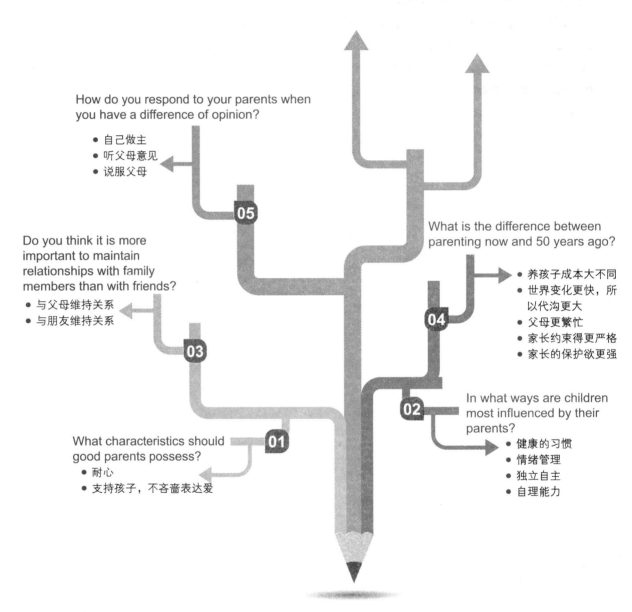

How do you respond to your parents when you have a difference of opinion?
- 自己做主
- 听父母意见
- 说服父母

05

Do you think it is more important to maintain relationships with family members than with friends?
- 与父母维持关系
- 与朋友维持关系

03

What characteristics should good parents possess?
- 耐心
- 支持孩子，不吝啬表达爱

01

What is the difference between parenting now and 50 years ago?
- 养孩子成本大不同
- 世界变化更快，所以代沟更大
- 父母更繁忙
- 家长约束得更严格
- 家长的保护欲更强

04

In what ways are children most influenced by their parents?
- 健康的习惯
- 情绪管理
- 独立自主
- 自理能力

02

父母类

01 What characteristics should good parents possess?

真 题	题 型	年 份
What should parents do to help their children to succeed in school?	口语第一题	2015/04/12

1.1 耐心

I think I have great parents because they are so patient with me. Patience is one of the most important characteristics for good parents. Parents who are patient respect, encourage and nurture[1] their children, rather than judge and blame them. When I was very little, I asked them a lot of hard questions. For example, "Where do babies come from?", a question that may be uncomfortable for a lot of parents. However, my parents never dismissed[2] my questions, made up stories[3], or tried to steer[4] the conversation elsewhere. They answered it directly, which helped me foster[5] healthy feelings and concepts about sex. It also encouraged my interest to explore the world. I am very grateful that I have parents who are very patient.

❶ nurture ['nɜːtʃə] v. 养育

❷ dismiss [dis'mis] v. 不予理会
❸ make up stories 编造故事
❹ steer [stiə] v. 引导
❺ foster ['fɒstə] v. 促进

1.2 支持孩子，不吝啬表达爱

My parents are the two best people I know. When I was growing up, my family wasn't well-off[6], as my father worked as a cashier[7] at a local supermarket. But we had what we needed. I've been fortunate enough to grow up with parents who support me in everything I do. They always make sure that I'm safe, healthy and secure, and they never forget to remind me how much they love me. They constantly affirm their affection[8], both verbally[9] and through their behavior. When I make an achievement, they're quick to offer enthusiastic praise. I remember when I was in primary school, they gave me a lot of encouragement by saying, "It's great that you cleaned your room without being asked" or "I'm so proud that you made it on the basketball team".

❻ well-off [wel-ɒf] adj. 富裕的
🔁 rich

❼ cashier [kæ'ʃiə] n. 收银员

❽ affection [ə'fekʃn] n. 喜爱
❾ verbally ['vɜːbəli] adv. 口头的

02 In what ways are children most influenced by their parents?

真　题	题　型	年　份
The most important thing people learned is from families.	口语 第一题	2015/11/21
What do you think is the most important thing that parents should teach their children? Please include details in your response.	口语 第一题	2016/04/23

2.1　健康的习惯

Parents play an important role in shaping children's habits. If you are struggling to get your child to eat healthier foods or stop watching so much TV, you can't expect them to do it on their own! Show them how! For parents, that means constantly eating healthy food such as vegetables, fruits, whole grain products, low fat dairy products, and lean meats in the house. Unhealthy food such as cakes, chocolate, cookies, doughnuts, ice cream, french fries, and potato chips, which are all high in calories, should surely be banned. Since children imitate everything that their parents do, they would naturally form a healthier life style. Furthermore, by taking a bike trip or a walk in the evening together, parents can show kids the benefits of exercising. After all, actions always speak louder than words.

2.2　情绪管理

❶ lose one's temper 发脾气

❷ scream [skri:m] v. 尖叫

❸ heated ['hi:tid] v. 激烈的，愤怒的

Children often handle stress in exactly the same way as their parents do. If a child loses his temper[1] quickly, there is a chance that it is the same way that their parents deal with anger. I think of the example of the mother who screams[2] at her children, "Stop yelling!" She might really want them to stop, but she is not teaching them how to communicate effectively. She is modeling the same bad behavior! On the contrary, if the child watches how his mother is able to manage her emotions even during heated[3] circumstances, she will follow her mother's lead and learn how to handle stress. So, parents should try to remain calm, take a deep breath and talk through the issue when they are faced with difficulties. They can talk to their child about what triggered[4] their anger and how to deal with it properly. Their children will know what to do the next time. Teaching by example is often easier and more effective than forcing children to obey rules by scaring, threatening, or tempting[5] them with rewards.

④ trigger ['trigə] v. 引发

⑤ tempt [tempt] v. 引诱

2.3 独立自主

The most important thing for parents is to put their children in the driver's seat and prepare them for adulthood. When I was in college, it was made clear to me that I would need to get good grades, and try for college scholarships in order to pay for my education. My parents couldn't afford it. Because I was paying so much of my future money for my college, I knew I had to get the most out of my education. So, I studied very hard, got several part-time jobs and spent money really meticulously[6]. Having to do a job while going to school can be hard, but it can also teach you something about time management[7]. I don't think that's a bad thing. Also, I am really thankful to my parents who gave me this real-world education about taking responsibility and learning the basics of saving and budgeting.

⑥ meticulously [mi'tikjuləsli] adv. 极为仔细地
⑦ time management 时间管理

2.4 自理能力

Parents need to teach their children basic living skills. My mom made me ride the metro[8] when I was nine years old. I was scared at first, but that feeling soon faded[9] as I became more confident. It is true that public transportation is a big risk for children, but it teaches them how to be independent, because their moms are not going to be there forever.

⑧ metro ['metrəu] n. 地铁
⑨ fade [feid] v. 逐渐变弱

Children need to know how to take care of themselves in the future. It would be too late if they start practicing when they're adults. For example, children can learn how to handle risks by climbing trees or taking the train, even if that means scraped knees and seeing the occasional weirdo[10]. To sum up, the job of parenting isn't just to protect kids. It's also to prepare them for life.

⑩ weirdo ['wiədəu] n. 古怪的人

03　Do you think it is more important to maintain relationships with family members than with friends?

真　题	题　型	年　份
Do you agree or disagree with the following statement: it is more important to maintain relationships with family members than with friends?	口语 第二题	2016/03/11

3.1　与父母维持关系

❶ ally ['ælai] *n.* 盟友

❷ be gonna do something = be going to do something

❸ overwhelming [ˌəuvə'welmiŋ] *adj.* 令人难以应付的

Yes. Friends come and go, but parents will always be there for us. They are my constant allies[1] and sources of support. I talk with my parents almost every week. Whenever I have questions or feel depressed, I call them. Last time, I failed my math test. I thought they were gonna[2] blame me, but instead, they said, "I know you're under a lot of pressure. It must be overwhelming[3] to manage all the courses. You seem stressed. Let's find a time to think things through and figure out how to make things easier." I am grateful to them, because they understand me and care about my feelings, not just my performance.

3.2　与朋友维持关系

❹ slip [slip] *v.* 下降

❺ take criticism 接受批评

❻ would rather do something

❼ bond [bɔnd] *v.* 增强信任关系

No. I seldom communicate with my parents. I just don't have much to say to them. I did ask them questions when I was a teenager, because I was not used to the busy school life, and my grades were slipping[4]. However, I didn't get the kind of support I wanted. They just constantly repeated: "You heard what your teacher said. You need to concentrate more on your class … Don't roll your eyes. You just can't take constructive criticism[5]." You know, I already felt pressured and was frustrated with myself. What they said not only increased my stress, but also made me want to avoid them, and worst of all, I have not sought their advice ever since. You know, I would rather talk[6] to my friends. We are equals and we understand each other. Instead of blaming me, my friends give me a lot of encouragement. Even though we are not bonded[7] by blood, I feel they are like my family.

04 What is the difference between parenting now and 50 years ago?

真　题	题　型	年　份
Since the world has changed so much in the past fifty years, the advice our grandparents give us is not useful.	口语 第二题	2015/09/17
The most important thing people learned is from families.	口语 第一题	2015/11/21

4.1　养孩子成本大不同

Nowadays, most parents can no longer shoulder[1] the bill for their children's college education without putting their own futures at risk. Parents are often sandwiched between caring for elderly parents and their own children while trying to meet their own needs. And the burden is getting heavier. Besides, it isn't just the cost of college that has risen, but the cost of raising children as well. Expenses for day care, sports, music lessons and cell phones are stretching[2] precarious[3] family budgets. They have already done a lot to raise their children. There is just no reason to make them pay for the college when their kids are already grownups. Today's parents need to ensure their own financial stability first. It's like putting on your airplane oxygen mask[4] before you put on your children's.

4.2　世界变化更快，所以代沟更大

Children communicate less with their parents because the generation gap is larger now than ever before. The world isn't what it used to be. Take myself for example. Sometimes, I feel tired of some cliché[5] parenting rules, because they are not so effective anymore. For example, my parents often say that if you go to college, you'll get a good job. This one makes me laugh. For teenagers, it's hilarious[6] to see that how their parents still think that a college degree always guarantees an awesome job. They don't know the fact that recent college graduates face the worst unemployment rate[7] in more than 20 years. The rules of the game have changed. Higher education no longer has the value it

❶ shoulder ['ʃəuldə] v. 承担

❷ stretch [stretʃ] v. 耗尽（钱或资源）

❸ precarious [pri'kɛəriəs] adj. 不稳定的，不稳固的

❹ oxygen mask 氧气罩

❺ cliché ['kliːʃei] n. 陈词滥调

❻ hilarious [hi'lɛəriəs] adj. 可笑的

❼ unemployment rate 失业率

⑧ dropout ['drɔpaut] *n.* 辍学者

⑨ make a living 谋生

⑩ tutorial [tju: 'tɔ:riəl] *n.* 指导说明

⑪ drawback ['drɔ:bæk] *n.* 缺点，障碍

⑫ interpersonal skill 人际交往能力

⑬ high-demand [hai-di'ma:nd] *n.* 高需求

⑭ disarray [,disə'rei] *n.* 混乱

once did. There are high school kids and college dropouts[8] making a living[9] on YouTube and Instagram by posting makeup tutorials[10] or playing video games. Things are just different today than they were decades ago, and some age-old advice just doesn't work anymore.

4.3 父母更繁忙

In this fast-paced and high-stressed society, parents are much busier than before. They have less time to look after kids. My father, who was a busy businessman, used to travel a lot when I was little. My mom, a nurse, also had a very busy schedule at the hospital and often had to take night shifts. So I was raised by my grandmother for most of my childhood. Although I love them very much, I wish that my parents had spent more time with me while I was little. I noticed that there are obvious drawbacks[11] of not having parents around during one's childhood. My experience tells me that children who do not have a strong bond with their father are often shy, unconfident, and usually suck at interpersonal skills[12] ; that children who do not have a strong connection with their mother are often insecure.

4.4 家长约束得更严格

Parents in the past tended to give children more freedom. For example, when I was a teenager, my parents seldom advised me about what to do with my life. They never forced me to pursue a career because it was in "high-demand[13]" or because "it pays well". This is why I have become the person I am today. However, nowadays, since the job market has become more and more competitive, parents pressure their children to pursue the routes they regard as the "best". The problem is the world moves much faster nowadays. Their advice might be wrong. One minute a college major is hot, and the next minute it's not. One minute a career field is brimming with opportunity, and the next minute it is in total disarray[14]. So, if parents love their kids, they should give them more freedom.

4.5 家长的保护欲更强

I think parents nowadays are a little bit more protective than before.

They closely watch their baby's breathing patterns and movements on baby monitors during all hours of the night to ensure their children are safe and sound. And when they grow up, they do not let their children cross the street alone until they are 9 years old. I remember when I was 10, my very loving mother wouldn't let me ride a bike because she was afraid that I might fall and get hurt. My parents never let me take public transportation alone when I was a teenager, because they thought I might be kidnapped[15]. The result was hilarious. I was convinced that every adult I didn't know was a murderer[16] waiting to attack me. I was afraid to walk into a store because I thought the cashier was a kidnapper. I was even nervous around adults with whom I am familiar, like the head of the family I babysat for. That is very sad, because children are not supposed to grow up always looking over their shoulders in fear[17].

Parents should rescue their bubble-wrapped kids by guiding them safely through a sequence of[18] activities that were once forbidden. For example, parents can teach children what type of behavior is considered unusual or inappropriate. They can also teach children how to recognize adults who are trustworthy—like policemen.

[15] kidnap ['kidnæp] v. 绑架，诱拐

[16] murderer ['mə:dərə(r)] n. 凶手

[17] look over one's shoulder 小心提防

[18] a sequence of 一系列的

05 How do you respond to your parents when you have a difference of opinion?

真　题	题　型	年　份
Since the world has changed so much in the past fifty years, the advice our grandparents give us is not useful.	口语第二题	2015/09/17

5.1 自己做主

I would like to make decisions by myself if we have different opinions. For example, when I was applying for[1] college, my mom thought I should choose finance as my major, because she thought that

❶ apply for 申请

would help me find better jobs and earn more money in the future. A lot of her friends who studied finance are very rich now. However, I didn't listen to her because I knew I wouldn't like it. I am really into music and I have a very beautiful voice. So I went with my own choice. I hope one day I can be a famous singer and shine on the stage.

5.2　听父母意见

I like to take account of[2] my parents' ideas, because sometimes their perspectives make more sense[3]. For example, and this is a true story, when I was in high school, I wanted to drop out[4] and pursue music as a career because I had a pretty good voice. But I am glad my parents stopped me because they were much older than me and they knew from experience that this was a bad idea. Now I work in a bank and have a pretty good salary. When I look back, I am still grateful for what they have done for me. I could have end up poorly if I had followed my own interest, and hadn't listened to them.

5.3　说服父母

I would try to persuade them. It is very important to maintain a pleasant relationship with parents, since family always provides us with the firmest support, no matter what. Besides, parents do have a great deal of influence on our mood. So, in order to make ourselves happy, we should make our parents happy. If my parents' opinion is too radical[5] or too conservative[6], the best solution is to tell them about my own perspective, and discuss the topic openly and thoroughly. If both sides are wise, we should be able to work things out with a little compromise[7] from both sides. Nonetheless, if we fail at reaching an agreement, I would then stick with[8] my own plan.

❷ take account of 考虑

❸ make sense 是明智的, 是合情合理的

❹ drop out 退学

❺ radical ['rædikl] adj. 激进的

❻ conservative [kən'sɜ:vətiv] adj. 保守的

❼ compromise ['kɔmprəmaiz] n. 折中，妥协

❽ stick with 继续坚持

第十九类　老师

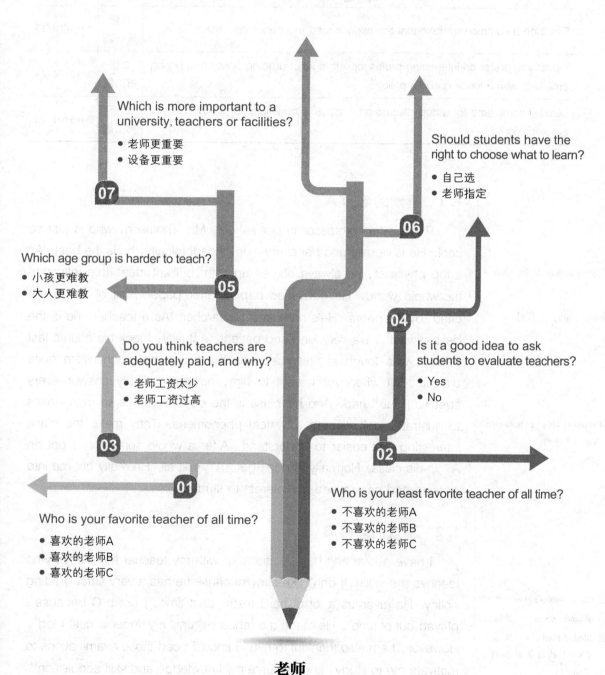

Which is more important to a university, teachers or facilities?

- 老师更重要
- 设备更重要

07

Should students have the right to choose what to learn?

- 自己选
- 老师指定

06

Which age group is harder to teach?
- 小孩更难教
- 大人更难教

05

Do you think teachers are adequately paid, and why?

- 老师工资太少
- 老师工资过高

04

Is it a good idea to ask students to evaluate teachers?

- Yes
- No

03

02

Who is your least favorite teacher of all time?

- 不喜欢的老师A
- 不喜欢的老师B
- 不喜欢的老师C

01

Who is your favorite teacher of all time?

- 喜欢的老师A
- 喜欢的老师B
- 喜欢的老师C

老师

第十九类　老师

01 Who is your favorite teacher of all time?

真　题	题　型	年　份
Describe a common mistake that the experienced teachers often make.	口语 第一题	2010/10/15
Would you prefer an interesting professor with a strict grading policy or a boring professor with a loose grading policy?	口语 第二题	2012/04/14
Leaving some time for group discussion in class is beneficial for study. Do you agree or not?	口语 第二题	2015/01/25

1.1　喜欢的老师 A

There is this professor in our school, Mr. Thomson, who is just so cool. He is literally good at everything. Academically, he is the best. As a top physicist, he always comes up with[1] brilliant ideas that influence the whole world. He publishes papers after papers, all of which are cited[2] by his peers. He's not just a researcher. As a teacher, he is the best as well. He's very kind and patient. Actually, I took his course last year. It was tough at first, because the things he taught were quite difficult. But whenever I went to him, he would kindly answer every specific issue I had. And his class is the best. He uses so many jokes to illustrate sophisticated[3] physical phenomena. They make the class interesting and easier to understand. After a whole semester, I got an A$^+$ in his class. Normally, I don't get "A" s at all. He really got me into working and he aroused my interest to study physics.

1.2　喜欢的老师 B

I have a love and hate relationship with my teacher Mr. Grey, who teaches me violin. I don't like him, because he has a very strict grading policy. He gives us a lot of hard tests. Last time, I got a C because I played out of tune[4]. He made me rehearse[5] until my finger almost bled[6]. However, I am also thankful to him. I know I need those examinations to motivate me to study, and evaluate my knowledge and skill acquisition[7]. If it weren't for him, I would never have a chance to become such a great violin player.

❶ come up with 提出，想出

❷ cite [sait] v. 引用

❸ sophisticated [sə'fistikeitid] adj. 复杂的

❹ out of tune 跑调
❺ rehearse [ri'hə:s] v. 排练
❻ bled [bled] v. 流血 (bleed 的过去时和过去分词)

❼ acquisition [ˌækwi'ziʃn] n. 习得

1.3 喜欢的老师 C

My history professor Mr. Grey is very good at teaching. For example, instead of just lecturing in a class, he always leaves us some time for class discussion. He understands it's hard to maintain students' focus and attention when all they hear is the professor talking. It helps to hear another voice. Last semester, we were asked to write a paper about a famous reformer for a history class. Most teachers I know are dictators[8]. They would just assign a topic for students at the end of class. However, Mr. Grey is different. He understands it's difficult for us to write something we are not interested in. So, he would ask smart questions for us to discuss at the end of class. For example, he would ask us who is the most admirable reformer, and which can pique[9] our interest and get us to think. Thanks to the discussion, I gained a lot of inspiration[10] about what to write.

❽ dictator [dik'teitə] n. 独裁者

❾ pique [pi:k] v. 产生（兴趣或好奇心）

❿ inspiration [ˌinspə'reiʃn] n. 灵感

02 Who is your least favorite teacher of all time?

真 题	题 型	年 份
Would you prefer an interesting professor with a strict grading policy or a boring professor with a loose grading policy?	口语 第二题	2015/01/10
Leaving some time for group discussion in class is beneficial for study. Do you agree or not?	口语 第二题	2015/01/25
Describe a common mistake that experienced teachers often make.	口语 第一题	2016/09/11

2.1 不喜欢的老师 A

I remember one of my seventh-grade teachers. Up to now, he is the most boring person I have ever met. Every day our class schedule was the same：read the chapter and copy down immense slides[1] for the

❶ slide [slaid] n. 幻灯片

rest of class. I just memorized a lot of information, took a test on it and then forgot everything. Imagine that cycle for an entire year. It was a nightmare. I would never want to relive that again.

2.2 不喜欢的老师 B

I had a teacher once. She had been teaching for 30 years, so she was very experienced. Everyone respected her a lot. However, sometimes I thought she was just too afraid to look foolish and make mistakes. She once accused one of my friends of not turning in their homework on time, but it turned out that she found the assignment in her bag. Instead of making a sincere apology to my friend, she was very cranky[2]. And my friend was very sad and disappointed. In fact, I think it is OK for teachers to talk about their errors, because we are humans, and humans make mistakes. If they refuse to do that, they will come off as very arrogant.

❷ cranky ['kræŋki] *adj.* 暴躁的

2.3 不喜欢的老师 C

I used to love studying history, but now my passion is gradually being ruined by my history teacher. Actually, her lectures are well intriguing[3], but she seems to be obsessed with[4] tests. I have to face examinations every week, and her grading policy[5] is just way too strict. Of course, I am not allowed to watch TV or play games before exams. The worst thing is that no matter how well prepared I am for my history test, when it comes to the judgment day, I screw it up[6]. I am well acquainted with[7] the feelings of remorse[8] and distress when these expectations are not met. The marks and grades keep my mind occupied with wild thoughts of failure. At the same time, I need to take peer pressure[9] and parental pressure because I am judged by my grade. I just can't discover my passion for learning and enjoy this subject anymore.

❸ intriguing [in'tri:giŋ] *adj.* 令人感兴趣的
❹ be obsessed with 痴迷于
❺ grading policy 评分政策
❻ screw up 弄槽
❼ be acquainted with 熟悉
❽ remorse [ri'mɔːs] *n.* 懊悔
❾ peer pressure 来自同辈的压力

03 Do you think teachers are adequately paid, and why?

真 题	题 型	年 份
Teachers should be paid at least as much as doctors, lawyers, or business leaders are paid.	口语 第二题	2013/11/19
It is generally agreed that society benefits from the work of its members. Which type of contribution do you think is most valued by your society: primary school teachers, artists or nurses?	口语 第一题	2015/06/13

3.1 老师工资太少

It is clear that nobody goes into teaching to get rich. And teachers deserve better pay, because teaching is the fundamental basis of every facet[1] of society. They literally create every other profession in the world. Without teachers, there would be no doctors, no police officers, no lawyers, and no musicians. Without teachers, there would be no society. So, it is crucial that schools are able to retain high-quality teachers. Also, teachers need to spend hours studying material, doing research and working on presentations before class to get fully prepared. And right after class, they have to answer questions and grade papers. It takes great patience. And a decent paycheck would enhance teacher's motivation to do those things.

❶ facet ['fæsit] *n.* 方面

3.2 老师工资过高

Many teachers are indeed overpaid. Ironically, most teachers feel just the opposite — that they are underpaid. Take many TOEFL training institutions for example. A lot of the teachers are still using lecturing materials that were designed 10 years ago, many of which are no longer applicable to the current test due to so many revolutions of question types. They are unwilling to **make the effort to keep up with the changes in real tests**. They are simply repeating the same lecture that they have done for decades, and they are demanding raises constantly at the same time. They should be eliminated in time.

04 Is it a good idea to ask students to evaluate teachers?

真 题	题 型	年 份
Many students are asked to evaluate their professors at the end of the semester. What are the advantages and disadvantages of this?	口语 第二题	2016/07/16

4.1 Yes

4.1.1 评估可以提高老师的表现

Getting feedback from students can improve teacher's performance. If they get negative feedback, the educators will begin to think about how this course could be improved. How can they make the course more interesting? They can correct their mistakes and get a better understanding of what students expect from them. And positive feedback can build teachers' confidence and encourage them to do a better job. Teachers who take this feedback seriously can surely be promoted faster than those who do not.

4.1.2 评估可以刺激老师之间的良性竞争

I heard from my teacher that at New Oriental, their evaluation results are publicly emailed to everybody monthly, so that anyone can see who the most popular teacher is and, who is the least popular. It reminds me of the announcement of examination results during high school. I think the benefit of this act is that it spurs[1] benign competition[2] among teachers, which will encourage all teachers to constantly improve. Of course, those who get low scores might get upset and eventually quit, but that will filter out[3] the unsuitable ones, which leaves the best[4].

4.2 No

4.2.1 打低分只是因为学生自己的分数低

No. Sometimes, good teachers get bad ratings because their courses are tough. There will always be someone who complains, or has a problem with the way the course has been taught. However, that

❶ spur [spə:] v. 激励

❷ benign competition 良性竞争

❸ filter out 过滤

❹ leave the best 留下最好的（老师）

shouldn't mean the professor is bad. Teachers should not become simply entertainers to have students like them. Their main goal is to have students learn the material and develop good habits, but the fear of bad ratings may stifle[5] pedagogical[6] innovation and encourage faculty to water down[7] course content.

4.2.2 评估只是评估谁更受欢迎

Evaluations reflect little about the effectiveness of learning. It's just a popularity contest. Sometimes, good teachers get bad ratings only because they are too strict with students. I used to hate a teacher who gave us strict deadlines. He never granted us any extensions no matter what happened. If we missed the deadline, he would punish us by giving us a very low score. As a result, he was not very popular among students, and his evaluations were not always positive. However, now I have grown up. I realize there are deadlines in life, and it is important to teach kids that deadlines are serious businesses. It may save them from prison for not filing their taxes. I finally understand my teacher's strict deadline policy, which taught us accountability and responsibility. And I feel bad about giving him a low rating just because he was so strict with us.

4.2.3 评估本身无法做到绝对公正

Most evaluations are biased[8]. Students in some experiments give higher scores to male teachers. Evaluations may also favor the white and the young, and punish[9] the less attractive. In addition to that, students judge things that instructors cannot control, such as class size or the food quality in the cafeteria. Small courses in a given topic always get better ratings than large ones, which shows that students prefer smaller classes. It has nothing to do with teachers' performance.

[5] stifle ['staifl] v. 压制
[6] pedagogical ['pedə'gɔdʒikl] n. 教学法的
[7] water down 降低，弱化

[8] biased ['baiəst] adj. 有偏见的

[9] To punish someone means to make them suffer in some way because they have done something wrong.

05 Which age group is harder to teach?

真　题	题　型	年　份
Which of the following activities would you be more interested in doing? Teaching children, teaching adults to use computers, or cleaning the city park?	口语第一题	2013/01/12
Do you agree or disagree with the following statement: it's easier to teach children in primary schools than students in universities?	口语第二题	2016/07/10

5.1 小孩更难教

❶ naughty ['nɔːti] *adj.* 顽皮的

❷ wrestle ['resl] *v.* 费力地拉

❸ projector cord 投影仪绳子

I think primary students are harder to teach. They are pretty[1] naughty sometimes. My friend Deepa used to teach in a primary school. She told me that the kids in her class interrupted her all the time. They walked around the classroom when they were supposed to be sitting down. And she had to wrestle[2] with a child who once tried to hang another student with a projector cord[3]. They are cute, but they are too little to learn how to become self-disciplined, whereas university students are much better at self-control. They have strong motivation to study. Thus, they actively take notes during classes, interact with teachers and engage in the group discussions.

5.2 大人更难教

❹ rampage ['ræmpeidʒ] *n.* 暴怒

I think it is easier to teach children in primary schools. They are born curious and playful. So, it's easier to motivate them to concentrate on class. I once was a teacher in a primary school. Sometimes, we played games together, which is an excellent way of introducing new concepts. They all found it very interesting, and loved to interact with me. Also, they were still young, so it was easier to bribe them with rewards as incentives to learn. But it's much harder to get and keep college students' attention and motivate them to study. Some of them are going through on a teenage rampage[4] where they just hate all forms of authority and don't give a damn about what teachers say.

06 Should students have the right to choose what to learn?

真 题	题 型	年 份
When choosing research paper topics, some teachers give students the freedom to choose topics that interest them; others assign topics to students. Which do you think is better and why?	口语 第二题	2013/06/08
Students doing their own personal reading is as important as, or more important than reading assigned by teachers.	口语 第二题	2014/04/19

6.1 自己选

I don't like rigid[1] teachers and inflexible requirements. I like options. I would definitely be more motivated if I could choose my own topic, because interest is the best teacher. Thus, I would be more likely to look for information I am interested in and be more active in focusing on finishing papers. I remember when I was in 8th grade, I was asked to write a paper about the world's modern architecture. However, I was just not into[2] this topic. I thought all those modern designs were very ugly, and I wanted to write a paper about the Summer Palace, one of the largest and the best preserved of the imperial[3] gardens in China. Unfortunately, I was not allowed to do that. So, I just rushed through this paper without doing any research online, and got a B at last. I only want to write when I have a choice about what to write.

6.2 老师指定

I think teachers should assign topics to students, because they are in the best position to ensure that topics they choose would have the most benefits to their students. It is true that students can have more inspiration and motivation to write about what they like. Also, it is easier to write about fields that they have more knowledge and interest in. However, some students would end up staying in their comfort zone forever. For example, if you get to choose a topic between earthquakes and tsunamis[4] in a geography class, it is likely you'd choose the easier

❶ rigid ['rɪdʒɪd] adj. 死板的

❷ be into something 对……感兴趣

❸ imperial [ɪm'pɪərɪəl] adj. 帝国的，皇家的

❹ tsunamis [tsu'nɑːmi] n. 海啸

one — earthquakes. As a result, there is a chance that you won't do well in the exam, because you don't have a thorough understanding of tsunamis. And exams test students on what is useful for their future, not what students are interested in.

Of course, teachers should assign topics. Students just aren't mature enough to know what is best for them. Yes, we do tend to perform better when we are absorbed in doing something. Yes, interest is our best teacher. But, teachers are experienced educators who have taught thousands of students, and know what is the best material to impart[5] to students at the most appropriate moment. Plus, teachers also know the importance of using curiosity to motivate students to learn. So they also choose interesting topics for students.

⑤ impart [im'pɑːt] v. 传授

07 Which is more important to a university, teachers or facilities?

真　题	题　型	年　份
A university should focus more on its facilities, such as libraries, computers or laboratoryies rather than on hiring famous teachers.	独立 写作题	2015/02/01
Do you agree or disagree that the success of a school depends on experienced teachers?	口语 第一题	2016/01/24

7.1　老师更重要

I think teachers are more important. When you ask people to remember a meaningful learning experience from high school, chances are they won't mention how big their student center was. Instead, working in groups, doing a tough project or learning with teachers — those are the lasting, meaningful learning experiences. So, you see, it's all about people. Just imagine that your school has the latest and highest quality science lab supplies, but there are no experienced teachers to tell you how to use the equipment to understand difficult scientific theories. Or your school has a very fancy library, which encompasses[1] a rich and varied universe of printed volumes[2] and digital resources. However, the teachers in your school fail to create a study atmosphere and stimulate your interest to make use of them to acquire knowledge. What a shame! So, it is obvious that teachers matter more to student achievement than any other aspect of schooling.

7.2 设备更重要

As the technologies such as artificial intelligence[3] continue moving forward, teachers' role in the learning process won't be as important as before. Students can learn almost everything they want on the Internet. There are just so many amazing resources on YouTube. You can learn cooking, music theories, photography, math, science, history, everything! You name it. So, in the future, teachers will not be the most important part of a college. What will be more important is facilities that facilitate the learning process, such as an amazing digitalized library, advanced laboratories, comfortable study lounges[4] and dorm rooms. These determine the quality of learning in our future.

❶ encompass [in'kʌmpəs] v. 包含
❷ volume ['vɔːljuːm] n. 书卷
❸ artificial intelligence 人工智能
❹ lounge [laundʒ] n. 休息室

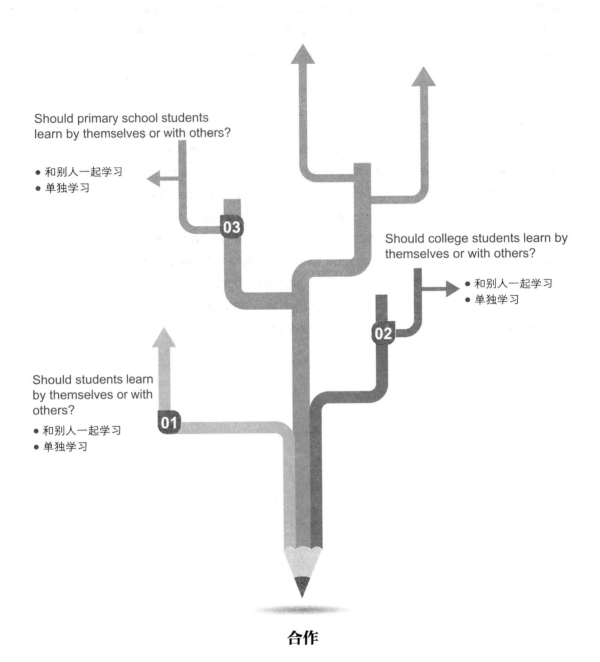

Should primary school students
learn by themselves or with others?

● 和别人一起学习
● 单独学习

03

Should college students learn by
themselves or with others?

● 和别人一起学习
● 单独学习

02

Should students learn
by themselves or with
others?

● 和别人一起学习
● 单独学习

01

合作

01 Should students learn by themselves or with others?

真　题	题　型	年　份
What is the most effective way to learn：taking notes, discussing with others or memorizing?	口语第二题	2012/09/29
Some students prefer studying with other students to prepare for an exam. Others prefer studying alone to prepare for an exam. Which way do you prefer and why? Include reasons and details in your response.	口语第二题	2012/10/27
Some students like to learn by themselves；others prefer to share their ideas with others. Which one do you prefer?	口语第二题	2013/11/22
Some people prefer to work independently；others prefer to work with others. Which do you prefer? Explain your answer in detail.	口语第二题	2016/03/26
Imagine if a professor wants students to learn as much as possible about a project in a short period of time, is it better to let students work in a group or study alone?	独立写作题	2016/11/13
Many schools require young children（aged 5 – 11）to work together in a small group instead of working alone for many of their activities.	独立写作题	2016/10/16
Imagine if a professor wants students to learn as much as possible about a project in a short period of time. Is it better to let students work in a group or study alone?	独立写作题	2016/11/19

1.1　与别人一起学习

1.1.1　高效

I like to collaborate with other people, because when I am working alone, time can so easily be wasted. I just can't get anything done. There are endless distractions, such as movies, music and video games. However, when I am collaborating with other people, I have to focus on the work. When participating in group work, I am not able to procrastinate[1] anymore. Take myself for example. I'm currently preparing for the TOEFL exam, and my Reading Comprehension instructor suggests memorizing[2] 50 words each day. When I was studying alone, I would persist at most[3] for 5 minutes. After that, I couldn't help unlocking[4] my phone, checking[5] if someone has sent me a message on WeChat. Then, I always fail to resist the temptation to

❶ procrastinate [prəuˈkræstineit] v. 拖延
同 delay

❷ suggest [+ ing form of verb]

❸ at most 最多（对应 at least，至少）

❹ unlock [ˌʌnˈlɔk] v. 解锁

❺ 分词表伴随

⑥ whose 引导的定语从句

⑦ marvel ['mɑ:vl] *v.* 大为
赞叹
🔄 admire

⑧ collide [kə'laid] *v.* 碰撞
🔄 hit

⑨ stuck [stʌk] *adj.* 陷入
的，困住的
🔄 fixed

⑩ prefer [+ to infinitive]

⑪ gossip ['gɒsip] *n.* 闲聊
🔄 talk about

⑫ which 引导的定语从句

⑬ browse [brauz] *v.* 翻看
（手机或书籍）

⑭ engaged [in'geidʒd] *adj.*
已订婚的

⑮ validity [və'lidəti] *n.* 可
信性
🔄 truth

⑯ efficacy ['efikəsi] *n.* 有
效性
🔄 effectiveness

⑰ stubborn ['stʌbən] *adj.*
顽固的
🔄 unyielding

⑱ compromise ['kɒmprəmaiz]
v. 妥协

play games, whose[6] icons are right next to WeChat. I would then play for hours, and marvel[7] at how fast time passes.

1.1.2　集思广益

When working with others, each of us can contribute different materials and perspectives. So, we have a variety of information to discuss and share with other people. When different ideas collide[8], better ideas emerge. For example, when I'm looking for ideas while writing a paper, I am often stuck[9] for hours. I feel helpless and do not know where to start. But if I work with others, when other team members share their ideas, I have a starting point to work on. I come up with my own ideas, and it just feels great that I can contribute something to the team.

1.2　单独学习

1.2.1　效率更高（不八卦）

I prefer[10] to work alone, since it's surely more efficient than working with others. When friends come to a meeting, they won't start to work immediately. Most people would prefer to chat for a while and soon the chat will turn into a gossip[11] which[12] will last for hours. Last week, I was attending a group discussion with my financial management classmates, and I had thought we could have everything done in two hours, but I proved completely wrong. Just when I was about to illustrate my plan for our group presentation, Jason interrupted while browsing[13] through gossip news on his iPhone. He was sitting quietly at first but suddenly screamed: Leehom got engaged[14]. Everybody else started to ask feverishly: really? Then, a heated discussion about the validity[15] of the news began, so we didn't get anything done that day.

1.2.2　效率更高（不用平衡意见）

Working alone guarantees maximum efficacy[16]. Although working with others means more ideas, sometimes too many ideas might not be a good thing, especially when team members are all stubborn[17] and won't compromise[18] easily. Last week when my group and I were choosing the background color for our PowerPoint, Jack and Tom had a huge disagreement. Jack argued that we should definitely choose black since it's elegant and serious, while Tom insisted that we should use yellow. The latter reasoned that black slides set a tone like that of a funeral, whereas yellow resembles the sun, which gives more positive energy. The worse thing was that the rest of the group members all chose sides and began to attack the other side. The argument lasted for two whole hours and still, we didn't even reach an agreement on this detail. If[19] I had been working alone, I would have been able to decide the color in less than a second.

⑲ if 充分条件关系句式的简单应用

1.2.3　不会有无本获利者

Although I do cherish[20] the opportunity to gain some leadership experience in group work, I still hate free-riders[21]. I have a habit of taking responsibilities onto my own shoulders, without assessing the gains and losses, so I often end up draining[22] all my own energy to do the work that originally belongs to others. I think a group of two or three people is ideal for collaborations. Any arrangement of more than three members would surely produce free-riders. When a large group forms, it is destined that some people will be more active and thus take more responsibilities and complete more work.

⑳ cherish ['tʃeriʃ] v. 珍惜
㉑ free-rider [fri:-'raidə] n. 无本获利者
㉒ drain [drein] v. 耗尽
🔁 consume

Free-riders will simply sit there and basically do nothing. Sometimes they will pretend to be working so that they won't get kicked out of the team. But this rarely happens, although everybody hates free-riders so much.

In the end, some smart free-riders might even steal your thunder[23] and get praised by the teacher, although you are the one who did all the hard work.

㉓ steal sb.'s thunder 抢风头

1.2.4　锻炼独立思考能力

Working alone is the best way to cultivate[24] independent thinking. I'm not an extremely smart guy, so sometimes I have to take a minute to think quietly to get my ideas to start flowing. But in group discussions, I never have this chance. There will always be a know-it-all[25] in every group, who instantly comes up with a solution to every problem. Although I don't have to struggle to think of the solution myself, I feel my own opportunity to practice and learn has been taken away. So, I guess that I am more suited to working alone since I can hone my skills without the distraction of others.

㉔ cultivate ['kʌltiveit] v. 培养
🔁 develop
㉕ know-it-all 假称或自称无所不知的人

02 Should college students learn by themselves or with others?

真 题	题 型	年 份
Imagine if a professor wants students to learn as much as possible about a project in a short period of time. Is it better to let students work in a group or study alone?	独立写作题	2016/11/13
Imagine if a professor wants students to learn as much as possible about a project in a short period of time. Is it better to let students work in a group or study alone?	独立写作题	2016/11/19

2.1　和别人一起学习

College students should surely learn with others since they are soon about to enter the workforce, where collaboration is the key to their survival. In companies, people who do not know how to cooperate with others or how to compromise will be weeded out[1] quickly. So, college students should seize the opportunity in school to learn how to work with both their peers and professors. Working with others is a great way to develop one's communication skills and leadership.

❶ weed out 清除，淘汰
🔁 eliminate, wipe out

2.2　单独学习

College students should cultivate their independent thinking skills. In a world where everybody cares so much about others' views, a strong mind is the key to success. Students should surely possess the ability to come up with their own opinions about current affairs, politics and work without the consultation of others.

03 Should primary school students learn by themselves or with others?

真 题	题 型	年 份
Many schools require young children (aged 5 – 11) to work together in a small group instead of working alone for many of their activities.	独立写作题	2016/10/16

3.1 和别人一起学习

Children should always learn with others, since, for primary school students, they are at a critical age to form their personality. In modern society, an extrovert[1] who enjoys working with others is more likely to succeed than an introvert[2] who is too shy to look others in the eye directly and confidently. So, to cultivate an outgoing character, schools should engage[3] children in group activities to show them that group work is fun. This period is extremely important for children because when they become teenagers, their traits[4] are more fixed and are difficult to change.

❶ extrovert ['ekstrəvə:t] *n.* 性格外向的人
❷ introvert ['intrəvə:t] *n.* 性格内向的人
❸ engage [in'geidʒ] *v.* 使从事
❹ trait [treit] *n.* 性格特点 ⓔ characteristic

3.2 单独学习

Children's communication skills are not yet fully developed at such a young age. As a result, children could end up hating collaborations if teachers force them to do too many group activities. Take myself for example. I was extremely afraid of both communication and public speaking when I was little. But there was this Chinese teacher, Mr. Zhou, who had an unexplainable love for group presentations. I mean, I was already hopeless just speaking in front of my whole class. But at the time, I also had to cooperate with my group members, who were all confident and knew what[5] they were doing. I became more and more diffident[6] as the class went on, and my personality pretty much just was formed badly because of these group activities.

❺ what 引导的宾语从句
❻ diffident ['difidənt] *adj.* 羞怯的 ⓔ shy, not confident

第二十一类　学习

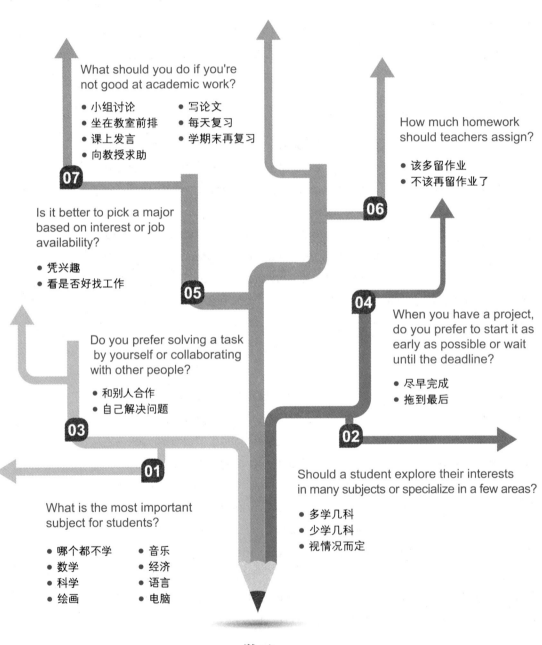

What should you do if you're not good at academic work?

- 小组讨论
- 坐在教室前排
- 课上发言
- 向教授求助
- 写论文
- 每天复习
- 学期末再复习

07

Is it better to pick a major based on interest or job availability?

- 凭兴趣
- 看是否好找工作

05

How much homework should teachers assign?

- 该多留作业
- 不该再留作业了

06

Do you prefer solving a task by yourself or collaborating with other people?

- 和别人合作
- 自己解决问题

03

When you have a project, do you prefer to start it as early as possible or wait until the deadline?

- 尽早完成
- 拖到最后

04

01

02

What is the most important subject for students?

- 哪个都不学
- 数学
- 科学
- 绘画
- 音乐
- 经济
- 语言
- 电脑

Should a student explore their interests in many subjects or specialize in a few areas?

- 多学几科
- 少学几科
- 视情况而定

学习

01 What is the most important subject for students?

真　题	题　型	年　份
Which new skill do you want to learn? 1) playing a musical instrument; 2) flying a plane; 3) playing a new sport	口语 第一题	2015/03/07
When do you think is the best time for one to learn a second language? Please use details to support your reasons.	口语 第一题	2015/09/05
Some universities require students to take foreign language classes, while others require students to take computer classes. Which do you think is more useful for students and why?	口语 第二题	2015/11/15
Which of the following classes would you like to take? 1) math, 2) painting, 3) science	独立 写作题	2016/12/03

1.1 哪个都不学

1.1.1 没时间

I don't think it's essential to study 学科名. School shouldn't put too much stress on students. Students should be exploring, playing, learning and discovering things on their own, rather than sitting in the classroom all the time. You know I am a college/high school student. I have to take a lot of classes, such as math, English and Chinese. It would drive me crazy if I had to learn all those courses in one semester.

1.1.2 没兴趣

The other thing is, although studying economics（可替换）might be a huge plus for students, it should not be a required course because not everyone has interest in it（可替换）. Take myself for example. I am really into[1] music（可替换）, I prefer to spend more of my time listening to music（可替换）. I just think economics（可替换）is not only boring but also useless.

❶ be into something 喜欢做某事

1.1.3 不重要

I don't really think knowing about economics is all that important. Some people claim that studying economics can help them make better investment decisions. That's just stupid. First of all, economics is a different subject from finance. It doesn't address personal investment decisions as you might expect. Second, even if it talks about principles in the economic market, it is not always correct. Hello, did any economist successfully predict the economic downturn in America in the recent decade? Finally, a lot of wise investment decisions in the business world depend on insider information and personal connections. All that learning economics gives you is something purely theoretical. You can boast[2] about it. But really, it has nothing to do with whether you make a fortune or not.

❷ boast [bəust] v. 吹嘘

1.2 数学

Students should surely take math since it provides the most flexible career options. With a mathematics background, students would be able to turn their hand to finance, statistics, engineering, computers, accounting or even education. This flexibility is extremely important nowadays, because there is a lot of uncertainty about finding jobs. In addition, learning math is more profitable. It is just a simple fact that a graduate from a math major can easily afford an apartment soon after graduation, whereas art majors might be still struggling to secure a job. Thus, for the sake of the career, math would definitely be a good choice.

1.3 科学

❸ be reliant on 依赖

Some of civilization's most prized and proud achievements are wholly reliant on[3] science. It contributes directly and efficiently to the development of society. Without science, none of the important revolutions, such as the industrial revolution, the information revolution and globalization, would have shown up on the stage of history. Also, studying science makes people's lives easier and more comfortable. We wouldn't have the chance to watch televisions, surf the Internet or take airplanes, if we knew nothing about science. So, students should study math and science and make this a better world for people to live in.

1.4 绘画

1.4.1 激发想象力

I think children should take painting classes, because they can boost[4] their creativity. In a painting class, children would be asked to create abstract art, such as a paining that represents their memories or emotions. It would obviously **make use of** one's imagination. And if children have practiced thinking creatively, it will come naturally to them in their future career.

❹ boost [bu:st] *n.* 促进
▫ improve

1.4.2 放松

Splashing[5] paint across a canvas is a good way to relax. Sometimes, pressures from life can be very tiring. I remember when I was a high school student, I **was under intense pressure** about the college entrance examination. So, I would draw to soothe[6] my mind. No tests, no homework — just color and shade. Whenever I immersed myself in painting, I could forget all those troubles from reality. A smile would naturally play around my lips whenever I saw the bright colors on my drawing.

❺ splash [splæʃ] *v.* 泼溅

❻ soothe [su:ð] *v.* 使镇定

1.4.3 建立自信

Painting is a great way to build children's self-esteem, because it is easier for them to **get a sense of achievement** when they are working in a non-competitive and relaxed environment. As students develop their skills in painting and drawing, they may feel good about their capabilities. I remember when I was little, when someone saw my artwork, I would gain immeasurable joy from seeing his or her reactions. I felt so proud to be unique and express my artistic style.

1.5 音乐

Through music study, students can learn the value of perseverance[7], which is a must for excellence. For example, when a child **plays the violin** for the first time, she knows that playing Mozart right away is impossible. It is only by hard work that a successful performance is possible. However, that Mozart concerto can eventually be conquered[8] if that child just keeps practicing, and masters the skills

❼ perseverance
[ˌpə:siˈviərəns] *n.* 坚持
不懈

❽ conquer [ˈkɔŋkə] *v.* 攻克

and techniques. This kind of spirit is essential to achieving success in this competitive world, because everything requires our perseverance.

1.6　经济

做出安全的投资决策

It's important to study economics, because so many things in the world are quickly changing. More people are losing jobs, the real estate market is surging[9], and jobs are being outsourced[10] to third-world countries. Knowing how the market works is important for our career, our investment decisions, and even retirement strategies. With expertise in economics, you can make profitable yet safe investments when others are feeling completely out of control.

1.7　语言

1.7.1　让出国旅游变得更简单

Mastering a language makes travel so much easier. Last year, I traveled to Japan with my friend Kayla. Unfortunately, she had a fever during the trip. The worst thing was that when we tried to find our way to the hospital, nobody understood what we were saying. I couldn't find people who spoke English or Chinese to tell us directions. It was a nightmare! I would never want to relive that experience again. So, this time, before going to Italy, I made sure I knew how to order certain foods and ask basic directions. Instead of asking everyone if they spoke English, I was able to figure things out on my own. I can get on the right trains and navigate in a new city with ease. It really gave me a sense of achievement[11].

1.7.2　不光要学，而且要尽早学

I think students should take language courses as early as possible, because it has already been established that children who learn a language when they are very young have a much better chance of not having a "foreign" accent when speaking another language. Also, the wonderful thing is that they will give things a try without worrying if it is correct or not. When I was little, I was eager to speak with foreigners. I wanted to see their responses when I used the new words I had just

❾ surge [səːdʒ] *v.* 剧增，飙升

❿ outsource ['autsɔːs] *v.* 外包

⓫ a sense of achievement 一种成就感

learned. I didn't worry about making mistakes at all. It was an exciting and empowering experience for me.

1.7.3 双语更具备竞争力

Multilingualism[12] is definitely a competitive edge[13]. In China, a lot of students who speak English well can go to the United States to receive a better education. In the U. S. , they can make use of modern facilities in labs, great resources in libraries, and interact with world-famous professors to enhance their learning experience. Thus, after they graduate, they have better chances of find decent[14] jobs. A world of global opportunities will open for them once they are fluent in English, because multilingualism is an ability that tells of a person's intelligence, flexibility and openness to diverse people.

⑫ multilingualism
[ˌmʌltiˈliŋgwəlizm]
n. 对多种语言的试用
（或熟悉）

⑬ edge [edʒ] n. 优势
🔁 advantage

⑭ decent [ˈdiːsnt] adj. 像
样的，得体的

1.8 电脑

It is vital[15] for students to learn coding because we are already living in a world dominated by software. Our telephone calls go over software-controlled networks; our television is delivered over the Internet; Instead of buying paper-based maps, we use Google Maps; we all shop on Amazon and TaoBao. The next generation's world will be even more digitalized. And learning computer-related courses is not about forcing students to become software engineers, but about instilling a basic understanding about the language of future machines, which is definitely beneficial for any future career. It combines mathematics, logic and algorithms, and teaches you a new way to think about the world.

⑮ vital [ˈvaitl] adj. 重要的
🔁 important

02 Should a student explore their interests in many subjects or specialize in a few areas?

真　题	题　型	年　份
Do you agree or disagree that students should take some additional courses so that they can get their credits more quickly?	口语 第二题	2016/03/19
Do you agree or disagree with the following statement：students should learn to draw or paint?	口语 第二题	2016/08/27

2.1　多学几科

2.1.1　学科之间是相互联系的

Taking a variety of courses is better because it gives you an opportunity to learn about subjects outside your field of study. Because so many fields of study **are related**, you never know when knowledge from one area will be helpful in another. Take people who work in advertising for example. The knowledge of psychology would be necessary **so that** they can understand consumers' minds. They can also benefit from taking courses in foreign languages, which enable them to communicate better with their foreign clients. All these courses will pay off[1] in their career.

2.1.2　多学几科探寻自己的兴趣所在

Students are supposed to[2] take a variety of subjects, because they are not mature[3] enough to decide what they want to learn and they need more time and opportunities to explore and figure it out. I **used to study** English when I was in college, but I took some elective courses[4] in education. It **turned out** that a little exploration turned up[5] my interest in education which I'd never considered studying before. I realized that I wanted to be a teacher in the future. If I hadn't taken those **elective courses**, I might never have realized what I am really interested in, and that would be a shame.

2.2　少学几科

2.2.1　没时间

I would like to focus on a single area, because I just don't have time and energy to learn everything. I major in engineering and it is tough. I have to finish 20 credits in one semester, all for compulsory courses[6]. Every day, I study until midnight in the library. I am always exhausted. It would **drive me crazy** if I had to learn courses outside my major field and that would definitely affect my academic performance in my own major. Therefore, focusing on one subject is a wiser choice for me.

❶ pay off 带来好结果

❷ be supposed to do something 应该做某事

❸ mature [mə'tʃuə] *adj.* 成熟的

❹ elective course 选修课

❺ turn up 找到，发现

❻ compulsory course 必修课

2.2.2 有助于事业进一步发展

I think single-subject study can contribute more to career development. We all start out broad and end at a specific area, from kindergarten where we're learning multiple subjects, to a Master's or PhD program where we're expected to master the most particular area of one topic. Suppose you work as a computer programmer in an IT company, and you specialize in coding. For your colleagues and boss, the most important thing is that you have a depth of knowledge in computer programming, and not in, say, economics or marketing. On the contrary, having only a breadth without focusing on a certain subject will make your employer think that you are not good at anything in particular. And that would definitely jeopardize[7] your chances of getting a promotion[8].

2.3 视情况而定

I think it depends on what you mean to accomplish, and we need to find a balance between breadth and depth. If you are trying to push the boundaries of human knowledge, depth is important. It's why PhDs can be very specific. You need to know nearly everything about a very specific topic. However, possessing only a depth of knowledge would make you an idiot[9] savant[10], fantastically capable at one thing and helpless in all other matters. You always need some of each. So we also need knowledge outside of our majors, which can help us get exposed to new ideas and new ways of thinking.

[7] jeopardize ['dʒepədaiz] v. 损害
[8] get a promotion 晋升
[9] idiot ['idiət] n. 笨蛋，白痴
[10] savant ['sævənt] n. 学者，专家

03 Do you prefer solving a task by yourself or collaborating with other people?

真 题	题 型	年 份
Some people prefer to work independently; others prefer to work with others. Which do you prefer? Explain your answer in detail.	口语 第二题	2016/03/26

3.1 和别人合作

3.1.1 高效

I like to collaborate with other people, because when I am working alone, time can so easily be wasted. I just can't get anything done. There are endless distractions, such as movies, music and video games. For example, I'm currently preparing for the TOEFL exam, and my Reading Comprehension instructor suggests that we memorize 50 words each day. When I was studying alone, I would persist[1] at most for 5 minutes. After that, I couldn't help unlocking my phone, playing a game for an hour and sighing with emotion that time passes so fast. However, when I am collaborating with other people, I am constantly engaged by the group and I am not able to procrastinate[2] anymore.

3.1.2 集思广益

When working with others, each of us can contribute different materials and perspectives. So, we have a variety of information to discuss and share with other people. When different ideas collide, even newer ideas emerge. For example, when I'm looking for ideas while writing a paper, I am often stuck[3] for hours. I feel helpless and do not know where to start. But if I work with others, when other team members share their ideas, I would have a starting point to work from. I would soon find my own ideas, and it just feels great that I can contribute something to the team. I'll never forget the praise in others' eyes when I tentatively stated my opinion on a group essay topic.

3.2 自己解决问题

3.2.1 效率更高

Sometimes group work is less productive because of too much gossiping and chattering, and too many different ideas. It's more fun, but less work gets done. Last week, I was attending a group discussion with my financial management classmates, and I thought we could have everything done in two hours, but I was proven completely wrong. Just when I was about to illustrate my plan for our group presentation, Jason interrupted while browsing through gossip news on iPhone. He was sitting quietly at first but suddenly screamed: LeeHom got engaged.

---

❶ persist [pə'sist] v. 坚持

❷ procrastinate [prəu'kræstineit] v. 拖延，耽搁

❸ stuck [stʌk] adj. 困住，卡住

Everybody else started to ask: really!? Then, a heated discussion about the validity of the news began, so we didn't get anything done that day.

3.2.2 不用平衡意见

Working alone surely assures maximum efficacy. Although working with others means more ideas, sometimes too many ideas might not be a good thing, especially when team members are all stubborn[4] and do not compromise[5] easily. Last week when my group and I were choosing the background color for our PowerPoint, Jack and Tom had a huge disagreement. Jack argued that we should definitely choose black since it's elegant and serious, while Tom insisted that we should use yellow. The latter reasoned that black slides set the tone of a funeral, whereas yellow resembles the sun, which gives a more positive energy. The worst thing was that most of the rest of the group members all chose one side and began to attack the other side. The argument lasted for two whole hours and still, we did not have an agreement on that detail. If I were working alone, I would have been able to decide the color in less than a second.

3.2.3 不会有无本获利者

Although I do cherish the opportunity to gain some leadership experience in group work, I still hate free-riders. I have a habit of taking responsibilities onto my own shoulders, without assessing the gains and losses, so I often end up draining[6] up all my own energy to do the work that should be done by others. I think a group of two or three people is ideal for collaborations. Any arrangement of more than three members would surely produce free-riders. When a large group forms, it is destined that some people will be more active and thus take more responsibilities and complete more work. Free-riders will seize the opportunity and do the minimum amount of work to prevent themselves from being kicked out of the team, which is an extremely rare case since most people would still tolerate free-riders despite disliking them. In the end, some smart free-riders might even steal your thunder[7] and get praised by the teacher, although you are the one who did all the hard work. I don't want to end up in a situation where others do less, but get praised.

④ stubborn ['stʌbən] *adj.* 顽固的，固执的

⑤ compromise ['kɒmprəmaiz] *v.* 妥协

⑥ drain [drein] *v.* 耗尽

⑦ steal sb. 's thunder 抢风头

04 When you have a project, do you prefer to start it as early as possible or wait until the deadline?

真 题	题 型	年 份
Which do you prefer：start a project as early as possible or wait until the due time?	口语 第二题	2016/09/25

4.1 尽早完成

I would start the project as early as possible so that I can be more prepared. Last semester, I made a heroic promise to myself—read my assignment on time, do the reviewing for my exams on time, and in general, stay on top of everything. However, not everything goes according to plan. Sometimes, I just couldn't be hard-hearted[1] enough to turn down[2] a ski trip invitation in the mountains; nor could I resist the temptation of watching talk shows and playing video games. In addition to that, I had a lot of errands[3] to do, such as going to the student union for a meeting. As a result, I fell behind with my schoolwork and I had one shot of espresso[4] and pulled an all-nighter[5] preparing for my history exam the day before the test. Although I finished all the reading materials in time, I was exhausted the next morning. I was not as quick or sharp as I normally am. And I just couldn't concentrate on the test. My performance was a disaster. I would never want to relive that again. So, next time, I will definitely start as early as possible.

4.2 拖到最后

Waiting until the last possible moment to do a task keeps me more focused. When I am rushing to meet a deadline, I am less likely to be distracted. I won't be answering the phone, checking emails, clicking on a news headline, or thinking about anything else except finishing the task. As a result, things get done faster. I am usually more productive before the due day. So, for me, procrastination is like an energy booster. Also, I think I am less stressed than people who start early. Some people allow their worries to keep them up at night and wake up

1 hard-hearted [ha:d-'ha:tid] *adj.* 无情的，冷酷的

2 turn down 拒绝

3 errand ['erənd] *n.* 差事

4 espresso [e'spresəu] *n.* 浓缩咖啡

5 pull an all-nighter 熬夜，通宵

tired, but I go to bed, sleep, and wake up early to finish that project. I don't want to spend 80% of my time worrying about what I am gonna do in the remaining 20% of the time.

05 Is it better to pick a major based on interest or job availability?

5.1 凭兴趣

I think it would be better to follow your heart and pick a major you love. Life is too short to pass up an opportunity to do what you love. My friend Kayla wanted to study music. However, forced by her parents, she chose finance. Now she works at Goldman Sacks[1] and she is getting paid a lot. But every time I run into[2] her, I can tell she is not happy because she does not like finance at all. Her real dream is to become a composer.

❶ Goldman Sacks 高盛（投资银行）
❷ run into 偶然遇见

5.2 看是否好找工作

I think it would be better to major in something practical unless it is the interest you are dying to follow. My friend Deepa has been playing piano for 16 years and she wanted to be a composer[3]. However, it is just so hard to make a living[4] as a musician today. The market is too competitive. She couldn't find a job after she graduated from conservatory[5]. So, she went to a lot of cities to find chances to perform at bars, restaurants or clubs. She worked super hard, but the money she earned was not enough to pay her rent. She even had difficulty paying for food in the end. At last, she gave up the dream of being a composer and found a job as an accountant[6].

❸ composer [kəm'pəuzə]
 n. 作曲家
❹ make a living 谋生，维持生活
❺ conservatory [kən'sə:vətri]
 n. 音乐学校

❻ accountant [ə'kauntənt]
 n. 会计师

06 How much homework should teachers assign?

6.1 该多留作业

1 assign [ə'saın] v. 布置（工作、任务等）

I think it's a good thing for teachers to assign[1] homework for students. It allows students to practice the skills they have learned during school. Of course, nobody likes practicing things. Musicians get bored practicing scales[2]; athletes get bored practicing their moves; and students get bored answering the same types of questions over and over again. However, practice does make perfect, and the more you work on your homework, the better you get. I often get good grades when I do my homework. When I do poorly on my assignments, I learn what my weaknesses are and discuss them with my teachers in office hours so I can prepare for my tests better.

2 scale [skeıl] n. 音阶

6.2 不该再留作业了

I don't think kids should be given a lot of homework. They already have seven hours of school. When I was a kid, I started school at eight and went home at four. That's a full day of school. Most adults work similar lengths of time at work and come home exhausted. I was just not able to concentrate on my work anymore at the end of the day. Also, students should have more time to do exercise. If they're busy in school during the day, and do a lot of homework when they get home, they'll be exhausted. A much better approach[3] is to do all the learning you need to do at school. When you go home, that's the time for you to play and go outside and get exercise.

3 approach [ə'prəʊtʃ] n. 方法

07 What should you do if you're not good at academic work?

真 题	题 型	年 份
Which of the following is the most effective way of learning: 1）studying from textbooks；2）having discussions with a group；3）reading articles written by others? Please use specific reasons to support your idea.	口语 第一题	2015/02/01
Which one do you prefer? Reviewing your notes after class and doing this throughout the whole semester, or just reviewing at the end of the semester?	口语 第二题	2015/06/27
When you have trouble doing assignments, do you prefer to seek help from classmates or professors?	口语 第一题	2015/07/12
What's the biggest problem during the course of being a student? How do you usually deal with it?	口语 第一题	2016/03/11
Some people prefer to work independently；others prefer to work with others. Which do you prefer? Explain your answer in detail.	口语 第二题	2016/03/26
Which do you prefer: starting a project as early as possible or waiting until the due time?	口语 第二题	2016/09/25

7.1 小组讨论

I like to collaborate with other people, because when I am working alone, time can so easily be wasted. I just can't get anything done. There are endless distractions[1], such as movies, music and video games. For example, I'm currently preparing for the TOEFL exam, and my Reading Comprehension instructor suggests that we should memorize 50 words each day. When I was studying alone, I would persist at most for 5 minutes. After that, I would unlock my cell phone and play games for an hour, and sigh with emotion that time passes so fast. However, when I am collaborating with other people, I am constantly engaged by the group and I am not able to procrastinate[2] anymore.

❶ distraction ［dis'trækʃn］
n. 使人分心的事儿

❷ procrastinate
［prəu'kræstineit］
v. 耽误，延迟

7.2 坐在教室前排

My biggest problem is that I just can't pay attention in class. My mind simply drifts away after listening to the lecture for a few minutes. Fortunately, I realize that when I sit in the front row, I am more focused on the class. I try to answer professors' questions and interact with them a lot. However, if I sit in the back, I get bored easily. So, I think teachers should let students sit in different seats.

7.3　课上发言

❸ drift［drift］v. 漂流，偏离

My biggest problem is that I just can't pay attention in class. My mind simply drifts³ away after listening to the lecture for a few minutes. Fortunately, I realize that speaking out in class is a good way to keep me concentrating, because I have to force myself to focus on the lecture to make sure I can say something relevant. If I just listen quietly and observe, I get bored easily and probably start sleeping.

7.4　向教授求助

❹ jot down 草草记下

❺ office hour 办公时间

❻ self-sufficient 自给自足

❼ enlightening［in'laitniŋ］adj. 有启发作用的

I would ask my professors for help. You know, I study math and it is really hard. Sometimes, I just don't want to admit that I am struggling to understand a concept or keep up with homework. As a result, I usually get stressed out when I spend hours struggling with just one problem. Last time, I was working on a homework assignment that was really confusing, so I jotted down⁴ little notes and asked the professor in office hours⁵ reluctantly. I was mad at myself at that moment because most of my life I've taken pride in being self-sufficient⁶. To my surprise, the professor pinpointed the problem immediately. It was really an enlightening⁷ talk to me! And that was definitely more efficient than studying alone. It made me realize that professors are there to help. Don't ever feel like you are bothering them, because they actually want us to come.

7.5　写论文

Writing papers is a great way to deepen students' understanding of course materials. Last semester I needed to write a paper on Kang Xi, an emperor of the Qing dynasty. Can you imagine how many books I read just to write this one paper? Ten! I read ten books to get this paper done. After tons of reading, I discovered more knowledge about the Qing dynasty, such as its culture, economic development, and foreign relations. Furthermore, it prompts[8] me to think more deeply about what I am learning. When I am writing, I have to make countless choices about my paper: what to read, how to organize ideas, how to check sources[9] So, I am forced to read thoroughly[10] and critically[11]. It allows me to have a better understanding of the subject.

⑧ prompt [prɔmpt]
v. 促进

⑨ check sources 检查信息源

⑩ thoroughly ['θɔ:rəli]
adv. 彻底地，认真仔细地

⑪ critically ['kritikəli] adv.
批判的

7.6 每天复习

I would review my notes after class and keep doing this throughout the whole semester, because repetition is the best way to learn. It's like playing a musical instrument. We know that skipping exercises always leads to poor performance, because when we learn something new, a pathway is created in our brain. And the more frequently we "travel through that pathway", the more likely we will be able to recall[12] the information later. For example, I took French in high school and I failed the test every semester. At that time, I blamed my teacher and his methods. Now I understand I should take responsibility for my poor performance. I only did the reviewing at the end of the semester. So, there was no way that I could have a large vocabulary. Actually, we don't need to study 8 hours every day. All we need to do is review for like 30 minutes every day and never give up until we've mastered it all. That's the key to excellence.

⑫ recall [ri'kɔ:l] v. 回想

7.7 学期末再复习

I would like to review at the end of the semester, because I am usually more productive[13] before the exam. I won't be answering the phone, checking emails, clicking on a news headline, or thinking about anything else except reviewing for the exam. As a result, things get done faster. So, for me, the deadline is like an energy booster[14]. Also, I think I am less stressed than people who review every day. I have the experience of reviewing notes[15] throughout the whole semester, but I forgot everything at the end of the semester. So, for me, it's just a waste of time.

⑬ productive [prə'dʌktiv]
adj. 多产的

⑭ energy booster 能量增强剂

⑮ review notes 复习笔记

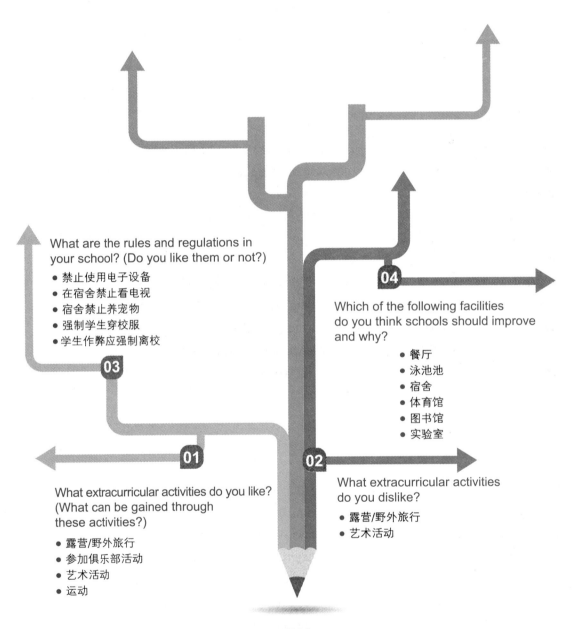

What are the rules and regulations in your school? (Do you like them or not?)
- 禁止使用电子设备
- 在宿舍禁止看电视
- 宿舍禁止养宠物
- 强制学生穿校服
- 学生作弊应强制离校

03

Which of the following facilities do you think schools should improve and why?
- 餐厅
- 泳池池
- 宿舍
- 体育馆
- 图书馆
- 实验室

04

01

What extracurricular activities do you like? (What can be gained through these activities?)
- 露营/野外旅行
- 参加俱乐部活动
- 艺术活动
- 运动

02

What extracurricular activities do you dislike?
- 露营/野外旅行
- 艺术活动

学校

01 What extracurricular activities do you like? (What can be gained through these activities?)

真　题	题　型	年　份
Some people think that it is an important part of children's education to go on field trips (e. g. museums). Others think a child's time is better spent in the classroom at school. Which do you prefer and why?	独立写作题	2013/10/05
Do you agree or disagree with the following statement: all students should attend social activities such as clubs or sports teams in school?	口语第二题	2015/04/12
These days, children spend more time on doing homework or participating in organized activities related to school or sports. However, they should be given more time to do whatever they want.	独立写作题	2015/07/12
Your university will sponsor one of the following activities for students, an outdoor camp night, a music festival to experience the local culture, or a computer game contest in the dorm. Which do you think is the best and why?	口语第一题	2015/09/17
Which kind of extracurricular activity would you like to attend if you have the chance: writing essays for a student newspaper, joining a hiking club, or working in the dormitory discipline committee?	口语第一题	2015/11/08
Your school used to offer three after-class activities: 1) sports, 2) art, 3) volunteering, but this year, the school's extra money can only offer one activity. Which one do you choose and why?	独立写作题	2015/11/08
Some college students like to join clubs and enjoy club activities; others like to spend their time studying another course or doing schoolwork. Which one do you think is better and why?	口语第二题	2016/05/07

1.1　露营/野外旅行

1.1.1　锻炼身体

Camping gives students a good opportunity to do various kinds of exercise. When you go out camping you can do lots of exciting activities like hiking, fishing, cycling[1], and climbing. For example, hiking is a very easy way to get fit. I went hiking in Xiang Mountain last week. By the time I got there, the Health app on my cell phone showed I had walked nearly 30, 000 steps, and I had burned 500 calories[2].

❶ cycling ['saiklɪŋ] n. 骑自行车

❷ calorie ['kæləri] n. 卡路里

1.1.2　放松

Camping really gives students a chance to **loosen up**. As a college student, I had lots of stress from schoolwork. However, when I went out camping, I took a break. I could forget all the troubles at school. My family went camping last weekend. There is a big beautiful lake near the camping site. I could sit by the lake by myself for hours, looking at the ripples[3] forming and disappearing on the surface of the lake, and feeling the breeze[4] blowing through the trees. It is so peaceful there.

❸ ripple ['ripl] *n.* 波纹

❹ breeze [briːz] *n.* 微风

1.1.3　远离电子产品

It gives me a chance to **detach** from electronic devices. I've become so **attached** to my phone and iPad that I've been to the point of checking them first thing when I wake up and last thing before I go to bed. That's not the life I want. When I go out camping, most places don't even have a Wi-Fi connection. So, I can touch the nature outside, talk with my friends more and leave my cell phone in my pocket.

1.2　参加俱乐部活动

1.2.1　获得社交和潜在工作的机会

Joining new clubs gives me the opportunity to expand my social circle[5]. And these connections will come in handy[6] when I'm looking for a job. Many clubs host several events with alumni or panel discussions with local professionals. These events can often lead to potential internships or employment opportunities in the future. For example, last summer, I met someone in a club. We started to talk and found out we are both really into[7] basketball, we started to hang out more and play basketball together. It turned out he is actually the recruitment[8] manager of a big company. And he offered me an internship at his company in the end.

❺ social circle 社交圈

❻ come in handy 方便

❼ be into 喜欢

❽ recruitment [riˈkruːtmənt] *n.* 招聘

1.2.2　放松

Joining a club gives me a chance to **loosen up**. As a college student, I have lots of stress from the schoolwork. When I have some time off, I really want to join some club activities with my friends. We can share our common interest like favorite sports or music while drinking a couple of beers, talking about some hot topics from recent news, or discussing our vacation plans for the school break.

1.3 艺术活动

1.3.1 创造力

Joining an art club helps students to **boost their creativity**. For example, in a painting class, children would be asked to create vivid images of houses, people, and places. Sometimes, they would even be asked to create abstract art, such as a paining that represents their memories or emotions. It would obviously make use of one's imagination. Furthermore, if children think creatively, it will become a habit and stay with them in the future.

1.3.2 放松

Joining an art club gives me the chance to loosen up. As a college student, I have lots of stress from school work. When I have some **time off**, I go to the art club to draw, to **soothe my mind**. My favorite painting style is water color painting[9]. I really like using vivid[10] colors to **express my feelings**. Whenever I immerse[11] myself in painting for several hours, I forget all these troubles from school.

❾ water painting 水粉画
❿ vivid ['vivid] *adj.* 生动的
⓫ immerse [i'mə:s] *v.* 沉浸

1.4 运动

1.4.1 做运动，减肥

Sports help me **keep in shape**. I couldn't help but notice that my belly[12] was starting to **stand out** when I looked at myself in the mirror last year, and it did not look great. So, I joined a sports team and started to do some exercise every day in order to keep myself **in good shape**. I have been running 2 miles daily, and my belly is under control now.

⓬ belly ['beli] *n.* 腹部

1.4.2 放松

Joining a sports club gives me the chance to **loosen up**. As a college student, I have lots of stress from schoolwork. During the weekends, I go to the sports club to do some running. I do some stretching[13] first to **warm up**. Then I compete with others in a five thousand meter running. When I focus on my breath and pace, I really can't think of

⓭ stretching ['stretʃiŋ] *adj.* 伸展

anything else. In this way, I forget all the troubles at school and feel refreshed.

02 What extracurricular activities do you dislike?

2.1 露营/野外旅行

2.1.1 没时间

I don't have time to go camping. I have so much schoolwork to do. For example, I am still struggling with my academic courses like physics, which is like a nightmare to me. I spend endless hours studying in the library, and stay up[14] all night googling information about these complex concepts. If I have some time off[15], I prefer to catch up on some sleep.

⑭ stay up 熬夜

⑮ time off 空闲时间

2.1.2 太累

It would be way too exhausted if I went camping. There was a time I went camping with my best friend Jay. It took us 5 hours to get to the camping spot. We were already extremely tired. So, by the time we set up the camp, made up our sleeping place, it was already mid night. We were not in the mood or energetic to enjoy the nature. We just went straight to[16] sleep. From that night, I swear I will never go camping again.

⑯ go straight to 直接

2.2 艺术活动

不感兴趣

I am not that into[17] art. It's so hard for me to appreciate a piece of art work. Once my best friend Jay and I went to an art museum together. He was shocked and amazed by these famous paintings, while I was standing there looking stupid. I thought about pretending to appreciate these masterpieces[18], and then I gave up the idea after like three seconds. These artworks just don't speak to me[19].

⑰ be into 喜欢

⑱ masterpiece ['mɑːstəpiːs]
n. 杰作

⑲ speak to someone 感同身受

03 What are the rules and regulations in your school? (Do you like them or not?)

真　题	题　型	年　份
It is important to have rules about the types of clothing that people are allowed to wear at work and at school.	独立 写作题	2013/08/24
Some schools prevent students from putting TVs in their dormitories. What are the advantages and disadvantages of this policy? Please include specific reasons and examples to support your answer.	口语 第一题	2015/05/09
Should universities allow their students to bring computers to class?	口语 第一题	2015/06/14
Do you think it is a good idea to let students keep pets in dorms?	口语 第一题	2016/01/09
Your School is planning to forbid the use of cell phones on campus. What do you think are the effects of the policy?	口语 第一题	2016/05/29

3.1 禁止使用电子设备

3.1.1 电子设备分散学生注意力

Most students are attached to[1] electronic devices all the time. Cell phones or laptops are major distractions for students in classes. One time when I kept checking information about a soccer game on my twitter, and I missed a lot in a review session. Of course, I didn't do well on the test and I was upset about my grades at the end of the semester. I would definitely focus more on my studies if our school forbade the use of electronic devices on campus.

❶ be attached to 沉浸在

3.1.2 电子设备的铃声干扰课堂

Cell phones can go off[2] anytime during class periods and that can disturb teachers and other students. Last week, someone's phone suddenly rang and the tone[3] was a cartoon voice. All the students in class started laughing, and the professor was pissed off[4]. It took almost 15 minutes till the whole class went back to being quiet. If this happens too much, I am pretty sure it will be a huge distraction for students who

❷ go off 失控

❸ tone [təʊn] n. 铃声

❹ pissed off 气疯了的，怒冲冲的

⑤ implement ['implimənt]
   v. 实施

⑥ eliminate [i'limineit] v.
   消除

⑦ scenario [si'nɑːriəu] n.
   情境

are really trying to pay attention in class. By implementing[5] a ban on such devices, these distractions could be eliminated[6] once and for all.

3.1.3 学生携带电子设备有利于紧急情况

Cell phones really **come in handy** in some emergency scenarios[7]. One time, a friend of mine was badly injured and it would have taken minutes to get back to the school to make a call. However, because one of the students had a mobile phone, We called the head-teacher immediately and the emergency services were contacted within seconds. Having mobile phones on campus could actually save lives.

3.1.4 学生携带电子设备方便查资料，提高学习效率

⑧ study aid 学习助手

⑨ boost study efficiency 提
   高学习效率

Because most cell phones have Internet access, students can use cell phones as an effective study aid[8]. For example, when teachers in class teach a complex concept, instead of struggling through the study material, students could just **pull out** their cell phones and **google** it. Looking at some beautifully designed video illustrations is just way better than looking at text descriptions in textbooks. It would definitely boost study efficiency[9] in class. Also, students can use cell phones to retrieve information from teachers. So, teachers won't waste too much time printing out the hand-outs. And students don't need to carry these papers to school every day.

3.2 在宿舍禁止看电视

3.2.1 看电视增强交流

⑩ be attached to 沉浸在

⑪ isolated ['aisəleitid] adj.
   隔离的

⑫ Super Bowl 超级碗
⑬ NBA finals NBA 总决赛

Most students are attached to[10] their electronic devices all the time. They barely talk with others and live an isolated[11] life. If there is a TV in the dorm, students will have more chances to talk with each other and share their feelings. We can talk about which characters we hate or love the most or predict what will happen in the next episode. When there is a major sports event like the Super Bowl[12] or NBA finals[13], students can gather and watch together, which surely will be more fun.

3.2.2　看电视可以放松身心

Joining a sports club gives me the chance to **loosen up**. As a college student, I have lots of stress from schoolwork. When I get back to my dorm, study is the last thing I want to do. Nothing beats lying on the bed and watching TV with my roommates. Last time, when finals were over, we finally got time to watch the last episode[14] of the series *Breaking Bad*[15]. That was the best memory for that semester. These troubles from school at that time didn't seem to matter at all.

❶ episode ['episəud] *n.*
剧集

❶ *Breaking Bad* 《绝命毒师》

3.2.3　看电视会干扰其他同学

Some students might not like watching TV. When they go back to their dorm, they want to take a nap[16] or continue studying. It is a huge distraction if someone else is watching TV at the same. Students may end up arguing with each other, or even fighting with each other. Everybody needs his/her own privacy and a personal schedule. We should respect each other's personal life.

❶ take a nap 打盹

3.2.4　看电视会导致成绩下降

When I live in a dorm with a TV, I get D minuses in my course work. I am really into TV shows. If I get the chance to lay in bed watching TV, I won't do anything else. One time, I supposed to do some review for the coming biology exam. However, I found out that the last season of *Breaking Bad* was showing on TV. Of course, I couldn't help but watch it for the whole afternoon and left the review behind. And I was really upset about my grades in the end. For those who cannot control themselves, throwing the TV out might be an idea worth trying.

3.3　宿舍禁止养宠物

3.3.1　养宠物可以放松身心

It is really easy for a college student to be overwhelmed[17]. They are busy with their academic work, internships, part-time jobs, and community services, etc. I think having a pet could help them get through these difficult and stressful situations. I used to spend lots of time with my dog before big exams. Watching him jumping and running really helped me loosen up and get ready for exams.

❶ overwhelmed
[,əuvə'welmd] *adj.* 不知所措的

3.3.2 没时间养宠物

Most college students just aren't mature and responsible enough to take care of pets. Already most of them are struggling with schoolwork and working part-time jobs. How much time could be left for taking care of pets? Pets need accompaniment, a lot. You have to spend time with them each day, walk them, play with them, and maybe talk to them. Many students decide to get a pet on a whim[18], but end up sending them away after just two months. So, just get one when you graduate.

⑱ whim [wim] *n.* 心血来潮

3.3.3 寝室小，没空间养宠物

Dorm rooms are small and an animal with its food, bed, cage or aquarium[19] will make it even smaller. So, with all the stuff packed up[20] in a small room, I don't think anybody will feel comfortable. If someone forgets to clean up the pet's mess, I am pretty sure no one will stand that smell and the whole dorm will become a nightmare.

⑲ aquarium [ə'kwɛəriəm] *n.* 养鱼缸
⑳ pack up 堆积

3.4 强制学生穿校服

3.4.1 帮助学生将注意力放在学习上

School uniforms help students shift their attention from what to wear to what to study. When all students are wearing the same outfit, they are less concerned about how they look and how they fit in[21] with their peers. Thus, they can concentrate on their schoolwork. When I was in my high school I was really embarrassed to wear my own clothes because other students thought they were ugly. Even though I didn't want to care much, it still distracted me from my studies. I started to lose concentration in class worrying about other students' opinions about my appearance.

㉑ fit in 融入

3.4.2 穿校服对学习没帮助

Actually, I think academic performance has nothing to do with school uniforms. When I was in middle school, our head teacher imposed a strict uniform policy, forcing students to wear school uniforms from Monday to Friday. The underlying intention behind this policy is that students could focus more on study, instead of clothing. However, the policy failed miserably. My classmates went out of their way to design ways to modify details on the uniform, so that they would look different, so that they would be idiosyncratic[22]. For example, some wore extra-large size, when they should have worn a medium; some used scissors to cut up the edges of their trousers.

3.4.3 学生有自己的个性，不应该强制穿校服

Children express themselves through clothing. School uniforms should not be required in public schools for children to wear. I grew up in a school that did not have dress codes[23], and since I was into[24] what was "stylish", I enjoyed choosing what to wear. Lots of kids use clothing as a fun, harmless way to express themselves. By expressing themselves, they have a better idea about who they are. This helps them to follow their passion and interests in the future.

3.4.4 穿校服不舒服

It is not comfortable. When I was in middle school, I had to cope with a tight collar[25] shirt and itchy[26] trousers that made me unfocused. In addition. I was not free to choose what type of clothing to wear according to the weather. When it was hot, instead of wearing something light and short, the school forced us to stick with the uniform. It was extremely awful, when you have to wear the uniform while bearing the summer heat in a classroom without an air conditioner[27].

3.5 学生作弊应强制离校

3.5.1 Yes

Punishment for cheating is the foundation of all schools. Everybody loves the easy way out[28]. If students know that cheaters are not punished, everybody soon enough becomes one. Come on! Many of my friends brag about their experiences of staying up all night in the library, reviewing for the finals, still getting "A"s after skipping class for the whole semester, but nobody would ever do that again if they knew they could cheat. A strict policy on cheating provides the fairness that everybody craves[29]. At the same time, the policy teaches students about honesty and integrity[30].

---

[22] idiosyncratic [ˌɪdɪəˈsɪŋkrætɪk] *adj.* 特质的

[23] dress code 着装要求
[24] be into 喜欢

[25] collar [ˈkɔːlə] *n.* 领子
[26] itchy [ˈɪtʃi] *adj.* 痒

[27] air conditioner 空调

[28] easy way out 解脱的方法

[29] crave [kreɪv] *v.* 渴望
[30] integrity [ɪnˈtegriti] *n.* 正直

③ despise [di'spaiz] v. 看不起

② dismissal [dis'misəl] n. 免职

3.5.2 No

Yes, cheating is bad. Cheating should be despised[31]. But cheating should not lead to one's dismissal[32] from school. Punishment for cheating should help students focus more on their studies. But a permanent dismissal from school sometimes means bye-bye to the education system. Kids who get dismissed might end up being beggars or even criminals. Schools should give students a chance to learn from their mistakes. So in my opinion, I think a temporary suspension from school, or giving a zero score to the student who cheated is more than enough.

04 Which of the following facilities do you think schools should improve, and why? (cafeteria, swimming pool, library, laboratory, school gym, dorm)

真　题	题　型	年　份
A university should focus more on its facilities, such as libraries, computers or laboratories, rather than on hiring famous teachers.	独立写作题	2015/10/24
Which one of the following should be done in order to improve the quality of life and study for the students? Repairing the swimming pool, building a new cafeteria, or improving laboratory equipment?	口语第一题	2016/03/13
The university will spend money on the dormitory to improve the students' quality of life. Which of the following do you think is best? Providing a room for quiet study, building an exercise room or providing a movie room?	独立写作题	2016/09/25

4.1 餐厅

吃得更健康

College cafeterias should serve delicious and healthy meals to help students form good eating habits. I can't even recall a single time that I have found a salad bar in my college cafeteria. All I remember is the greasy[1] fast food, like fries, fried chicken, and burgers. After eating this several times, I was just sick of these junk foods, and went out to eat. However, if college students are introduced to healthier foods like fruits and salads which contain more vitamins and minerals, they are more likely to maintain these healthy eating habits.

❶ greasy ['gri:si] *adj.* 油腻的

4.2　游泳池

4.2.1　锻炼身体，减肥

A swimming pool allows every student to enjoy aquatic[2] activities. Swimming also helps students keep in shape. I couldn't help but notice that my belly was starting to stand out when I looked at myself in the mirror last year, and it did not look great. So, I started to take some swimming lessons on campus. It then became my favorite sport. It works most muscle groups in my body, improving flexibility and increasing muscle strength. My body is in much better shape now.

❷ aquatic [ə'kwætik] *adj.* 水上的

4.2.2　安全

Swimming can be a dangerous and life-threatening experience if students are not trained in water safety. A bigger swimming pool can provide more opportunities for students to learn the fundamentals of swimming during a PE class. And these fundamentals will assure students of a safe aquatic experience. When I visited my cousin in Denver last summer, my mind was blown by their swimming classes. As they have lots of indoor and outdoor swimming pools, their classes are well structured. Once they learned to float, the instructor would move on to breathing lessons, and taught them how to hold their breath properly underwater. Then students would learn how to paddle[3] and float. These trainings may someday save lives.

❸ paddle ['pædl] *v.* 划水

4.3　宿舍

改善环境

Most colleges have poor facilities in dorms, so they should surely be improved. My college dorm only had a basic set of two twin-sized beds, two desks, a mirror, and a tiny sink to wash hands. There was no TV in the dorm room and my college had imposed a monthly limit on the downloads and uploads. As a result of these extremely poor conditions, we often had to go off campus to satisfy our need for entertainment. Had the school prepared all these necessities for students, we would have had a much more pleasant life in college.

4.4 体育馆

4.4.1 放松

④ overwhelmed [ˌəuvəˈwelmd]
　　adj. 不知所措的

It is really easy for a college student to be overwhelmed[4]. They are busy with their academic work, internships, part-time jobs, and community services, etc. So, having a place to get rid of this stress is really important. After studying in the library the whole day, I always come to the school gym to do some exercise. When I stay focused during my workout, I can get my school work off my mind. No matter how awful I feel before I hit the gym, I always come out fresh. Also, an effective workout can always put me to sleep quicker at night, which in turn reduces stress.

4.4.2 锻炼身体

Working out in a gym with fine equipment just feels great. Last year, I couldn't help but notice that my belly was starting to stand out, when I looked at myself in the mirror, and it did not look great. I tried to do push-ups in my dorm room. But, it is not quite an ideal work out environment, so I figured I needed a better site. Then, I tried the school gym with my friends. I could just do way more in a school gym. I could do some lifting to warm up first, and then I would move to the pull up station to do some overhand pull-ups. It really helped to boost strength and build muscle more quickly. After repeating for half an hour, I would do some stretches to cool down. It helps to increase blood flow and relax all my muscles.

4.5 图书馆

4.5.1 改善图书馆环境

⑤ insulated [ˈinsjuleitid]
　　adj. 隔音的

Our library has been used for 50 years. It is way too old to provide good study conditions for students. The whole building is not insulated[5] well. You can hear clearly what is happening outside. When someone is walking on the stairs, they start creaking. It makes it hard for students to concentrate on their work. There is no Wi-Fi inside the library, which means you have to use your personal hotspot on your iPhone for Internet access, which costs tons of money. The library system is outdated. It takes forever to find the right books or materials. Without further improvements, nobody will be willing to go to the library.

For those who don't want any distractions when they want to get things done, a library seems to be the only choice. Trust me that studying anywhere else will be time-wasting nightmares. When I study in my dorm room or in a lounge, I get muddled[6] on the Internet, talk on the phone, listen to music, watch TV, and read everything but my assignments. Worst of all, I have an endless stream of time wasters pulling me down with them. My roommates talk about ball games and won't shut up till midnight. My friends come to my room to hang out, because they are always bored. When you realize that you didn't accomplish a single thing at the end of the day, you know you need to find somewhere else to study.

❻ muddle ['mʌdl]
v. 混日子

4.5.2　在图书馆学习有效率

If we had a big library, we wouldn't have to study anywhere else. When I study in my dorm, I talk on the phone, listen to music, read everything but my assignments. My roommates talk about ball games and won't shut up till midnight. However, the library creates a complete separation between students' personal lives and their academic lives. Everybody in the library has a big bubble around them that protects them from annoying outside influences. It is the last place on campus where your friends are going to come in and chat you up. Once you sit in a library, the quiet atmosphere will force you to shut your phone off and keep focusing on your school work. I really can't find anywhere else to provide me this uninterrupted and highly effective study time.

4.6　实验室

4.6.1　学习更有效

There are several scientific theories and concepts that are difficult to explain directly from books. The knowledge that students attain in classrooms would be ineffectual unless they observe the whole process of real chemical reactions. A lab is the perfect place for students to understand complex concepts better. For example, teachers can show students the burning of magnesium. When it reacts with oxygen to produce the oxide, it can be shown that there has been an increase in mass. The results can be used to find the formula of magnesium oxide[7]. However, if the lab is underfunded, students won't be able to see amazing experiments, and thus cannot effectively learn the topic.

❼ magnesium oxide 氧化镁

4.6.2　启发学生的是灵感

A lab with the latest and most advanced materials and supplies is able to contribute a lot to scientific advances yet to come. Advances and developments in the field of medical science and technology would not take place if schools did not prepare brilliant and dedicated scientists and researchers. Students develop interest in scientific research in science labs. When they observe various things and carry out different experiments, their reasoning skills are honed and they start thinking deeply about those theories and concepts. Schools thus play a vital role in bringing up the next generation of engineers and doctors.

第二十三类　课外

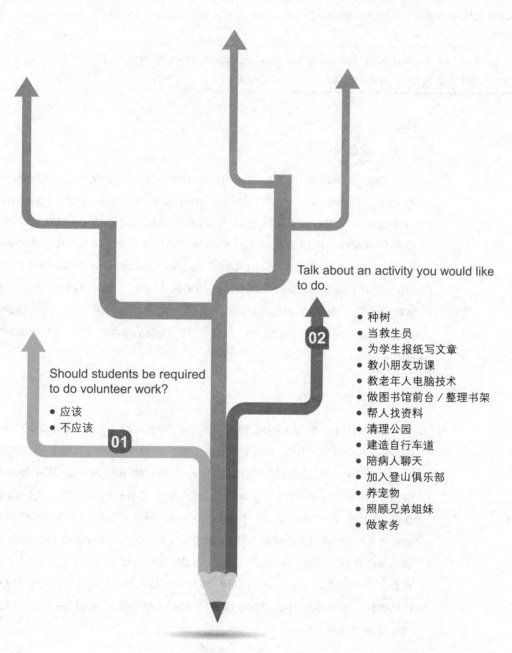

Talk about an activity you would like to do.

- 种树
- 当救生员
- 为学生报纸写文章
- 教小朋友功课
- 教老年人电脑技术
- 做图书馆前台／整理书架
- 帮人找资料
- 清理公园
- 建造自行车道
- 陪病人聊天
- 加入登山俱乐部
- 养宠物
- 照顾兄弟姐妹
- 做家务

02

Should students be required to do volunteer work?

- 应该
- 不应该

01

课外

01 Should students be required to do volunteer work?

真　题	题　型	年　份
Should schools require their students to participate in 40-hour-long community work?	口语第一题	2015/09/05
Do you think it's a good idea that some schools require students to finish 40 hours of community service each year?	口语第一题	2016/05/07

1.1　应该

Yes. Volunteering can help students gain new experiences and insight. It allows students to get involved in things they have never engaged in, and to develop skills that couldn't be learned in a classroom environment. Last semester, I volunteered as a lifeguard[1] in a swimming pool. Thanks to this job, I picked up[2] vital skills. I was trained in first-aid[3] and water-based rescues. So, I can potentially help save someone's life. In addition, it makes your resume more appealing. Employers surely tend to hire graduates with lots of volunteer experience.

❶ lifeguard ['laifɡɑːd] *n.* 救生员
❷ pick up 学会；获得
❸ first-aid [fəːst-eid] *adj.* 急救的

1.2　不应该

I don't think students should be required to do volunteer work because they simply don't have time. You know, I am a college student. I have to study constantly to keep an appealing GPA and find time to attend a hundred group meetings in a week. I just don't want to devote my last few spare hours to volunteer work. Last semester, I spent a couple of months completing my school's volunteer requirements at a local hospital. Actually, I did not care about it at all, and I only showed up so that the volunteer coordinator would sign my time sheet[4]. It meant nothing to me. So, I don't think students should be forced to do volunteer work.

❹ time sheet 考勤表

02 Talk about an activity you would like to do.

真 题	题 型	年 份
Which of the following would you choose to do in summer vacation? Working at the front desk of a public library, painting in a community art center, or being a life guard in a community swimming pool?	口语 第一题	2012/07/15
Which kind of extracurricular activity would you like to attend if you have the chance? Writing essays for a student newspaper, joining a hiking club, or working in the dormitory discipline committee?	口语 第一题	2013/01/26
What kind of activity do you think can help children cultivate a sense of responsibility? 1) Have a pet; 2) do house chores; 3) help take care of their younger sisters or brothers. Use specific details and examples in your response.	口语 第一题	2013/07/21
The university is recruiting volunteers to help the community protect the environment. If you are recruited, which of the following three tasks will you choose to do? 1) pick up trash and litter on the street; 2) plant trees and flowers to green the town; 3) Teach children about protecting the environment	口语 第一题	2013/10/12
Talk about one activity you will do in the near future and explain why.	口语 第一题	2013/12/07
Talk about an interesting activity you recently participated in. Did everyone involved enjoy the activity? Give details and examples in your response.	口语 第一题	2013/12/14
Talk about an activity you participated in recently. Did everyone have a good time?	口语 第一题	2013/12/15
Which of the following community services would you choose to do? Working with children, cleaning the city park, or planting a campus garden?	口语 第一题	2014/09/27
Which of the following hospital volunteer work would you be interested in doing? Talking to patients, reading to patients or taking care of their families?	口语 第一题	2014/12/06
If there is a community activity, would you like to play with children, or do the gardening?	口语 第二题	2015/03/07
What should we do to help the elderly in our community?	口语 第一题	2015/08/22
If you had to volunteer for a project, which one would you choose? Cleaning up the city, creating bicycle trails, or planting trees?	口语 第一题	2015/10/25
If you were to do a volunteer job in the community, which one of the following jobs would you choose? Clean up the park, plant trees, or build a bicycle lane?	口语 第一题	2016/06/04
Which of the following would you choose to do in summer vacation? Working at the front desk of a public library, painting in a community art center, or being a life guard in a community swimming pool?	口语 第一题	2016/09/25

2.1 种树

I would like to plant trees, because it can help reduce air pollution. Air quality has become so poor in recent years, because factories and cars put too much carbon dioxide[1] and other harmful gasses into the air. People get different kinds of diseases because of that. However, trees can take in the carbon dioxide for their own food — then turn it into oxygen for us to breathe! Also, they clean the air by absorbing harmful gasses and trapping other pollutants. So, we need trees now more than ever! Also, they can save a lot of energy. In my school, there is a big and leafy shade tree. It keeps us cool during the summer. We don't even need to turn on the air conditioner.

I recently read on social media that the cheapest way for governments to improve air quality is to plant trees. So, if I ever have time to do volunteer work, planting trees would be my top choice. They said that tree leaves are great for trapping dust and other harmful particles in the air. Also, there are no maintenance[2] costs because rains would wash dust and particles to the ground, which makes the leaves clean again, and thus ready to absorb more harmful particles.

❶ carbon dioxide 二氧化碳

❷ maintenance ['meintənəns] n. 维护

2.2 当救生员

I want to be a lifeguard in a swimming pool, because of the lifelong skills I can acquire. For example, I will be properly trained in first-aid and water-based rescues. I can potentially help save someone's life. Also, it pays better than most of the summer jobs available to teens. A lot of my friends who work as library assistants only get 8 dollars an hour, but being a life guard can earn 20 dollars an hour. Money isn't everything, but there's no doubt that earning more is better.

2.3 为学生报纸写文章

I would like to write essays for a student newspaper, because it's a very flexible job. The best thing about this job is that I can work at home instead of working at an office. I can sit in bed with a cup of tea and take a break whenever I feel tired. I just hate the feeling of being stuck in the office, staring at my cell phone and waiting to leave for dinner.

Also, working in a newspaper office earns more. A lot of my friends who work as library assistants only get 8 dollars an hour, but writing essays for student newspapers earns way more than that. Money isn't everything, but there's no doubt that earning more is better.

2.4 教小朋友功课

I want to be a tutor and help kids with their homework. Actually I have done this before. I was once a tutor and taught a little kid, Jason, math. He used to be really poor at math. The perfect score for each math test was 100; he normally got a score of 50. I quickly pointed out his problems. He was smart, but he didn't receive adequate training in his third grade. So whenever he came across problems related to third-grade knowledge, he would stumble. Then I helped him focus on that part and he soon got improved. I think I am a really good teacher. I want to do it again.

2.5 教老年人电脑技术

I would like to teach senior citizens[3] computer skills because it can help them connect better with their children. For example, my mom has just realized how useful computers are. My mother and I live in different cities. So we seldom see each other. But now, after teaching her how to use a computer, we can still communicate with each other by using face-time or Skype. Now, we Skype every night using computers. I tell her what's going on at school so that she doesn't worry about me so much. Also, teaching old people computer skills can make their lives easier. For example, they don't need to go to the bank anymore. They can manage their personal finances through computers. All they need is a computer and some online banking apps, and they can know exactly how much money they have.

③ senior citizen 老年人

2.6 做图书馆前台/整理书架

I would choose to work at the front desk of a public library, because I am really into[4] reading. So, if I'm a library clerk, I guess I'll be able to

④ be into something 喜欢某事

⑤ get access to 可以适用

⑥ get sued 被起诉

⑦ malpractice [ˌmælˈpræktis]
n. 渎职，玩忽职守

⑧ wander [ˈwɔndə] v. 心
不在焉

get access to[5] all the books in the library. Also, I get to see all of the new materials a while before they go on the shelves. Also, it would be very peaceful and stress-free. If I make a bad decision, nobody dies. I won't get sued[6] for librarian malpractice[7]. If I let my attention wander[8] for a while, I don't have to worry about some piece of machinery taking my hand off or anything like that.

2.7 帮人找资料

I would like to help people find materials. Last semester, I had to write a paper about China's emperor Kang Xi. I knew nothing about him so I needed to read a lot of books to get the paper done. However, when I went to the library, I found that the computer system for finding books was really difficult to navigate. There were just tons of books and I couldn't find the right one. I wasted a lot of time on that. So I hope I can be a librarian who is able to help students with their research projects. I would feel good after helping them.

2.8 清理公园

⑨ incentive [inˈsentiv] n.
激励某人做某事的诱因

⑩ sustain [səˈstein] v. 维
持，支撑

⑪ passerby [ˌpɑːsəˈbai] n.
路过的人

⑫ strew [struː] v. 散播

I would like to clean up the park, so that there is more incentive[9] for people to exercise. Now, kids have less time to do enough physical activities. They spend more time watching TV, surfing the Internet and playing video games, rather than playing outside. It raises the risk of health problems. I think beautiful parks can encourage people to go outdoors and sustain[10] healthy lifestyles. Even a small and inexpensive park may attract passersby[11] to come in and therefore start walking or exercising. If the park is not clean, nobody will want to come and exercise anymore. Even more, if the running track is strewn[12] with litter, people may get hurt when running through the park.

2.9 建造自行车道

⑬ gasoline [ˈæsəliːn]
n. 汽油

⑭ carbon dioxide 二氧化碳

I would like to build a bicycle lane since riding bikes is a great form of green transportation. As we all know, cars consume gasoline[13] and create carbon dioxide[14] emissions, but riding a bike doesn't require fuel at all. It is pollution-free. Plus, parking lots for bicycles do not take up as much space as cars. One parking spot for a car alone can easily fit up[15] to 20 or more bikes. So, if we build bicycle lanes to promote green travel, our city surely will become a better place.

Also, if riding a bicycle is convenient and safe enough, everybody will join the trend[16]. Who doesn't like to be green and fit at the same time? But, we have to build some great bicycle lanes first. Once the lanes are ready, everything else will follow naturally. Take my own experience for instance. I hadn't ridden a bike for like 10 years until the government somehow built a bicycle lane from my residence area to my school, overnight. I was amazed and couldn't help myself but try out the MoBike that I have always wanted to try. I lost about 30 pounds. It also greatly improved my circulation[17]. After about a week of bike riding, I noticed that my cheeks had become naturally rosier.

2. 10　陪病人聊天

Chatting with the elderly and patients teach students responsibility and how to look after for others. I used to walk with patients in wheelchairs around the hospital during my time volunteering in the surgical[18] services department. I would talk to them about anything not related to hospitals and medicine. It was a great way to get their minds off their situation, and helped comfort them emotionally. Sports, news, places they've traveled, their opinions on things, music, these are all great conversation starters, and help immensely[19] in connecting with patients. So, when my family or friends get sick, I know what to do to make them feel better.

2. 11　加入登山俱乐部

Climbing mountains provides people with great sense of achievement. I can't think of any other activity more fundamentally human than walking upright on two feet. It's an extension of something we all do naturally every day. The initial learning curve[20] is almost non-existent. I have never heard of somebody quitting this sport, because it's not demanding at all. All you really need is persistence. Also, it is a great way to connect with Mother Nature[21]. I just love to sit or walk along rivers or lakes；to appreciate the good view of waterfalls, green vegetation[22], and even wildlife；and to listen to the singing of beautiful birds. It just feels great to get out of our spiritless[23] city.

---

⑮ fit up 填满

⑯ trend [trend] *n.* 趋势

⑰ circulation [ˌsɜːkjəˈleɪʃn]
n. 循环

⑱ surgical [ˈsɜːdʒɪkl] *adj.*
外科的

⑲ immensely [iˈmensli]
adv. 极大地

⑳ initial learning curve 最初的学习曲线
㉑ Mother Nature 大自然

㉒ vegetation [ˌvedʒɪˈteɪʃn]
n. 植被
㉓ spiritless [ˈspiritləs] *adj.*
无精打采的

2.12 养宠物

2.12.1 培养责任感

Having a pet teaches children about responsibility and how to care for others. For example, feeding a pet is something concrete that all students can understand. They know what it feels like to get hungry and they understand that food is the cure for hunger. When their pet "attacks" the food and gets satisfied, they know what they are doing is really important. They come to see that their parents are doing the same for them as what they are doing for their pets. They will be more willing to get involved in family activities like helping parents with chores[24]. They will be more responsible for their own tasks.

2.12.2 放松

I would like to have a pet because it can help me relieve stress[25]. You know, I am a senior in college and it is a pretty stressful environment. I have to take a lot of classes and tests and I really want to get ahead. Sometimes, I feel isolated[26] and overwhelmed[27], especially before exams. However, when I spend time with my dog, I can forget about all those troubles in the real world. He is like my best friend! Watching him jumping and running really makes me feel happy and relaxed. So, I think it would benefit students a lot if they can keep pets in the dormitory.

2.13 照顾兄弟姐妹

It will help students form a sense of responsibility and caring. Kids will grow up one day. Skills they learn from taking care of younger sisters or brothers will come in handy[28] when they become parents and start taking care of their own babies. My elder brother used to take care of me when I was little. I was not a quiet kid and used to be naughty all the time. I used to break glasses, mess up sheets, and play with fire. It was my brother who kept me out of trouble when my parents were busy. Now he has three kids, and I am not surprised at all that he takes good care of them well. I know he learnt quite a lot when he took care of me.

24 chore [tʃɔ:] n. 家务

25 relieve stress 释放压力

26 isolated ['aisəleitid] adj. 孤立的

27 overwhelmed [,əuvə'welmd] adj. 不知所措的

28 come in handy 派上用场

2.14 做家务

Students can learn some practical skills from doing house chores. When I was little, my father would ask me to try to fix broken toys. That was actually the first time I touched a screw driver[29] and a hammer. Although I didn't know how to use these tools in the beginning, eventually I got better, after father's patient explanations. And these skills really come in handy since I've grown up. Because of my father, I never feel worried about a broken pipe, an air conditioner, or an electrical failure in my house. I can fix everything by myself.

㉙ screw driver 螺丝刀

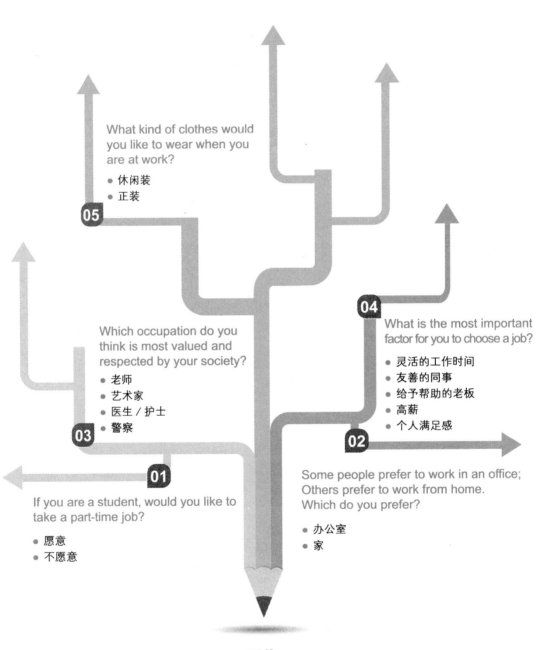

What kind of clothes would you like to wear when you are at work?

● 休闲装
● 正装

05

Which occupation do you think is most valued and respected by your society?

● 老师
● 艺术家
● 医生 / 护士
● 警察

03

04

What is the most important factor for you to choose a job?

● 灵活的工作时间
● 友善的同事
● 给予帮助的老板
● 高薪
● 个人满足感

02

01

If you are a student, would you like to take a part-time job?

● 愿意
● 不愿意

Some people prefer to work in an office; Others prefer to work from home. Which do you prefer?

● 办公室
● 家

工作

01 If you are a student, would you like to take a part-time job?

真　题	题　型	年　份
Some people believe that it is important for young people to have a part-time job as a work experience, while others think they should spend more time on their studies. What is your opinion and why?	口语 第二题	2012/04/20
Some people believe that it is important for young people to have a part-time job as a work experience, while others think they should spend more time on their studies. What is your opinion and why?	口语 第二题	2013/04/14
Do you think it's a good idea for students to work for a year before entering university?	口语 第一题	2013/09/29
Your friend is planning to work for a year before entering university. Give your opinion about his plan.	口语 第一题	2013/10/20
Do you agree or disagree that people should work for some time before they find a permanent job?	口语 第二题	2014/03/01
After high school, students should have at least one year to work or travel. It's better than attending university straight away.	独立 写作题	2016/03/13
Do you agree or disagree one of your friends, who is planning to work part-time while studying on campus?	口语 第一题	2016/11/26

1.1　愿意

1.1.1　学习时间管理

Having part-time jobs can help students learn something about time management. Nowadays, a lot of students are procrastinators[1]. They always wait until the last minute to do their homework. If they have a job, they know they only have a few hours to do their homework, so they won't put things off anymore. They'll be more efficient and manage their time better.

❶ procrastinator
[prəu'kræstineitə] *n.* 拖延症患者

1.1.2　获得工作经验

Students can gain some work experience by doing part-time jobs, because it can teach them skills every employer is looking for, such as commitment, time management, teamwork and leadership. Last year, I applied for the position of communication assistant in an advertising company. However, I didn't get the offer, because I was told that the employers want candidates who had work experience. However, unfortunately, when I was in college, all I did was study. So, it's necessary for students to have part-time jobs, which can build up their resume and give them a better shot[2] at finding decent jobs when they graduate.

② shot [ʃɔt] *n.* 机会
⊡ chance

1.1.3　探索职业发展兴趣

For high school students, having part-time jobs can help them find their interests and further explore their future career options. I wanted to study education and be a teacher. So, in my gap year, I took a position as a teacher in a primary school, teaching students coding. However, this experience was torture for me. I was not good at communicating with kids. They were too naughty[3]. As a result, I changed my mind about studying education and chose computer science as my major in the end. So, by taking a part-time job, students can know what they like or don't like, whether it's sitting in an office or going on business trips. It'll save them lots of time and effort choosing majors and looking for jobs.

③ naughty [ˈnɔːti] *adj.* 淘气的

1.2　不愿意

1.2.1　没时间

I don't want to take a part-time job, because I may not be able to balance my work and study and that would affect my academic performance. I remember when I was a college student, I often worked until midnight in a local restaurant and had chemistry class the next morning. So, I felt exhausted and couldn't concentrate on the class. As a result, I failed chemistry. I regret that, because I know I could have got better if I had focused more on study. As a student, study has to be my priority[4].

④ priority [praiˈɔrəti] *n.* 优先处理的事

02 Some people prefer to work in an office, others prefer to work at home. Which do you prefer?

真　题	题　型	年　份
Some people prefer to work in an office; others prefer to work at home. Which do you prefer?	口语 第二题	2014/03/15

2.1　办公室

2.1.1　效率更高

I prefer to work in the office, because it has the working atmosphere that I need so much. When I am working at home, time can so easily be wasted and I can't get anything done. There are just so many distractions, such as movies, music, video games, roommates and family. However, if I am in the office, it's a totally different story. I am forced to sit in my quiet cubicle[1], with only my work to focus on. Also, there are so many hard. working colleagues, I feel ashamed if I just sit there and do nothing.

> ❶ cubicle ['kju:bikl] *n.* 格子间

2.1.2　便于交流

Working in the office is better, since we can communicate more easily with our coworkers, and most of the office work today involves collaborations. For example, I'm working with two of my colleagues on a book that we are writing together. We are all lazy, and thus tried to communicate through WeChat without coming to the office. But sadly we found out that this didn't work. Some complicated operations in Excel and Word must be explained face-to-face. Eventually, we decided that the easiest way to get things done is to meet weekly at the office, and work the remaining parts at home.

2.2　家

2.2.1　节约通勤时间

I prefer to work from home, because it can reduce my commuting time and fuel costs. I live in Beijing. It's a super big city. It would take me more than two hours to go to my work place. If I am allowed to work from home, I can save myself at least two hours and I can use that time to have a big breakfast. And if I can have a big breakfast, I can concentrate better on my work.

2.2.2　招揽各地人才

❷ disability [ˌdɪsəˈbɪləti] *n.* 残疾

With flexible location policies, employers are able to hire talent from across the country and even the whole world. Stay-at-home parents, retired professionals, and professionals with disabilities[2] are all brought into the workforce through flexible work options. And it is priceless for an employer to find talents that fit best his or her company.

03　Which occupation do you think is most valued and respected by your society?

真　题	题　型	年　份
It is generally agreed that society benefits from the work of its members. Which type of contribution do you think is most valued by your society? Primary school teachers, artists, or nurses?	口语第一题	2015/12/05

3.1　老师

❶ respected [rɪˈspektɪd] *adj.* 受到广泛尊重的
❷ literally [ˈlɪtərəli] *adv.* 确实地
❸ facet [ˈfæsɪt] *n.* 方面

I think teachers are the most respected[1] job, because teachers literally[2] create every other profession in the world. Without teachers, there would be no doctors, no police officers, no lawyers, and no musicians. Teaching is the basis of every facet[3] of society. Without teachers, there would be no society. Also, teachers need to spend hours studying material, doing research, and working on presentations before the class to get fully prepared. And right after class, they have to answer questions and grade papers. It takes great patience.

3.2　艺术家

I admire artists. They create a lot of masterpieces that give us relaxation and enrich our emotions. Listening to a peaceful piano piece relaxes us after a long day at work; an exciting symphony keeps us motivated at work; more importantly, when disappointed in love, we feel much better after listening to pop music, as if the singer is directly comforting and encouraging us. My favorite artist is Beethoven. Through his pieces, I can feel his despair, his sorrow, his fight against fate, and his passion in life. I personally relate to[4] his experiences and feel inspired by his masterpieces.

❹ relate to 与……息息相通

3.3　医生/护士

I think being a doctor is the most challenging job because doctors need to give up a lot of things. They need to say goodbye to sound sleep, health, fitness goals, etc. My friend Deepa works at hospital. She does not have a lot of time to hang out[5] with us. There are lots of sunny weekends when we are having a barbecue while Deepa is taking care of her patients. Also, just as saving lives can be rewarding, the responsibilities that come with being a doctor can be stressful and they may accidentally kill someone. So, a doctor needs to be mentally strong to deal with all those difficulties, such as making a mistake, losing a patient, or fearing the loss of one.

❺ hang out 闲逛

3.4　警察

I think being a police officer is the most challenging job because policemen need to give up a lot of things. They need to say goodbye to sound sleep, health, fitness goals, etc. My friend Deepa works in police station. She does not have a lot of time to hang out with us. There are lots of sunny weekends when we are having a barbecue while Deepa is patrolling the neighborhood and investigating crime. Also, just as saving lives can be rewarding, the responsibilities that come with being a police officer can be stressful, and they may accidentally kill someone. So, a police officer needs to be mentally strong to deal with all those difficulties, such as making a mistake or fearing the loss of a life.

04 What is the most important factor for you to choose a job?

真　题	题　型	年　份
Talk about a positive experience you recently had working with another person. Explain why this experience was important to you.	口语 第一题	2013/03/24
When you are at work, which of the following factors do you think is the most important to you? Having flexible schedules, having friendly coworkers, or having a helpful boss?	口语 第一题	2015/03/14
Which would you choose：a higher pay job with longer hours or an average paying job with normal work hours? Explain your choice, using specific reasons and details.	独立 写作题	2016/07/09

4.1　灵活的工作时间

　　A flexible schedule enables people to balance work and life in a better way. It can help them meet their family needs, personal obligations, and life responsibilities more conveniently. For example, if you have a flexible schedule, you can go to a parent-teacher conference during the day to fulfill your obligations as a mom or dad. You can also take your yoga class in the middle of the day to develop a good habit of exercising, or be home when the maintenance man[1] comes. I personally feel very satisfied when I am empowered to structure my work and personal life according to my needs.

4.2　友善的同事

　　Having friendly coworkers can create a fertile[2] ground for teamwork, and is far better than a sterile[3] workplace that spawns[4] competitiveness and mistrust. I am a designer and the staff in our office all get along[5]. When we are doing projects together, each of us usually brings different materials and perspectives. So we have a variety of information to discuss and share with other people. And this can force me to think thoroughly and engender[6] more creativity. I feel supported. The work culture is upbeat[7] and fun. However, if I am surrounded by a bunch of

[1] maintenance man 维修工

[2] fertile ['fɜːtail] *adj.* 肥沃地

[3] sterile ['sterail] *adj.* 贫瘠的
 🔲 deficient in originality or creativity; lacking powers of invention

[4] spawn [spɔːn] *v.* 引发

[5] get along 相处融洽

[6] engender [in'dʒendə] *v.* 引起

[7] upbeat ['ʌpbiːt] *adj.* 乐观的
 🔲 cheerful

mean and unfriendly people, I don't think I will be in the mood for work. The longer I stay around such people, the more my health will suffer.

Also, work sometimes brings us a lot of stress, so it would be nice if there was someone that you could count on and talk to. I am glad my coworker Jack is also my friend. Sometimes, I complain to him about my new boss. And he can totally understand what I am going through and come up with brilliant ideas to help me solve the problem. In addition, we usually have lunch breaks together where we don't talk about work and just relax.

4.3　给予帮助的老板

As for me, all I want is a helpful boss because they are usually good listeners and wise decision makers. You know, I used to have a very authoritative boss. He is a very poor communicator. My coworkers and I once suggested that we should update the look of our cell phone so we could attract more customers. However, instead of reading the proposal, our boss just said no because he thought that we should focus more on technology. None of us challenged his opinion because we knew he was very arrogant. We didn't want to make a very bad impression on him or jeopardize[8] our chances of getting a promotion[9]. The result was our competitor changed the look of their cell phone and earned a lot of money. So, I really hope I can have a helpful boss who is willing to listen to other people's advice.

⑧ jeopardize ['dʒepədaiz]
　　v. 损害，危及
⑨ get a promotion 升职

4.4　高薪

I prefer a higher paid job, because career decisions are not decisions about what I love most. Career decisions are about what kind of life I want to set up for myself. I am a computer programmer, but I love playing video games more than coding. I can get a sense of accomplishment from playing video games, and it makes me feel very happy. The problem is that I don't get paid for playing computer games and I need money to live a decent life. For example, I want to buy an apartment for my parents in Beijing, but the house prices are very high. It's best if I work as a computer programmer during the day and spend my spare time pursuing my passion.

4.5　个人满足感

I would like to choose a job from which I can gain personal satisfaction. My friend Deepa works at IBM and she is getting paid a lot. However, every time I run into[10] her, I notice that she is not happy and she looks very tired. She told me that she does not like computer programming at all and she was not keen[11] on working in the IT Industry. So, I think life is too short to pass up an opportunity to do what I love. Also, if I love my job, I will keep learning and improving. This will not only set me on the path toward success, but also help me get through the daily grind[12]. My life will be more fulfilling[13].

[10] run into 碰见

[11] be keen on something 热衷于某事

[12] grind [graind] n. 苦差事
[13] fulfilling [ful'filiŋ] n. 令人满足的

05 What kind of clothes would you like to wear when you are at work?

真　题	题　型	年　份
It is important to have rules about the types of clothing that people are allowed to wear at work and at school.	独立写作题	2013/08/24
Some people believe it's better to wear formal clothes at work, while others believe it's better to wear casual clothes. Which do you prefer?	口语第二题	2014/11/29

5.1　休闲装

I prefer to dress casually for the following reasons. First, some work places don't require employees to suit up[1]. Take my company for example. I work in an IT company. All my colleagues are in jeans and T-shirts. Even my boss dresses casually. So, it would be very weird if I were the only one who dressed in a very formal style. Second, suits and ties look professional, but they are not very comfortable, especially those slim fit[2] shirts. I just can't breathe when I am in them. Also, formal clothing is more expensive than casual clothing. It would cost me at least 200 dollars to buy a decent suit. T-shirts and jeans are way cheaper

[1] suit up 穿戴整齐（指西装或制服）

[2] slim fit 修身款

than that. In addition, suits need to be ironed[3] every day, which is very troublesome. So, I don't want to waste my time and energy in dressing formally.

③ iron ['aiən] *v.* 熨平

5.2 正装

I would like to dress formally, because the first impression is very important. And I think I can create a positive professional image by dressing appropriately. I have a friend who works in Human Resources[4]. She told me that a candidate dressed in a suit and tie is going to make a much better impression than a candidate dressed in jeans and a T-shirt. They show their respect to this job. So, I would choose a suit in a dark color, such as navy or black. And I would wear a conservative blouse, which is not too tight or revealing[5]. If I wear a skirt, I would make sure it is of a moderate length.

④ Human Resources 人力资源

⑤ revealing [ri'vi:liŋ] *adj.* 袒胸露背的

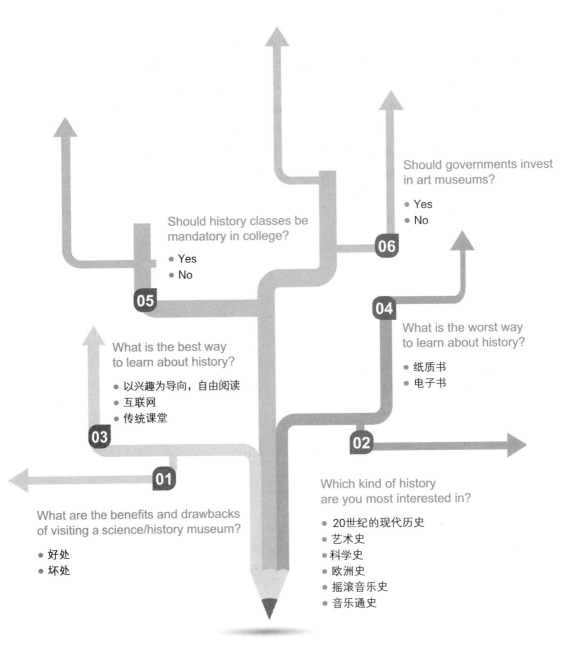

Should governments invest
in art museums?

- Yes
- No

Should history classes be
mandatory in college?

- Yes
- No

What is the worst way
to learn about history?

- 纸质书
- 电子书

What is the best way
to learn about history?

- 以兴趣为导向，自由阅读
- 互联网
- 传统课堂

05

04

06

03

02

01

What are the benefits and drawbacks
of visiting a science/history museum?

- 好处
- 坏处

Which kind of history
are you most interested in?

- 20世纪的现代历史
- 艺术史
- 科学史
- 欧洲史
- 摇滚音乐史
- 音乐通史

历史

01 What are the benefits and drawbacks of visiting a science/history museum?

真　题	题　型	年　份
Which one of the following classes would you choose? 1）science history；2）art history；3）European history	口语第一题	2012/06/17
Which of the following ways is the best to get to know Italian culture? 1）watching Italian movies；2）learning Italian cooking；3）attending Italian lectures or history classes	口语第一题	2012/07/22
Visiting museums is the best way to learn about a country.	独立写作题	2014/09/29
All university students should be required to take history courses no matter what their field of study is.	独立写作题	2015/01/07
If you are a teacher of a tutor group and you are going to take students on a study trip，where would you take them to? A science museum, a local farm, or a theatre performance?	口语第二题	2015/10/25
Which of the following three classes will you choose to fit into your schedule? 1）Musical History；2）World Economics；3）Environmental Science	口语第一题	2015/11/14
Which one of the following history courses should be added? History of science, art history, or modern history of the 20th century?	口语第一题	2016/01/23
Some people think that it is an important part of children's education to go on field trips（e. g. museums）. Others think a child's time is better spent in classrooms at school. Which do you prefer and why?	口语第二题	2016/03/27
When you're visiting a city you've never been to, how would you like to tour around? A. sign up for a well-organized trip；B. visit history museums；C. walk along the streets	口语第一题	2016/05/11
Which of the following is the best way to learn about a city? Joining an organized trip；visiting the museums；or taking walks in the streets of its cities?	口语第一题	2016/05/22
If you are a teacher of a tutor group and you are going to take students on a study trip，where would you take them to? A science museum, a local farm, or a theatre performance?	口语第一题	2016/05/29
Some people think that it is an important part of children's education to go on field trips（e. g. museums）. Others think a child's time is better spent in classrooms at school. Which do you prefer and why?	口语第二题	2016/06/07
Which of the following classes do you think can attract the most students? 1）sound engineering；2）history of rock music；3）film studies	口语第一题	2016/12/11

1.1　好处

1.1.1　学习效果比课堂更好

First things first, students learn history better in museums than in classrooms. When I was in elementary school, I got excited on all field trips, as long as we could leave our classroom and go outside. When students are relaxed and light-hearted, the learning experience comes naturally, and memorizing all the difficult material is no longer that troublesome[1]. Also, many museums now utilize advanced technologies such as Virtual Reality[2], Augmented Reality[3], or 4D movies to demonstrate interesting yet important phenomena or events, which would definitely enhance students' learning experience.

1.1.2　满足好奇心

I loved going to science museums when I was little. I guess the primary drive behind my obsession is curiosity. Kids are always curious about everything. My parents told me that my favorite word during my childhood was "why". I would ask questions like "Why does the sun rise in the east?" "Why can't we breathe underwater?" "Why can't we fly?" etc. Although most questions can be answered by my parents, an interactive demonstration in the science museum is often way better than pure verbal explanation. I can still recall vividly the intriguing experiences: the demonstration of static electricity by a glass ball, the two differently shaped trajectories which demonstrate Newtonian Theory, the augmentation of sound which can travel more than 50 meters by concentrating through two huge concave planes.

I still remember all the interesting demonstrations: the experiment which proves Newtonian Theory[4] with two iron balls rolling down from a shelf, the amazing phenomenon that static electricity can cause, and the gathering of sound by huge concave[5] plates.

1.1.3　可以发朋友圈

I love to visit museums because I can show off amazing photos on social media apps afterwards. When I travel to a new place, there are a few places that I would definitely explore, and museums are one of them. Normally, each museum has its most precious treasure. Sometimes it is a golden Buddha[6], a traditional Chinese screen made of the purist Jade,

① troublesome ['trʌblsəm] *n.* 麻烦的
② Virtual Reality 虚拟现实
③ Augmented Reality 增强现实

④ Newtonian Theories 牛顿定律
⑤ concave [ˌkɒnˈkeiv] *adj.* 凹的

⑥ Buddha ['budə] 佛

or a mummy of a prestigious Pharaoh from Egypt. I take pictures of these treasures, and show them off on WeChat[7]. One time, I posted a picture of me sitting on a set of traditional redwood furniture from the Ming Dynasty[8], and I got 200 likes instantly.

❼ WeChat 微信

❽ Ming Dynasty 明朝

1.2　坏处

1.2.1　费时间

Travelling to museums is time-consuming. Generally, museums are built in suburban areas where no public transportation is available. As a result, people with no cars might have to first take a bus to a nearby station and then walk to the museum on foot, which often takes more than an hour. Students nowadays are simply too busy to squeeze time out of their schedule, which is already packed with various activities such as lessons in piano, violin, or guitar; sports such as golf, ice-hockey or ballet; or cram schools, test preparation courses, and so on. Taking time out of their already packed schedule will surely cause great damage to their academic performance. Besides, computerization has allowed us to teach history in a much more efficient and absorbing way than before, given the advent of iPads, online videos, and artificial intelligence.

1.2.2　没意思

I hate travelling to museums because it's dull, but in real life, sometimes you have to. For example, last month my friend Foosen visited Beijing, and he asked me to take him to the Museum of Fine Arts. I had only been there once when I first came to Beijing in my freshman year, and it was full of boring and unintelligible art which drove me crazy. But again, he is my dearest friend, so I couldn't turn his sincere request down. So, I went with him reluctantly on a Saturday morning, when I am usually still in bed, and began our exhausting tour. He, in sheer contrast to me, is very into arts. He would constantly stand in front of abstract modern art and would stare at it for minutes. I, on the other hand, had to pretend that I was also interested, and to give him a smile of understanding when he gave me a look that asked if I was getting the underlying meaning of the art. Thank god there was a coffee bar in the middle of the museum. I might have passed out in front of that high-end art if we didn't rest there for half an hour before we continued the torment tour which lasted for a full day.

02 Which kind of history are you most interested in?

真 题	题 型	年 份
Which one of the following classes would you choose? 1) science history；2) art history；3) European history	口语 第一题	2012/06/17
Which of the following ways is the best to get to know Italian culture? 1) watching Italian movies 2) learning Italian cooking 3) attending Italian lectures or history classes	口语 第一题	2012/07/22
Which of the following three classes will you choose to fit into your schedule? 1) Musical History；2) World Economics；3) Environmental Science	口语 第一题	2015/11/14
Which one of the following history courses should be added? History of science, art history, or modern history of the 20th century?	口语 第一题	2016/01/23
Which of the following classes do you think can attract the most students? 1) sound engineering；2) history of rock music；3) film studies	口语 第一题	2016/12/11

2.1 20 世纪的现代历史

I'm not interested in any kind of history, actually. If I must choose, I'd pick modern history, since I'm more familiar with it. I learned a little about modern history in high school. Because of that, I have a basic understanding about the intricate timeline and complicated characters such as Abraham Lincoln[1], Joseph Stalin[2], and Chairman Mao. Without such basic knowledge, reading a history book can be an extremely wearisome and daunting experience. For instance, my GRE instructor in New Oriental suggests that we should read about art history since it is a frequently asked question in the test. So I followed his advice and started to read *A Brief History of the Arts*.

Frustrated by the difficult vocabulary and strange names, I only made it to Page 4. I regrettably put the book down, and never picked it up again.

As I have aged, I have gradually become interested in history, especially modern history. I want to know the answers to questions like：why is the world the way it is now；what was it like a decade, or a century ago；who won the cold war；what caused the disintegration of the Soviet

❶ Abraham Lincoln 亚伯拉罕·林肯

❷ Joseph Stalin 斯大林

Union[3]; or how did the United States become the leader of the world? In order to answer these intriguing questions, we have to learn modern history.

❸ Soviet Union 苏联

2.2　艺术史

I have never truly grasped the purpose of learning art history. Not everyone is an artist, so why bother to learn the history of a subject with which they will never get involved? I have always hated those people who constantly brag about their "erudition[4]" of arts. For example, a friend of mine, Jason, can tell you the exact dates when Mozart[5] composed his symphonies[6], but he cannot distinguish the most distinguishable music with his ears. To me, these people are just forcing themselves to remember the things they are not even interested in, for the mere purpose of being "erudite[7]."

❹ erudition [ˌeru'diʃn] *n.* 学问
🔲 knowledge
❺ Mozart 莫扎特
❻ symphony ['simfəni] *n.* 交响曲
❼ erudite ['eruːdait] *adj.* 博学的

2.3　科学史

I am currently very interested in science history, because I just finished reading *A Brief History of Human Kind*, written by Yuval Noah Harari. It is the best book that I have read so far in 2017. It discusses a lot of absorbing topics concerning the history of science: from the emergence of fictive language to the Cognitive Revolution, which happened 70,000 years ago; to the extinction[8] of Neanderthals[9]; to the agricultural revolution; and finally to the scientific revolution. There are way too many interesting topics within the scientific revolution: the emergence of mathematics, religion, philosophy, history, physics, chemistry, etc. I especially like a saying in the book which goes: "The day when we admit that we are ignorant[10] is the day when we begin to flourish[11]".

❽ extinction [ik'stiŋkʃn] *n.* 灭绝
❾ Neanderthals 尼安德特人（欧洲原人）
❿ ignorant ['ignərənt] *adj.* 无知的
⓫ flourish ['flʌriʃ] *v.* 繁荣

2.4　欧洲史

I am most interested in European history, especially the history of England, because I am obsessed with[12] the popular TV drama *Game of Thrones*[13], whose author publicly acknowledged that he used the real history of England — The War of Roses — as the blueprint for its storyline. So I found several books about the war, and was astounded

⓬ be obsessed with 沉迷于
⓭ *The Game of Thrones* 《权力的游戏》

by the similarities of the names of the Great Houses. For example, the most powerful house in the TV series is called House of Lannister, while its counterpart in real history is called House of Lancaster; and the rival of House of Lannister in real history is called House of York, whereas in the series it is called House of Stark. Even the climax in Season 5 is inspired by the key point in the War of Roses, in which one of the protagonists, Jon Snow, was rescued right before he was about to be crushed by the enemy, by the reinforcements summoned by his sister.

I know basically nothing of European history. Here are the only European countries that I know the names of: England, Germany, France, Italy and Spain. The reason that I know their names is because of the world cup of soccer. I once went to a restaurant which has a game session in which customers are asked to guess which country has the flag that is shown on the TV screen. Out of the 10 flags shown, I knew only one: Japan.

2.5　摇滚音乐史

I am most interested in the history of rock music, since I am a die-hard[14] fan. I want to know how rock music evolved[15] from its original form in the 50s into the various genres of today. My electric guitar instructor sometimes tells me about the history of rock music. He says that it is heavily influenced by blues, rhythm and blues and country music. So I am currently learning all these different genres of music.

The only type of music that I listen to is pop music. To be honest, I can't really tell the difference between jazz, blues, and soul musics. And I only have a very vague[16] idea about what rock music is. I believe it is an outdated music that was once very popular in the 80s in America. And that's all I know about it.

> Rock music is a genre of popular music that originated as "rock and roll" in the United States in the 1950s, and developed into a range of different styles in the 1960s and later, particularly in the United Kingdom and the United States. It has its roots in 1940s' and 1950s' rock and roll, itself heavily influenced by blues, rhythm and blues and country music. Rock music also drew strongly on a number of other genres such as electric blues and folk, and incorporated influences from jazz, classical and other musical sources.

⑭ die-hard [ˈdaihɑːd] adj. 死忠

⑮ evolve [iˈvɔlv] v. 进化

⑯ vague [veig] adj. 模糊的

Musically, rock has centered on the electric guitar, usually as part of a rock group with electric bass guitar and drums. Typically, rock is song-based music usually with a 4/4 time signature using a verse-chorus form, but the genre has become extremely diverse. Like pop music, lyrics often stress romantic love but also address a wide variety of other themes that are frequently social or political in emphasis. Rock places a higher degree of emphasis on musicianship, live performance, and an ideology of authenticity than pop music.

https://en. wikipedia. org/wiki/Rock_music

Well, I still don't know what I am interested in, but at least I know for sure that I'll never take a class in the history of rock music. To begin with, most of my friends and families don't even know what rock music is, not to mention its predecessor or history. The genre[17] that we, younger generations, are interested in is pop music, such as *Jay Zhou*, *Mayday*, and *Phoenix Legend.* Elderly people tend to like elderly pop singers such as *Lijung Deng*, *Yuqing Fei*, etc. So, why would I bother to learn this boring subject when nobody even knows anything about it?

2. 6 音乐通史

I am extremely interested in Music History, since I want to know more about the story and background of the best musicians such as Mozart[18], Michael Jackson[22], Beethoven[19], Bach[20], and Madonna[21]. I have often heard music terms such as Medieval[23] Music, early Renaissance[24] Music, or Baroque[25] Music, but have no idea which of the musicians mentioned above belongs to which genre. Since I learned philosophy courses online, I have a basic understanding of the timeline of each period. But still, I would like to get a rigorous education about such matters. Then, I can better understand their masterpieces[26].

I know nothing about music, let alone music history. My schedule has been crazily packed since I was in elementary school. All of my free time has been filled with extracurricular activities such as piano lessons, dance classes, and badminton courses. And I am currently in my junior year in college, which is the time for me to look for an internship. Meanwhile I have to start planning my application for graduate school.

⑰ genre ['ʒɑːnrə] *n.* 类型

⑱ Mozart 莫扎特
⑲ Beethoven 贝多芬
⑳ Bach 巴赫
㉑ Madonna 麦当娜
㉒ Michael Jackson 迈克尔·杰克逊
㉓ Medieval [,medi'iːvəl] *adj.* 中世纪的
㉔ Renaissance [rə'neisəns] *n.* 文艺复兴
㉕ Baroque [bə'rəuk] *adj.* 巴洛克的
㉖ masterpiece ['mɑːstəpiːs] *n.* 大师作品

So I just have no time now for music history.

Actually, I once took a general music history class in high school, because I have always been enthusiastic about music. However, the class turned out to be a disaster. Instead of listening to beautiful pieces like I thought we would, we had tons of lectures going through the trivialities (unimportant stuff) such as dates of birth, dates of death, dates of first symphony composed, most famous five pieces composed in somebody's 20s, 30s, 40s, etc. Plus, we had tons of assigned readings each week. What's worse, we had to write a final paper about our favorite composer. Because of this terrible experience, I will never take any class about general music history again.

> Music history, sometimes called historical musicology, is the highly diverse subfield of the broader discipline of musicology that studies music from a historical viewpoint. In theory, "music history" could refer to the study of the history of any type or genre of music (e. g. , the history of Indian music or the history of rock). In practice, these research topics are often categorized as part of ethnomusicology or cultural studies, whether or not they are ethnographically based. The terms "music history" and "historical musicology" usually refer to the history of the notated music of Western elites, sometimes called "art music" (by analogy to art history, which tends to focus on elite art).
>
> The methods of music history include source studies (esp. manuscript studies), paleography, philology (especially textual criticism), style criticism, historiography (the choice of historical method), musical analysis, and iconography. The application of musical analysis to further these goals is often a part of music history, though pure analysis or the development of new tools of music analysis is more likely to be seen in the field of music theory. Some of the intellectual products of music historians include editions of musical works, biography of composers and other musicians, studies of the relationship between words and music, and the reflections upon the place of music in society.
>
> https://en. wikipedia. org/wiki/Music_history

03 What is the best way to learn about history?

真 题	题 型	年 份
All university students should be required to take history courses no matter what their field of study is.	独立写作题	2015/01/07
If you are a teacher of a tutor group and you are going to take students on a study trip, where would you take them to? A science museum, a local farm, or a theatre performance?	口语第二题	2015/10/25
Some people think that it is an important part of children's education to go on field trips（e. g. museums）. Others think a child's time is better spent in classrooms at school. Which do you prefer and why?	口语第二题	2016/03/27
If you are a teacher of a tutor group and you are going to take students on a study trip, where would you take them to? A science museum, a local farm, or a theatre performance?	口语第一题	2016/05/29
Some people think that it is an important part of children's education to go on field trips（e. g. museums）. Others think a child's time is better spent in classrooms at school. Which do you prefer and why?	口语第二题	2016/06/07

3.1 以兴趣为导向，自由阅读

The best way to learn about history is, of course to read based on one's own preference. History is a profoundly wide-ranging subject. The only way for one to learn history well is to use her interest as a guide. So, the first step is to read about general history, then pinpoint[1] the exact period which interests you the most. After that, just purchase the best book that elaborates[2] on that particular period on Amazon[3] or TaoBao[4].

3.2 互联网

The best way is surely through the Internet. With the popularization of online video sites like YouTube, there are just way too many great quality online videos now. I would recommend an excellent history channel on YouTube to every one: The Crash Course. I came across a video accidentally when I was doing some research for my history paper

❶ pinpoint［'pinpoint］*v.* 精确定位

❷ elaborate［i'læbərət］*v.* 详细解释，阐述

❸ Amazon 亚马逊

❹ TaoBao 淘宝

⑤ exceedingly [ik'si:diŋli]
adv. 非常

⑥ incorporated
[in'kɔ:pəreitid] *adj.* 合
并的

⑦ intriguing [in'tri:giŋ]
adj. 有趣的

⑧ Ecology [i'kɔlədʒi] *n.*
生态学

⑨ Anatomy [ə'nætəmi] *n.*
解剖学

⑩ Physiology [ˌfizi'ɔlədʒi]
n. 生理学

⑪ Astronomy [ə'strɔnəmi]
n. 天文学

in college, which is exceedingly[5] engaging because the video incorporated[6] cute cartoons to explain an abstract historical event. And it turns out that *The Crash Course* not only covers World History and the History of the United States, it also covers other intriguing[7] topics such as Chemistry, Biology, Ecology[8], Psychology, Big History, Literature, Anatomy[9] and Physiology[10], Astronomy[11], Intellectual Property, U. S. Government & Politics, Economics, Philosophy, Physics, and Games.

The Crash Course

We create free, high-quality educational videos used by teachers and learners of all kinds. That's all we want to do. After 200,000,000 views, it turns out people like this. And our videos aren't just for schools; the majority of our viewers, around 60% – 70%, watch Crash Course without being currently enrolled in an associated class.

Tons of awesome courses in one awesome channel! Nicole Sweeney teaches you sociology, Carrie Anne Philbin teaches you computer science, Craig Benzine teaches film history, and Mike Rugnetta is teaching mythology!

Check out the playlists for past courses in physics, philosophy, games, economics, U. S. government and politics, astronomy, anatomy & physiology, world history, biology, literature, ecology, chemistry, psychology, and U. S. history.

https://www.youtube.com/user/crashcourse/about

3.3　传统课堂

The best way is still the traditional learning form: lectures in class. There is a reason why people have to go to school. Even with the assistance of advanced technologies, people still have to be guided by experienced teachers. I'm not saying that no one can be self-taught. I admit that there are geniuses, but for most people, we have to have a great teacher to avoid detours[12] during the course of study.

⑫ detour ['di:tuə] *n.* 绕路

04 What is the worst way to learn about history?

真　题	题　型	年　份
All university students should be required to take history courses no matter what their field of study is.	独立 写作题	2015/01/07
If you are a teacher of a tutor group and you are going to take students on a study trip, where would you take them to? A science museum, a local farm, or a theatre performance?	口语 第二题	2015/10/25
Some people think that it is an important part of children's education to go on field trips (e. g. museums). Others think a child's time is better spent in classrooms at school. Which do you prefer and why?	口语 第二题	2016/03/27
If you are a teacher of a tutor group and you are going to take students on a study trip, where would you take them to? A science museum, a local farm, or a theatre performance?	口语 第一题	2016/05/29
Some people think that it is an important part of children's education to go on field trips (e. g. museums). Others think a child's time is better spent in classrooms at school. Which do you prefer and why?	口语 第二题	2016/06/07

4.1　纸质书

I hate to use paper-based textbooks to learn history. For example, when I started to learn US history, I was often confused about the names of different states. The problem was aggravated by the names that are no longer in use such as *New England.* As a result, I often had to pause and put my textbook down, pull out my iPhone, and start to google those strange geographical names that I was unfamiliar with. In contrast, when I switched to Kindle, I realized that everything could be done so easily. Whenever I encounter unfamiliar words, I can simply tap that word, and an built-in dictionary pops out automatically and shows me the information that I need. It can also provide a quick link to Wikipedia.

4.2　电子书

I hate using electronic textbooks. I guess I'm just a traditional guy. I miss the sensation of flipping through real paper-based books, the freedom to write whatever jumps to my mind on wherever I want on the page, the ease with which I can underline the key points that will be on our final exam, and also the smell of new books.

05　Should history classes be mandatory in college?

真　题	题　型	年　份
All university students should be required to take history courses no matter what their field of study is.	独立写作题	2015/01/07

5.1　Yes

History, of course, should be mandatory in college. For one thing, college students are mature[1] enough to interpret the outcome of historical events and learn from them. For another thing, students should at least have a basic understanding about world history, and the history of their own country. Without this knowledge, their friends and coworkers might regard them as uneducated.

5.2　No

History should never be mandatory. What's the point of forcing students to memorize facts that are of absolutely no importance to them? Students would surely forget those boring materials as soon as the final exam is over. My own experience shows that when students become more mature as they age, they naturally become interested in history and will subsequently look for books to read, without telling them to do so. In contrast, a compulsory[2] course in history might extinguish[3] students' potential interest in the subject.

❶ mature ［mə'tuə］ adj.
成熟

❷ compulsory ［kəm'pʌlsəri］
adj. 必修的
❸ extinguish ［ik'stiŋɡwiʃ］
v. 压制

06 Should governments invest in art museums?

真 题	题 型	年 份
It is more important for the government to spend money on art museums and concert halls than on recreational facilities such as swimming pools and playgrounds.	口语 第一题	2015/10/10
It is more important for the government to spend money on art museums and concert halls than on recreational facilities such as swimming pools and playgrounds.	口语 第二题	2015/11/28
Your city is going to build new places to attract more visitors. Among the following three options, which do you think is the best? A local history museum, a modern art and film museum, or a children's science museum?	口语 第二题	2016/10/10

6.1 Yes

Governments should definitely invest in art museums. Take China for example. The government has invested tons of money in the construction of art museums such as the Grand National Art Museum, which has stimulated immense[1] interest in the public. Without the governments' promotion of the arts, the public would take a much longer time to appreciate the beauty of music and arts. Promotion by the government would serve as an initiative[2] to attract the public to the domain[3] of arts. Otherwise, the public might spend all of their disposable[4] income on entertainment such as movies or fancy restaurants.

6.2 No

The government should never invest in art museums, for it might be detrimental[5] to the free development of the arts. Accordingly, there is no way that a government is simply providing free funds for artists only for the purpose of promoting the aesthetic[6] judgement of the public. More often than not, artists are controlled by the government once they accept financial subsidies. For example, in the famous US TV series *House of Cards*[7], President Underwood hired a writer to compose a novel to promote himself for the next election. The author had more than a few divergences[8] with Underwood, and was constantly pressured by the latter to change the plot of the book. Although in this ficticious story, the writer insisted on his own design, that is just a story. In reality, artists who do not obey the will of the government will surely be eliminated[9].

❶ immense [i'mens] *adj.*
巨大的

❷ initiative [i'niʃiətiv] *n.*
主动权

❸ domain [dəu'mein] *n.*
领域

❹ disposable [di'spəuzəbl]
adj. 可以任意处理的

❺ harmful ['hɑ:mfəl] *adj.*
有害的

❻ aesthetic [i:s'θetik] *adj.*
美学的

❼ *The House of Cards*《纸
牌屋》

❽ divergence [dai'və:dʒəns]
n. 分歧

❾ eliminate [i'limineit] *v.*
消除，排除

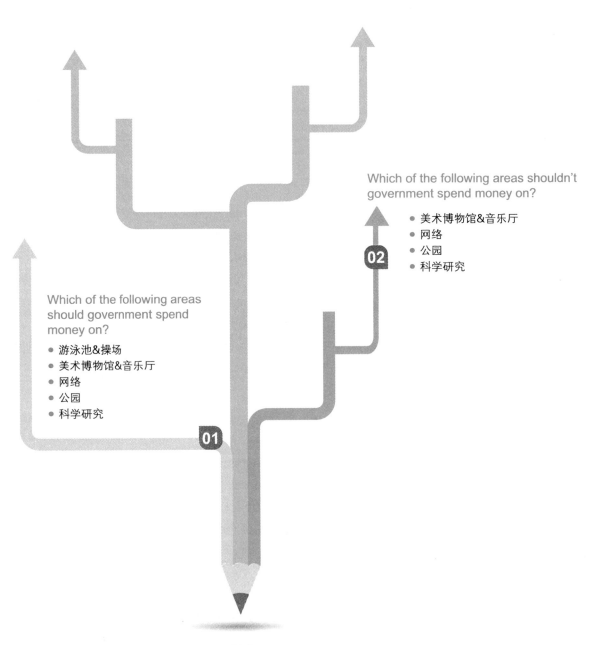

Which of the following areas shouldn't government spend money on?

- 美术博物馆&音乐厅
- 网络
- 公园
- 科学研究

02

Which of the following areas should government spend money on?

- 游泳池&操场
- 美术博物馆&音乐厅
- 网络
- 公园
- 科学研究

01

政府

01 Which of the following areas should government spend money on?

1.1 游泳池 & 操场

真　题	题　型	年　份
It is more important for the government to spend money on art museums and concert halls than on recreational facilities such as swimming pools and playgrounds.	口语 第一题	2015/10/10
It is more important for the government to spend money on art museums and concert halls than on recreational facilities such as swimming pools and playgrounds.	口语 第二题	2015/11/28

In modern society, governments are all focusing their money on road construction, the Internet and space exploration. As a result, almost no money is being spent on recreational facilities such as swimming pools and playgrounds. I admit that an investment in our infrastructure can boost our economy and enhance our work efficiency. But ordinary citizens also have to have a life besides their work. After all, we work to live better, and we surely have to have ways to relax and spend time with our family. Sadly, most governments today are not allocating sufficient funds on these areas, so people often have to drive for hours to find a nice swimming pool; and there are just no playgrounds in residential areas any more because governments are charging too much on real estate developers. As a result, nobody is willing to build a playground for children. Instead, most developers erect as many buildings as possible to maximum profits.

1.2 美术博物馆 & 音乐厅

真　题	题　型	年　份
In times of an economic crisis, in which area should governments reduce their spending? 1) arts, 2) scientific research, 3) parks and public gardens	独立 写作题	2015/09/14

提高艺术鉴赏力

It is extremely important for governments to allocate enough resources to support art museums and concert halls. Most people around the world don't need to worry about food and shelter[1] any more. So, it's governments' job to fulfill people's psychological needs after they have accomplished the mission of satisfying their physical needs. Arts are extremely important to everyone. Without arts, the world would be a less beautiful place. People should not just focus on work and become mercenary[2] businessmen. Instead, people should take their attention from work sometimes to relax and enjoy the beauty of life, and artists are the ones who keenly[3] capture the amazing details in life and present it to the masses. However, without the support of governments, brilliant artists are often unappreciated[4] and eventually likely to sink into oblivion[5]. For example, Vincent Van Gogh sold only one painting in his lifetime. But all of his paintings were deemed[6] invaluable[7] after his death. If the government had supported talented artists like him, maybe there would be a lot more masterpieces[8].

- **1** shelter [ˈʃeltə] *n.* 庇护所
- **2** mercenary [ˈmɜːsinəri] *adj.* 唯利是图的
  🔲 greedy
- **3** keenly [kiːnli] *adv.* 敏锐的
- **4** unappreciated [ˌʌnəˈpriːʃieitid] *adj.* 不被欣赏的
- **5** sink into oblivion 被遗忘
- **6** deem [diːm] *v.* 视作，认为
  🔲 consider
- **7** invaluable [inˈvæljuəbl] *adj.* 无价的，非常珍贵的
- **8** masterpiece [ˈmɑːstəpiːs] *n.* 大师之作

1.3 网络

真题	题型	年份
Government, rather than individuals, should cover Internet fees.	口语第一题	2015/11/28
Internet is as important as other service, such as building roads that government should make Internet access to all the citizens at no cost.	独立写作题	2016/04/23
Internet is as important as other services, such as building roads, that government should provide Internet access to all the citizens at no cost.	独立写作题	2016/05/22
Internet is as important as other services, such as building roads, that government should provide Internet access to all the citizens at no cost.	独立写作题	2016/07/03

1.3.1 省钱

Of course, the government should make Internet access available to everyone at no cost. Although people are getting wealthier nowadays, most are still far from becoming financially free. We, ordinary people, have to worry about basic fees including utilities, transportation, food, clothing, and entertainment. The Internet fee for residential broadband service, although not too much, still accounts for at least 5% of our monthly income, which is not a small number; not to mention the Internet fee incurred by mobile phones, which can easily surpass 1,000 yuan per month. Take my own sad experience for instance. During winter vacation, I went to study TOEFL at New Oriental, an English training school. We had to watch online videos on YouTube to practice our listening skills, but the Internet in our dormitory was just too slow. So I turned on my hotspot on my iPhone because it was way faster. Unfortunately, in China, we still don't have unlimited data plans. I had 500 Megabytes left, and I forgot to purchase the additional 1 Gigabyte data pack which cost 80 yuan at the time. In the end, my data usage for that month amounted to 8 Gigabytes, and because I had not purchased the additional data pack beforehand, I had to pay the service provider 200 yuan per Gigabyte of data. My bill skyrocketed to almost 2,000 yuan that month and I went on eating instant noodles for a whole month.

1.3.2　提高网络连接速度与质量

Not only should governments make free Internet access available to everyone, it should also improve the quality of Internet connections. In China, the use of Internet is growing fast, but in most residential areas, the quality of the Internet is barely satisfactory. And because ordinary citizens can do little about it, government should surely make some moves to help. Take myself for example. I recently moved into a high-end apartment adjacent to my company. The Internet connection in my neighborhood is a district broadband network, in which the residents of a building share a certain amount of bandwidth. This means that during evening hours, when everybody is watching online videos and video chatting through WeChat with their friends, the speed of the Internet becomes extremely slow. I even have trouble opening a basic website like BaiDu. What's more frustrating, I found out that I cannot access my company's email server, which means that I cannot communicate with my coworkers at home. As a result, I have to arrive at my company early in the morning and leave work only after I am done replying to all the emails at work. This is just so inconvenient. Had the government invested more in the construction of high quality Internet, none of these unfortunate things would have happened.

1.3.3　推广到贫困地区

Government should pay for the Internet because Internet access is just like a highway or a health care program. The private market cannot sufficiently provide these options, because as private entities, they will always be seeking the highest reward and making their own profits. They're going to leave out less wealthy areas and places that are more remote. So, this is where the government should step in, to make sure that everyone has this access, just the same way everyone can get health care.

1.3.4　帮助适应网络普及化

It's no secret that more services are being provided online. Perhaps more importantly, more services are being provided only online. In a world faced with a constant battle to cut costs, online solutions not only make things easier and more accessible, but also save a lot of money. For example, companies today no longer have to spend a lot of money inserting an advertisement in newspapers or placing it on billboards along the road. All they have to do is post their job openings online. Thus, public funds would be better spent on Internet infrastructure and digital literacy.

1.4　公园

真　题	题　型	年　份
In times of an economic crisis, in which area should governments reduce their spending? 1) arts, 2) scientific research, 3) parks and public gardens	口语第一题	2015/09/14
People can solve important problems by themselves or with the help from their family members, so there's no need for the government to help them.	独立写作题	2016/05/07
People can solve important problems by themselves or with the help from their family members, so there's no need for the government to help them.	独立写作题	2016/05/29

1.4.1　给人们提供休息的地方

Governments should focus more on parks and gardens, which is another area where governments do not pay much attention, and I guess the reason is simple: it is not profitable to invest in gardens and parks. However, it is the governments' job to preserve and maintain beautiful parks, and to provide people with a tranquil and pleasant place to take a walk. For example, in Beijing, there are plenty of famous parks which have great scenery and buildings from the past. I personally like TianTan Park the best, also known as the Temple of Heaven. In my childhood, my grandmother would often bring me to the park to play. I have great memories of places such as the Echo Wall, and the Hall of Prayer for Good Harvests, which is a magnificent triple-gabled circular building, where the Emperor prayed for good harvests. It would be such a shame to see the park sink into oblivion due to the lack of maintenance and government promotion for parks like this.

1.4.2　绿化环境

The government should definitely list cleaning the environment as its priority, at least this is the case in Beijing. Air quality is a big problem for decades. Chemical haze is becoming a huge problem for both the government and citizens. For example, I recently moved to a new apartment, which was just refurbished. Because I am extremely sensitive to smells of new furniture and paints, I have to open the window constantly. Otherwise, I cannot bear the smell. However, when the air quality index is above 300, I would suffer regardless of whether the window is open. If I keep the windows open, the chemical haze will flow into my room and I will begin to cough violently. If I shut the windows to keep out the smog, I will be choked to death by harmful chemicals emitted from the new furniture and paints. I guess it is a blessing that it has been raining for the past few days so that the air quality is still bearable. But, the government should really spend money to address the smog problem.

1.5　科学研究

真　题	题　型	年　份
In times of an economic crisis, in which area should governments reduce their spending? 1）arts, 2）scientific research, 3）parks and public gardens	独立写作题	2015/09/14

1.5.1　攻克绝症

The government should allocate enough funds to medical research so that incurable diseases can be cured. Researchers predict that Alzheimer's Disease is likely to become curable in ten years. My great-grandfather had Alzheimer's Disease in his final years. He couldn't recognize his wife, sons, daughters and grandchildren. He sometimes would drink a bottle of perfume, thinking that it was mineral water. The whole family suffered a lot because of the disease. If the disease becomes curable, a lot of families could enjoy more time with their beloved elder relatives, create more memories and hear more of their stories from the past. However, without the support of the government, despite the current existence of Non-Governmental Organizations, money for modern research centers is still a big problem. So the government should definitely allocate enough funds to research.

1.5.2　使科技突破创新

Major scientific breakthroughs always revolutionize the way people live, so governments must invest in and pay sufficient attention to scientific research. For example, the current concern of Beijingers is chemical fumes, and the reason the problem is so serious is that factories would incur astronomical[9] costs if they were required by the government to install purification equipment, which would surely make these factories unprofitable. If, however, scientists are able to discover a new chemical material that can absorb all the harmful particles created during the manufacturing process, and if this new chemical material is extremely affordable, and can be produced in big batches, this would surely solve the environmental problem. People would be able to go out on the streets without wearing masks, and we could all throw our air

⑨ astronomical
[ˌæstrəˈnɒmɪkl] *adj.* 巨大的（天文数字的）

purifiers away and enjoy the freedom to open our windows at any time we want.

02 Which of the following areas shouldn't government spend money on?

2.1 美术博物馆＆音乐厅

2.1.1 投资艺术无法让所有人都收益

Considering the economy, I think the Government should abandon the arts because few people can benefit from them. Last year, I went to the Getty museum, which is one of the most famous museums in Los Angeles. It is adorned[10] by a beautiful lawn, which has sculptures, hedges, flowerbeds etc. Inside the museum, there are many great paintings and gorgeous[11] pictures. However, I just couldn't understand those art works at all. They are just too abstract for me. And I think most people are just like me. Art is not helpful or necessity for the general public, who are ultimately those who have to pay taxes. So, I would like to see funding in areas that can benefit everyone, such as science and education.

⑩ adorn [əˈdɔːn] v. 装饰
🔟 decorate

⑪ gorgeous [ˈɡɔːdʒəs] adj. 美丽的
🔟 elegant

2.1.2 政府不宜资助艺术，会影响艺术的独立性

It's not a good thing for arts organizations to become dependent on the governments' money. Just imagine museums and theaters that are sponsored by the government. They're likely to be more responsive to the likes and dislikes of bureaucrats. I once sat through a show called Red Star — an awful mix of contemporary circus[11] and dance that could only exist through state funding. Looking back, I can't think of one government funding show that was any good, while every day the world of commercial entertainment throws up work that is new, vibrant, creative and exciting without any need for government help. So, governments should reduce the spending on arts to protect the true artistic endeavor[12].

⑪ circus [ˈsəːkəs] n. 马戏团

⑫ endeavor [inˈdevə] n. 努力
🔟 effort

2.2　网络

解决饥荒和健康更重要

In a world where some people still can't afford basic necessities like food and medicine, demanding that the Internet should be free is a bit ridiculous. It is a gorgeous service, but for many people there are far more pressing needs. For example, millions of people across the world still have no access to fresh air and safe drinking water because of environmental issues. Tens of thousands of people are homeless. So many children are not able to get educations due to lack of money. A lot of them haven't even heard about the Internet, not to mention how to use it. So, it is not hard to see that what they need are the basic necessities of life, rather than free Internet.

2.3　公园

2.3.1　为烧烤提供场地

One of my favorite ways to relax during the weekend is to invite my friends to the parks in my community and have a nice barbeque together. I enjoy every part of this activity: from the start when we drive to a supermarket to pick out foods, including various kinds of kebabs, vegetables, fruits, and beverages. I have a thing for tasty beverages such as Tsingtao beers, Jianlibao soda water, and Wong Lo Kat; to the part when we gather in the park and prepare to light up the grill; to the part where we start enjoying the food under the sunlight on the grass in the park; and finally to the part when we play games such as soccer and Frisbee. So, I wish the government could spend more money building more high-quality parks for people to have barbecues and picnics in.

2.3.2　政府建的公园太烂

I have been to a lot of parks funded by the government. Unfortunately, all of them are disappointing. The parks themselves are roughed up and dirty, and you don't expect the shops to be open for business. The entertainment facilities are old and outdated. Also, there is staff to take your money when you come into the park, but you're going to have a hard time finding employees elsewhere. So, governments shouldn't be counted on to build parks and public gardens. This is especially true when it comes to the economic crisis and people in panic. In this critical moment, the government's role is not to provide slides, but rather to create job opportunities and boost the economy.

2.4 科学研究

2.4.1 不确定性大，收益慢

There is too much uncertainty in investing in scientific research, especially during times of economic crisis. Think about it. Scientific research does not guarantee a cure or a fix to a problem and can take years to progress. Inventing a vaccine[12] to that virus could take decades. Given the current state of things, governments may feel obliged to spend money on things that can achieve immediate and more reliable results, such as education, existing healthcare techniques and maintenance of infrastructure. Science sadly is not immediate enough.

⑫ vaccine ['væksi:n]
n. 疫苗

2.4.2 私有公司应负责投资科学研究

Government doesn't need to spend a lot of money on scientific research, because private companies have funded science very generously. According to a research, 16 major American oil and chemical companies have invested in pure science. And the more a firm invests in basic science, the more its productivity grows. So the funding of science is not supposed to be a political decision; it is economically determined.

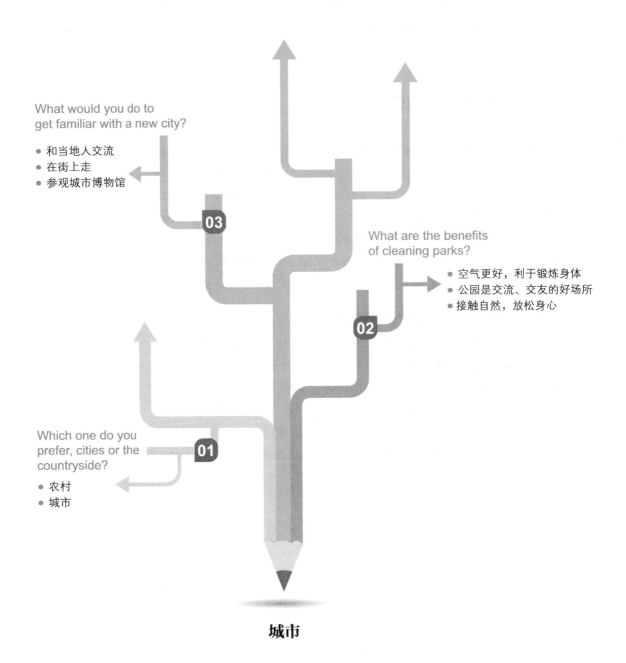

What would you do to get familiar with a new city?

- 和当地人交流
- 在街上走
- 参观城市博物馆

What are the benefits of cleaning parks?

- 空气更好，利于锻炼身体
- 公园是交流、交友的好场所
- 接触自然，放松身心

Which one do you prefer, cities or the countryside?

- 农村
- 城市

城市

01 Which one do you prefer, cities or the countryside?

真 题	题 型	年 份
Do you agree or disagree with the statement that people from small towns are kinder and more helpful than people in big cities?	口语 第二题	2015/03/28
Describe two cities you visited before and tell the differences.	独立 写作题	2014/12/06
Some people prefer to take a vacation in cities；others prefer to spend their vacations in the countryside. Which do you prefer? Explain why.	口语 第二题	2014/11/23

1.1 农村

1.1.1 人更友善

People in the country are both more friendly and warmer, because they have a rather small social circle[1] and thus know each other very well. They grow together, go to school together, maybe even work on the same farm after they graduate. In the countryside, when people bump into[2] each other, they stop, smile, wave, say hello and ask how things are going. In contrast, people in big cities don't even make eye contact with their neighbors when they are passing by. They are just too busy with their own stuff like how to pay back their housing loans[3], how to get promoted at work or how to avoid getting set up on a blind date[4] by their parents. They don't really have time to be nice to a total stranger. That's why there are so many cold-looking people in cities.

People in the cities have less friendly traits[5]. People are always bustling[6] like bees. Although people in the city live closer to each other, most of the dwellers don't even know their neighbor's names. I lived in an apartment in Boston for 2 years, and I never met my neighbor in person. I only heard his voice or the music from his apartment. But there was this time he came home early in the morning and I was about to take off to work. I saw "him" for the very first time. We said hello, and it turned out my neighbor was actually a woman who has deep voice. People in the city are busy minding their own business. Sometimes I feel isolated[7] and cold.

❶ social circle 社交圈

❷ bump into 碰到

❸ housing loans 住房贷款
❹ blind date 相亲

❺ trait [treit] n. 特点
❻ bustling ['bʌsliŋ] adj. 忙乱的
🔁 busy

❼ isolated ['aisəleitid] adj. 孤立的

1.1.2　环境好

The environment is much better in rural areas than it is in the city. People in the country are living healthier lives. There isn't so much traffic in rural areas. As a result, country folks don't suffer from polluted air. Another benefit would be less noise from cars honking, construction sites, and police sirens[8] zooming by your house at night. It is very annoying when you have to get up early the next morning and are trying to sleep. Country folks produce their own food. They grow plants, fruit and vegetables, and raise animals. So the food is organic and safe. People can also enjoy nature more. They can run with their dogs in the field without worrying about getting lung cancer, swim in a lake instead of a swimming pool full of chemicals, build tree houses as large as they want, and hang out with their friends inside without the need to turn on air purifiers[9].

1.1.3　花销少

Things are much cheaper in the country. You can have a fancy meal for less than 20 bucks. A movie can cost only about five bucks. And no one cares if you're wearing a fashionable brand of clothing, whereas city dwellers[10] surely judge you if you do not wear a Louis Vuitton bag to a fancy party, and you will never receive an invitation again. You can also buy a big house with multiple bedrooms, bathrooms and garages at a fairly cheap price. If you choose the countryside, you could even build your own swimming pool. However, it may cost you over a million dollars for a house with the same setting in a city.

1.2　城市

选择多

Living in the city means I have more choices. People in the city are surrounded by amazing culture. Museums, galleries, and libraries are easily accessible and most of them are free. If I want to go shopping, I have lots of options. I can buy cheap food at a local grocery store[11] within walking distance or I can go to fancy shopping malls to get clothes or electronics. As for the education, there are more top-ranking

⑧ siren ['saiərin] *n.* 警笛

⑨ air purifier 空气净化器

⑩ dweller ['dwelə(r)] *n.* 居住者
回 resident

⑪ grocery store 杂货店

schools, which hire famous professors, possess fancy dorms and facilities, and invest tons of money each year in labs, etc. Also, there are more job opportunities. As there are many more companies in cities than in countries, I can more easily choose a career that matches my interests.

02 What are the benefits of cleaning parks?

真 题	题 型	年 份
Your city is planning to spend more on one of the following three projects. Which do you think is the most important: expanding tourism, building city parks, or improving the public transportation system?	口语 第一题	2012/03/18
Which of the following volunteer activities do you think is the most beneficial to the environment, cleaning the city, planting trees or recycling?	口语 第一题	2012/07/22
Which of the following community services would you choose to do: working with children, cleaning the city park, or planting a campus garden?	口语 第一题	2012/10/14
Which of the following community services would you be more interested in doing and explain why: cleaning the city park, planting flowers and trees, or building a bicycle lane?	口语 第一题	2012/10/19
Which of the following activities would you be more interested in doing? Teaching children, teaching adults to use computers or cleaning the city park?	口语 第一题	2013/01/12
If you had to volunteer for a project, which one would you choose? Cleaning up the city, creating bicycle trails, or planting trees?	口语 第一题	2015/10/25
Which of the following community services would you be more interested in doing and explain why: cleaning the city park, planting flowers and trees, or building a bicycle lane?	口语 第一题	2016/06/04
If you were making a donation, which of the organizations would you make your donation to: environmental protection group, city library, or animal shelter?	口语 第一题	2016/08/21

2.1　空气更好，利于锻炼身体

Parks clean the air in the city and provide citizens with a place to exercise in. A tree can absorb three tons of carbon dioxide[1] during its lifetime. So even on bad days, the air in the park would still be fresh in the morning. If parks are being taken good care of, they are great places to jog, take a walk or simply sit on the grass and enjoy the sunshine. However, if the park is not clean, people will choose to go to the gym, which is expensive, and whose air is just unbearable.

❶ carbon dioxide 二氧化碳

2.2　公园是交流、交友的好场所

Parks are great places for local residents to meet new people. We can have picnics with friends and family on a sunny day, sitting on the grass, enjoying the companionship[2] of others. We might also meet neighbors who we have never talked to before. Chances are high that we could become good friends after sharing a homemade sandwich together. Kids, too, can make some friends after playing a friendly soccer game. Parents might be standing beside the football court, cheering for their kids, while chatting pleasantly with other parents.

❷ companion [kəm'pæniən]
   n. 同伴，朋友

2.3　接触自然，放松身心

Parks offer people a place to truly immerse themselves in nature. They offer people a place to escape the noise and crowds of urban life. Also, parks are great places for concerts. Many pop stars now choose outdoor venues[3] as their stages. People can enjoy great music and fresh air at the same time. I know a lot of my friends who prefer sitting on the grass to plastic seats in a stadium.

❸ venue ['venju:] n. 场地，场馆
   ▣ outlet

03 What would you do to get familiar with a new city?

真　题	题　型	年　份
Your city is going to build new places to attract more visitors. Among the following three options, which do you think is the best? A local history museum, a modern art and film museum, or a children's science museum?	口语 第一题	2012/03/24
Which of the following is the best way to learn about a city? Joining an organized trip, visiting the museums, or taking walks in the streets of the city?	口语 第一题	2012/09/22
When you're visiting a city you've never been to, how would you like to tour around? A. sign up for a well-organized trip; B. visit history museums; C. walk along the streets	口语 第一题	2013/03/17
If your friend is moving to another city, what would be your suggestion for him? Give details and examples for your explanation.	口语 第一题	2015/01/10
One of your friends just moved to a new city. What suggestions do you have to help him fit in?	口语 第一题	2015/12/05
Do you agree or disagree with the following statement? It is important to learn the history of the city you live in.	口语 第二题	2016/07/10

3.1 和当地人交流

I will talk to locals to get to know the city well and help me settle down quickly. A city is more than buildings and pavement. Local people have lots of cultural experiences. So I can get more information about the city from talking with them. When I came to work in Denver 2 years ago, the first thing I did was to ask my colleagues, who are locals, where to eat. From their recommendations, I got to know a very popular Asian restaurant which has the best Chinese food I have ever tasted in the US. It is much better than searching it online or reading some travel magazines, because some articles and information may be wrong or outdated[1].

❶ outdated [aut'deitid] *adj.* 过时的

3.2 在街上走

I will walk along the street to learn more about the city and see how the city is organized. By learning its transit and traffic nodes[2], I can

❷ node [nəud] *n.* 节点

③ commute［kə'mjuːt］ *n.*
通勤

④ time off 空闲时间

⑤ evolve［i'vɒlv］*v.* 进化

⑥ household［'haushəuld］
n. 一家人

⑦ ceremonial［ˌseri'məuniəl］
adj. 仪式的

⑧ artifact［'ɑːtifækt］*n.* 人
工制品

⑨ engraving［in'greiviŋ］*n.*
雕刻品

⑩ erudite［'eruːdait］*n.* 博
学的
▣ knowledgeable

figure out the shortest way to commute³. So I don't need to worry about being late for work when I get up in the morning. I can check out the malls and movie theatres. So I will know where I can chill when I have some time off⁴. Furthermore, walking in the street offers me a good chance to discover some local markets in the city. These markets are always filled with food like BBQ, tasty snack bars, and ice cream vans. Once I spot these places, I can't move my legs until I taste them all.

3.3　参观城市博物馆

Museums show you the history of the city and how it evolved⁵. If I want to explore a city, a museum is always the first place to go. When I first visited Beijing, I went to the Palace Museum. I was amazed by the architecture, art collections and photos. It showed me how the city served as the home of the Emperor and his household⁶ for almost five centuries, and how it eventually became the ceremonial⁷ and political center of the Chinese government. The museum has thousands of rooms with millions of artifacts⁸ inside. It tells me everything I want to know about the city.

We must know a city's history if we want to truly understand its culture. This is especially true for big cities such as Beijing, London, Boston, and the list goes on. For example, I went on a trip to Boston several months ago. I could experience the weight of its history from the ancient buildings along its busiest streets, many of which had elegant engravings⁹ of angels and goddesses on them. But I did not know what they stood for and why they were there. So I went to the museum of fine arts. There, with the help of a patient and erudite¹⁰ guide, I slowly began to understand the pride and intelligence carried by its residents.

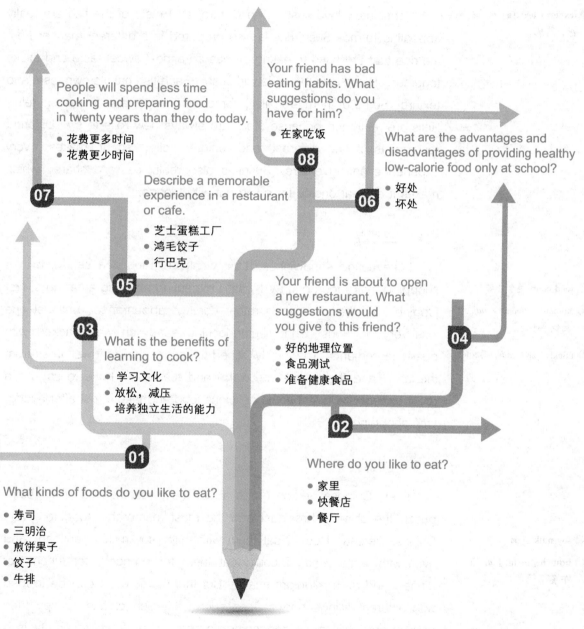

People will spend less time cooking and preparing food in twenty years than they do today.
- 花费更多时间
- 花费更少时间

07

Your friend has bad eating habits. What suggestions do you have for him?
- 在家吃饭

08

What are the advantages and disadvantages of providing healthy low-calorie food only at school?
- 好处
- 坏处

06

Describe a memorable experience in a restaurant or cafe.
- 芝士蛋糕工厂
- 鸿毛饺子
- 行巴克

05

03

What is the benefits of learning to cook?
- 学习文化
- 放松，减压
- 培养独立生活的能力

Your friend is about to open a new restaurant. What suggestions would you give to this friend?
- 好的地理位置
- 食品测试
- 准备健康食品

04

02

01

What kinds of foods do you like to eat?
- 寿司
- 三明治
- 煎饼果子
- 饺子
- 牛排

Where do you like to eat?
- 家里
- 快餐店
- 餐厅

饮食

01 What kinds of foods do you like to eat?

1.1 寿司

❶ texture [ˈtekstʃə] n. 质感，质地

I absolutely love sushi. The texture[1] and taste of the fish are really appealing to me. Sushi rice is also prepared in a different manner from the rice that I'm used to eating. It has an almost sweet taste and sticks together. I also love the variety in sushi. Each fish has its own taste and texture. Some of them are oilier, some are firmer. I also love sushi rolls! Rolls are really fun because there are always new rolls to try. Different restaurants serve different and unique rolls, so it makes every experience an adventure. Sushi is also really easy to share, which makes it a great choice for going out with friends.

1.2 三明治

❷ food court 美食广场

❸ homely [ˈhəumli] adj. 相貌平平的

❹ thickly [ˈθikli] adv. 厚地

I like eating sandwiches. Last week, I grabbed a sandwich in a shopping mall's food court[2]. I wasn't expecting anything amazing at first judging from the sandwich's rather homely[3] appearance, but that one was very delicious. That simple-looking sandwich was packed with quality ingredients. The thickly[4] sliced turkey tasted like it was fresh from the farm, and the bread was warm and toasted. I have to say it's a great experience to eat some delicious food and take a rest after a long-time shopping.

1.3 煎饼果子

❺ soy milk 豆奶

❻ brunch [brʌntʃ] n. 早午餐

Every Chinese person brags about the awesomeness of Jianbing-guozi, the ultimate breakfast and the most memorable food for every Chinese person. I could eat them with milk, soy milk[5], jianlibao, and even with white wine. I could eat them for brunch[6], for lunch, for dinner, and for a midnight snack. But there's more. It can be topped with different fillings and sauces such as green onions, crispy fried cracker and chili sauce depending on personal preference. The taste is divine!

1.4 饺子

Well, every Chinese person loves dumplings, despite the vast territories of China. And dumplings provide gourmets[7] with possibly endless choices and combinations of tastes and flavors. For example, my favorite flavor of dumpling is with pork and cabbage filling. I just love the amazing taste of high-quality pork mixed with the crispy[8] and crunchy[9] texture of cabbage. In recent years, people have started to develop new flavors such as fish and scrambled eggs[10], tomatoes and eggs, or beef and carrots, etc.

❼ gourmet ['ɡuəmei] n. 美食家

❽ crispy ['krispi] adj. 酥脆的
❾ crunchy ['krʌntʃi] adj. 脆的
❿ scrambled eggs 炒鸡蛋

1.5 牛排

Nothing could compete with the satisfaction that a perfect steak can provide. To be honest, I hated beef when I first tried it. The meat was too thick, too raw, and too tasteless. Even when I "drowned" the steak into a "lake" of steak sauce, the food was still inedible. Then, one of my friends took me to a steak house, one of the best in town, and my attitude toward steak changed overnight. The meat was soft, chewable, and cooked just to the appropriate point. Moreover, it tasted a thousand times better than pork. I couldn't put my fork and knife down until I finished all of the steak, and it tasted so good that I had to keep myself from licking[11] the leftovers[12] on my plate.

⓫ lick [lik] v. 舔
⓬ leftover ['left'əuvə] n. 剩余食物

02 Where do you like to eat?

真 题	题 型	年 份
Do you prefer to cook home or eat outside?	口语 第二题	2012/04/20
Some people prefer to prepare meals at home; others like to eat out in restaurants. Which do you prefer? Explain with details and examples.	口语 第二题	2014/10/26
Some people prefer to eat at fast food restaurants; others prefer to eat at regular restaurants. Which do you prefer? Explain your answer in detail.	口语 第二题	2014/11/15

2.1　家里

2.1.1 省钱

One of the most important benefits of dining at home is that I can save a lot of money. Meat, vegetables and other ingredients from supermarkets or grocery stores[1] are very affordable. However, if I dine at a fancy restaurant, I may end up spending at least $100.00 for a candle-lit dinner. That is just too expensive for me! With this amount of money, I can actually prepare up to three or four ordinary meals at home, buy that great pair of skinny jeans, or just have a little more spending money[2].

2.1.2 健康

Eating at home is one of the best ways to promote a healthy lifestyle. If I eat at home, I often make myself an omelet[3] or a bowl of salad, because I care a lot about my own health and I only use low-fat and low-calorie ingredients[4]. However, when I am dining out, I will be exposed to greater temptation to eat tasty, but unhealthy food, such as fried chicken, cheesecake, and hamburgers. Those foods contain too much fat, and they can be detrimental[5] to our health if they are consumed on a regular basis. Besides, if I eat out with my friends, I can totally forget that I am on a diet.[6] So for me, the best way to overcome temptation and stay faithful to my diet plan is to stay away from such situations and eat salad at home.

2.1.3 促进家庭关系

Eating at home offers an excellent opportunity for family bonding. Children and parents are all very busy nowadays. Soccer practices, dance rehearsals, meetings, and other scheduling conflicts make family time so precious. Sometimes, parents are feeding their kids breakfast bars during the morning commute[7] and grabbing dinner at the drive-thru window[8]. They seldom have a chance to talk to each other, but eating at home enables family members to share their days with each other, relax, laugh, discuss social issues and strengthen family relationships.

---

❶ grocery store 杂货店

❷ spending money 零花钱

❸ omelet［'ɔmlit］ n. 煎蛋卷

❹ ingredient［in'griːdiənt］ n. 配料

❺ detrimental［,detri'mentl］ adj. 有害的

❻ on diet 节食

❼ commute［kə'mjuːt］ n. 通勤

❽ drive-thru window 免下车窗口

2.2 快餐店

I like to eat in fast food restaurants, because it saves me a lot of time. You know I am a college student. I have to take a lot of classes and tests. Right now, I have 5 papers due next week. And I spend most of my time in the library, working on my papers. So, you see, I just don't have time to cook for myself. If I do, I need to go to the supermarket to get fresh food, and then spend at least two hours in the kitchen preparing food. After eating, I need to wash the dirty dishes[9]. It is so time-consuming[10]! However, if I eat in a fast food restaurant, I can save myself the trouble of preparing the food and I have more time to get my papers done.

⑨ wash dishes 洗盘子
⑩ time-consuming 浪费时间的

2.3 餐厅

I like to eat in restaurants because of the cozy[11] atmosphere and hospitable[12] waiters. Just imagine, after a long week, on a Friday night, all I want to do is have a nice and relaxing dinner[13]. You get to your favorite restaurant and get seated at a lovely table. They are playing jazz music, which is soothing[14] and calming. In addition, there is candlelight, which makes the restaurant elegant and romantic. You would definitely feel very relaxed and refreshed.

⑪ cozy ['kəuzi] adj. 舒适的，惬意的
⑫ hospitable ['hɔspitəbl] adj. 热情好客的
⑬ all I want to do is do sth.
⑭ soothing ['suːðiŋ] adj. 抚慰的

03 What is the benefit of learning to cook?

真　题	题　型	年　份
Which of the following ways is the best to get to know Italian culture? 1) watching Italian movies；2) learning Italian cooking；3) attending Italian lectures or history classes	口语 第一题	2012/07/22
People will spend less time cooking and preparing food in twenty years than they do today.	独立 写作题	2015/03/25
For getting a better understanding of nutrition and health, your school decides to open cooking classes；do you think this is a reasonable decision?	口语 第二题	2016/09/10

3.1 学习文化

Cooking is a wonderful way to learn about a certain country's culture because we all love eating. I used to have an Italian roommate. We talked a lot, and I realized we had so many things in common, such as cooking. You know we are all foodies[1]. Moreover, she began to teach me how to make pasta[2], which is a traditional Italian cuisine[3]. Through our collaboration, I got to know a lot of Italian customs[4] and learned a lot of new words, such as spaghetti[5] and pasta. I felt that my knowledge about Italy had increased a lot in just a few hours. I just can't wait to go to Italy to try the authentic[6] food there and learn more about Italian culture.

3.2 放松，减压

Cooking helps to ease stress and release tension. Take myself as an example. When I am melting butter, chopping onions, peeling[7] garlic or stirring a pot of sauce, I can forget all those troubles in the real world. Cooking has become almost a therapy for me.

It is even more gratifying when other people praise my dishes. Last week, I invited my friends to my place to have dinner together. I just love having people around and making them feel welcomed. I served them spaghetti. According to my friends, I successfully took homemade pasta to the next level. I felt very happy. So, for me, cooking is an easy way to unwind[8] in the midst of a busy life.

3.3 培养独立生活的能力

Mastering cooking is super important, if you want to become truly independent. Once I wanted to make myself an omelet. It was my first time cooking, but I had seen my mom do it, so how hard could it be? I chopped[9] the onions on the work surface[10]. Then came the tomatoes. Unfortunately, disaster struck and I cut my finger. There was no bleeding but it was just painful. Then, I spent a long time deciding how much salt I should put on my omelet[11], all the while the omelet was sizzling[12] in the pan. Finally, I got a burnt omelet! And I felt ashamed of myself since I was already 20 years old at that time. However, after learning how to cook, I enjoy it very much because it gives me a sense of independence, freedom and self-sufficiency. I can make whatever I want to eat.

① foodie [ˈfuːdi] *n.* 美食家，吃货

② pasta [ˈpɑːstə] *n.* 意大利面食

③ cuisine [kwɪˈziːn] *n.* 菜肴

④ custom [ˈkʌstəm] *n.* 风俗习惯

⑤ spaghetti [spəˈɡeti] *n.* 意大利面

⑥ authentic [ɔːˈθentik] *adj.* 真的，地道的

⑦ peel [piːl] *v.* 剥

⑧ unwind [ˌʌnˈwaind] *v.* 放松

⑨ chop [tʃɒp] *v.* 切

⑩ work surface 工作台

⑪ omelet [ˈɔmlit] *n.* 煎蛋卷

⑫ sizzle [ˈsizl] *v.* 发出咝咝声

04 Your friend is about to open a new restaurant. What suggestions would you give to this friend?

真 题	题 型	年 份
If one of your friends wants to run a restaurant, what is your opinion or advice on food and location?	口语 第一题	2016/10/11

4.1 好的地理位置

When it comes to the success of a restaurant, location is everything. It is even more important than the food it serves. Just imagine you have the best Beijing Duck in your city, but if a customer has to walk eight blocks[1] from the nearest parking garage[2] or subway station to get to your place, they might choose to visit your competitors who are more accessible[3]. So it's important to find a spot[4] that is easily accessible and has enough parking.

4.2 食品测试

It's best to test the food before opening the restaurant. I would suggest a small party which invites close friends to come over to try the food. Thus, the owner can get honest feedback on the taste and the pricing. It is possible that the owner of the restaurant might love the taste of a certain dish, but customers don't. It would be difficult to make money under these circumstances.

4.3 准备健康食品

I hope my friend will serve some healthy foods for customers. Nowadays, people eat a lot of junk food, such as hamburgers, fried chicken, and French fries. They contain too many calories. Because of that, people not only gain a lot of weight, but also get all kinds of "fat diseases". Thus, it would be best if my friend can serve foods that are both delicious and healthy.

❶ block [blɔk] n. 街区
❷ garage ['gærɑːʒ] n. 车库
❸ accessible [əkˈsesəbl] adj. (地方) 易于进入的
❹ spot [spɔt] n. 地点，场所

05 Describe a memorable experience in a restaurant or cafe.

真 题	题 型	年 份
Describe a memorable experience in a restaurant or cafe.	口语 第一题	2015/09/17

5.1 芝士蛋糕工厂 The Cheesecake Factory

A memorable experience I've had at a restaurant was at The Cheesecake Factory. My friends threw me a birthday party[1] there. The atmosphere of the restaurant was very relaxing. It was playing jazz music, which was soothing and calming. And there was candlelight, which made the restaurant feel elegant and romantic. All my friends felt very relaxed too. Also, the service there was impeccable[2]. Waiters took food orders very fast. And they came to our table and sang Happy Birthday for us because they overheard[3] our conversation. The most fantastic thing was that the cheesecake there was divine[4]! It was so rich and creamy. I would love to return to this restaurant and would advise my friends to try it.

5.2 鸿毛饺子 Hongmaojiaozi

There is a dumpling restaurant, Hongmaojiaozi, right across the street from my school. My classmates and I often eat lunch there. It's not a fancy restaurant, but it's fast, clean, and the food is good. We always have a great time there, chatting light-heartedly, and enjoying the great food and the warm jiaozitang, the dumpling soup. The environment somehow just relaxes me and my friends, and we have so many good memories there.

5.3 星巴克 Starbucks

There is a Starbucks right across from our library that we love to go to. Every afternoon, when my friends get bored, thirsty or tired, they suggest that we take a walk to Starbucks to buy something refreshing. In the hot summer, we would buy iced lattes or Frappuccinos[5]. My

① throw a party 举办派对

② impeccable [imˈpekəbl] *adj.* 无瑕疵的，没有缺点的

③ overhear [ˌəuvəˈhiə] *v.* 无意中听到

④ divine [diˈvain] *adj.* 极妙的，极好的

⑤ Frappuccino [ˌfræpəˈtʃinəu] *n.* 星冰乐

personal favorite is the Iced Shaken Peach Green Tea, which tastes amazing. In winters, we buy espresso, hot chocolate or hot tea. We have a lot of interesting and memorable talks in the course of the walk.

06 What are the advantages and disadvantages of providing healthy low-calorie food only at school?

真 题	题 型	年 份
Your school is planning to provide healthy low-calorie food only. What are the advantages and disadvantages?	口语 第一题	2012/02/05
The university dining hall is changing its food service to include more healthy food with lower calories. What do you think are the advantages and disadvantages of this change?	口语 第一题	2013/10/12

6.1 好处

The advantage of including more healthy food is obvious. It can change students' eating habits. Students love eating junk food, which have already led to obesity[1] and other diseases. For me, I just can't resist the temptation of eating junk food! I usually eat hot dogs in the morning, chicken burger at lunch, and French fries in the evening. Those foods contain too many calories, and I have gained a lot of weight because of that. So I think it's a good thing if school only provides low-calorie foods, which will force me to eat in a healthy way.

❶ obesity [əuˈbiːsəti] *n.* 肥胖症

6.2 坏处

The disadvantage is that it may cause a decrease in the University dining hall's total revenue[2]. Healthy food does not taste as good. Sometimes it's boring and flavorless. For example, salad is healthy, but I hate eating it. Eating salad, for me, is like eating grass. It's torture since I am a meat lover. So I may choose to go off campus to buy the food I like, such as fried chicken and steak. And the dining hall's revenue would definitely be affected if more and more students chose to eat off campus.

❷ revenue [ˈrevinjuː] *n.* 收入，收益

07 People will spend less time cooking and preparing food in twenty years than they do today.

真　题	题　型	年　份
People will spend less time cooking and preparing food in twenty years than they do today.	独立写作题	2015/03/7

7.1　花费更多时间

I think people will spend more time preparing food since we are getting more health-conscious. Nowadays, there are a number of serious health issues, such as diabetes[1] and heart diseases, and there is enough evidence to support the fact that we are what we eat. As a result, I am more concerned about the safety of the food I eat and the water I drink. I worry about the effects of food additives[2], pesticides[3], pollutants and genetically modified foods[4] on my body. So now when I am going shopping, I take more care to read nutritional facts[5] and seek out products with health benefits. And I pay more attention to having a well-balanced and diversified diet. Sometimes I even grow my own vegetables to make sure they are not polluted. So I believe that people will spend more time preparing food.

7.2　花费更少时间

History has proven that people will spend less time cooking in the future because of technology. For instance, microwaves can boil milk in 30 seconds. Electric pressure cookers[6] can cook rice in 10 minutes. People who lived 50 years ago could never have imagined that we could cook that fast. So there are many reasons to believe that more technology will be available in 20 years. I have heard that some scientists are working on a kind of medicine, which people can eat instead of food and then can have all the nutrients we need, such as carbohydrates[7], protein[8], and fat.

① diabetes [ˌdaiəˈbiːtiːz] n. 糖尿病

② additive [ˈædətiv] n. 添加剂

③ pesticide [ˈpestisaid] n. 杀虫剂

④ genetically modified food 转基因食品

⑤ nutrition facts 营养表

⑥ electric pressure cooker 电高压锅

⑦ carbohydrate [ˌkɑːbəuˈhaidreit] n. 碳水化合物

⑧ protein [ˈprəutiːn] n. 蛋白质

08 Your friend has bad eating habits. What suggestions do you have for him?

在家吃饭

Eating at home is one of the best ways to promote a healthy lifestyle. Most foods that are served in restaurants contain high amounts of fat and calories, and they can be detrimental[1] to your health if they are consumed on a regular basis. If you eat at home, you can choose your own low-fat and low-calorie ingredients to prepare your meals. Also, I would ask him to practice the art of distraction. When he gets the urge to eat something he shouldn't, he should tell himself that he'll wait 15 minutes before he gives in. Chances are he'll get busy doing something else and forget about it. Moreover, eating slowly is a good way to control your diet. It gives people's brain enough time to process the chemicals sent from their stomachs, saying "OK, I am very satisfied."

❶ detrimental [ˌdetriˈmentl]
　　adj. 有害的，不利的

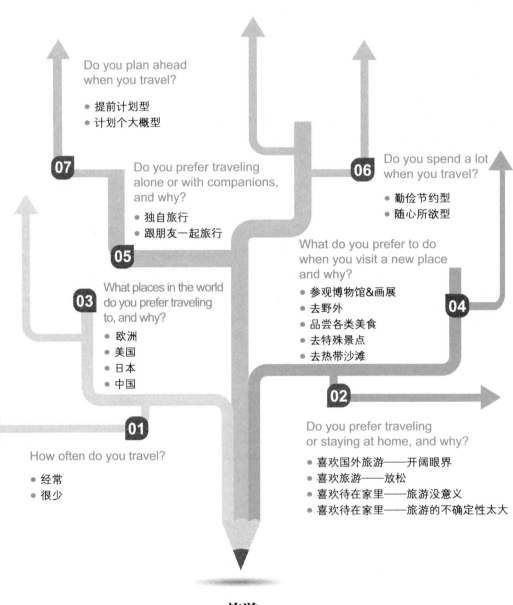

Do you plan ahead
when you travel?

- 提前计划型
- 计划个大概型

07

Do you prefer traveling
alone or with companions,
and why?

- 独自旅行
- 跟朋友一起旅行

05

Do you spend a lot
when you travel?

06

- 勤俭节约型
- 随心所欲型

What do you prefer to do
when you visit a new place
and why?

- 参观博物馆&画展
- 去野外
- 品尝各类美食
- 去特殊景点
- 去热带沙滩

04

03

What places in the world
do you prefer traveling
to, and why?

- 欧洲
- 美国
- 日本
- 中国

02

01

Do you prefer traveling
or staying at home, and why?

- 喜欢国外旅游——开阔眼界
- 喜欢旅游——放松
- 喜欢待在家里——旅游没意义
- 喜欢待在家里——旅游的不确定性太大

How often do you travel?

- 经常
- 很少

旅游

01 How often do you travel?

真　题	题　型	年　份
Which do you prefer with the same rate of pay, an interesting and challenging job with less vacation time, or a job with more vacation time but less fun?	口语第二题	2013/03/16
After high school, students should have at least one year to work or travel. It's better than attending university straight away.	独立写作题	2015/01/31
Do you agree or disagree with the following statement: traveling to new places should be a pleasant memory instead of a time-consuming and energy-burning task?	独立写作题	2016/05/22

1.1　经常

I travel a lot. My frequent-flyer mileage[1] is so high that I can get a free plane ticket from China to the U. S. Whenever I am off work, I like to go somewhere exotic.

❶ frequent-flyer mileage 航空公司累计里程数

1.2　很少

I seldom travel. The few times I had to go somewhere, I had business conferences[2] to attend. Otherwise, I just stay in my city.

❷ conference ['kɔnfərəns]
  n. 会议
  🔲 meeting

02 Do you prefer travelling or staying at home, and why?

真　题	题　型	年　份
When going on vacations, some people prefer to go camping in tents; others prefer to stay in hotels. Which do you think is better?	口语第二题	2013/06/08
It is better to spend money on travel and vacation than to save money for the future.	口语第二题	2015/05/30
If you have some extra money, which would you prefer to spend it on? 1) some practical things, like clothes or electronics; 2) some experiences, like vacations and concerts	口语第一题	2015/10/31

2.1　喜欢国外旅游——开阔眼界

I enjoy travelling, especially to foreign countries. It opens up my horizons, and allows me to see a different world, which I could only get a glimpse[1] of through books and movies. In fact, travelling is so much better as a way of knowing a place than reading or watching movies. Through the latter media, I can only get second-hand opinions. On a trip, I can truly relish[2] the beauty of nature, feel the power of history, and embrace the shock of culture[3].

2.2　喜欢旅游——放松

Travelling helps me relieve the stress and anxiety of work. As a (job name), I am under constant pressure. Hence, whenever there is an opportunity, I like to leave everything behind, turn off my phone, and enjoy total freedom and abandonment in a place where nobody knows me. It is a moment of complete rejuvenation[4]. I don't have to suck up to my boss or fake smile to clients. I get to be me, the ruler of my own world.

2.3　喜欢待在家里——旅游没意义

I don't think travelling offers anything that is unique and irreplaceable. If I would like to taste exotic foods or meet exotic people, my town, Beijing, a metropolis[5], is already able to provide them, with its various restaurants and bars. If I would like to visit a place of interest, VR technology provides an alternative. If I would like a complete break from work and a total refresh of energy, a local spa and message can more than make up for the absence of a beach.

2.4　喜欢待在家里——旅游的不确定性太大

I don't travel a lot, because I don't enjoy unpredictability. In a strange place, not everything is under my control. I have to get accustomed[6] to local conventions, and sometimes it is not enjoyable. Accidents often happen, and not in a good way. Suitcases may get lost, passports may be stolen, planes may get delayed, and hotel rooms may turn out to be much smaller than they appeared in booking. Also, I work, so the only time I'm able to travel is during vacations. Unfortunately, that

1 glimpse [glimps] *n.* 一瞥

2 relish ['reliʃ] *v.* 享受
〓 enjoy

3 shock of culture 文化冲击

4 rejuvenation [ri,dʒu:vi'neiʃn] *n.* 重生
〓 rebirth

5 metropolis [mi'trɔpəlis] *v.* 大都市
〓 big city

6 get accustomed to 习惯于
〓 get used to

is the period when everyone else is traveling. As a result, wherever I choose to go, it gets excessively crowded. To be frank, fighting for a spot in a restaurant with 30 other people or lining up outside the ticket office under the summer heat for 2 hours completely kills the mood.

03 What places in the world do you prefer traveling to, and why?

真 题	题 型	年 份
While traveling, some people prefer to go to new places; others prefer to visit familiar places. Which do you think is better? Explain why.	口语 第二题	2012/04/28
When traveling, do you prefer to stay in one place for a long time or spend less time but visit more places? Explain your answer in detail.	口语 第二题	2013/04/20
When going on vacations, some people prefer to go camping in tents; others prefer to stay in hotels. Which do you think is better?	口语 第二题	2013/06/08
Some people prefer to go straight to their destination while traveling; others prefer to spend more time looking around on the way. Which do you prefer?	口语 第二题	2014/11/09
Some people prefer to take a vacation in cities; others prefer to spend their vacation in the countryside. Which do you prefer? Explain why.	口语 第二题	2014/11/23

3.1 欧洲

I love going to Europe. I have been there many times, and don't mind going there many times more. It is rich in culture, and yet also has incomparable natural beauty. From the ancient Acropolis and the Colosseum, to the relatively younger Eiffel Tower and Louvre Palace, I am completely humbled by the masterpieces of extraordinary artists and architects that our world is honored to have. On the other hand, I would never ever forget the thrilling moment of seeing the aurora on a freezing night in Scandinavia.

3.2 美国

I must say there is nothing better than going to the U. S. , and in the

① metropolis [mi'trɔpəlis]
  n. 大都市
  ▫ big city
② shopaholic [,ʃɔpə'hɔlik]
  n. 购物狂
  ▫ love shopping so much
③ innumerable [i'nju:mərəbl]
  adj. 无数的
  ▫ countless
④ cuisines [kw'zi:n] *n.* 烹
  饪方法（菜系）
  ▫ food

⑤ antiquity [æn'tikwiti] *n.*
  古老
  ▫ the old
⑥ modernity [mə'də:nəti]
  n. 新潮
  ▫ the new
⑦ welding ['weldiŋ] *n.* 结合
  ▫ marriage
⑧ mesmerize ['mezmeraiz]
  v. 迷住
  ▫ fascinate

⑨ gourmet ['ɡuəmei] *n.*
  美食家

U. S. , there is nothing better than New York. For anyone in love with modernity, it has everything a metropolis[1] has to offer. Just from the airplane, I was already marveling at the number of skyscrapers there are. For a shopaholic[2], a week in Manhattan, the fashion capital, is when my dreams come true. With the endless stores and their innumerable[3] fashion wear, I had only my credit card to worry about. After an exhausting shopping experience, an evening that starts with a fine dinner would be another pleasant trouble. All those Michelin Restaurants with cuisines[4] from all nations in the world make choosing more difficult than ever. For a rich and lovely evening time, a Broadway musical is also a must-see. Last but not least, New York, with all the museums and galleries, is also a paradise for anyone that is a fan of culture.

3. 3　日本

Japan is by far my favorite spot for a trip. It is a perfect combination of antiquity[5] and modernity[6], a successful melding[7] of nature with culture. Whereas a tour in the Himeji Castle might bring back all the movie scenes of shoguns and samurais, a ride on the Shinkansen awakens me to an extremely orderly and civilized modern society. While in one moment I might be mesmerized[8] by the cherry blossoms on Fuji Mountain, in the next I will be tasting sashimi and ramen, kneeling on a tatami mat. This is a place where I can never get bored.

3. 4　中国

Why do I have to go somewhere other than China, my home country, for a thrilling trip? Its vast land and diverse landscapes provide everyone with endless options. If you are a fan of culture and history, a month spent in Beijing and Xi'an would not be enough to exhaust all the palaces and museums. If you love the outdoors, a backpacking trip in Tibet would be a huge challenge to even the best athletes in the world. If you are a gourmet[9], then it is a sin if you have not been to Szechuan or Canton. Still, what I've just listed is less than the tip of the iceberg. For a person who has already travelled to more than 30 provinces and over a hundred cities in this country, I still have tons of work to do before I can call myself a travel expert in China.

04 What do you prefer to do when you visit a new place and why?

真　题	题　型	年　份
While traveling, some people prefer to go to new places; others prefer to visit familiar places. Which do you think is better? Explain why.	口语 第二题	2012/04/28
Which do you prefer? Traveling to foreign countries when you are young or when you are older? Give specific reasons or examples to support your decision.	口语 第二题	2013/03/03
When traveling, do you prefer to stay in one place for a long time or spend less time but visit more places? Explain your answer in detail.	口语 第二题	2013/04/20
When going on vacations, some people prefer to go camping in tents; others prefer to stay in hotels. Which do you think is better?	口语 第二题	2013/06/08
Some people prefer to go straight to their destination while traveling; others prefer to spend more time looking around on the way. Which do you prefer?	口语 第二题	2014/11/09
Some people prefer to take a vacation in cities; others prefer to spend their vacation in the countryside. Which do you prefer? Explain why.	口语 第二题	2014/11/23

4.1　参观博物馆 & 画展

Museums and galleries are often my favorite places. I enjoy culture. On the streets, the big cities all over the world have gradually become identical, with overpasses and skyscrapers. What's unique about a place is often preserved in its museums, where all the memories are preserved intact. In the outside world, everything is but a transient[1] fad. In a museum, all the moments are sealed in a time capsule. Everything is juxtaposed[2] together to tell a story of lasting significance[3]. In a history museum, I get to see the crests[4] and falls of dynasties, the shift in political entities, and the progress in craftsmanship. In an art museum, I am able to understand how the concept of art itself evolves, from totems[5] of godly power and the celebration of divinity[6], to the capture of reality, and eventually to the unqualified[7] expression of emotion and soul. In a science museum, I am in awe of the progress human intellect has made, from a stage of almost complete crudity[8] to a level of

❶ transient ['trænziənt]
adj. 短暂的
≈ momentary

❷ juxtapose ['dʒʌkstəpəuz]
v. 并列
≈ lay out

❸ a story of lasting significance
意义重大的故事
≈ an important story

❹ crest [krest] *n.* 顶峰
≈ rises

❺ totem ['təutəm] *n.* 象征
≈ symbol

❻ divinity [di'vinəti] *n.* 神明
≈ gods

❼ unqualified [ʌn'kwɔlifaid]
adj. 无保留的
≈ sincere

❽ crudity ['kru:dəti] *n.*
无知
≈ ignorance

⑨ subordinate [sə'bɔ:dinət]
　　n. 奴隶
　　■ salve

immense possibility, from the subordinate[9] of nature, to the conqueror of oceans and mountains, and even of outer space.

4.2　去野外

⑩ excursion [ik'skə:ʃn] *n.*
　　逃离
　　■ a leave

⑪ laborious [lə'bɔ:riəs]
　　adj. 费力的
　　■ exhausting

⑫ repletion of energy 补充
　　能量
　　■ brings back energy

Being an urban resident, I share every problem with my fellows in the city, pollution, noise, and endless work. Taking an excursion[10] from the modern concrete jungle and into the wild nature, I am able to possess a moment of complete abandonment and rebirth. Hiking in the woods or in the mountains may sound laborious[11], but to a person engaged in endless brainwork in the office, this shift is actually repletion of energy[12]. The sweat and exhaust make me forget every trouble I had to go through, and allow me to see my life with a fresh view. Also, the fresh breezes and the exercise themselves are a lift of my health and strength.

4.3　品尝各类美食

I love food. Whenever I choose a travel destination, the main thing I care about is its food. It does not have to be those fancy Michelin Restaurants. I can just walk aimlessly on its little streets, and try out little snacks in every side shop. Of course, there have been terrible disasters. But it makes the whole trip worthwhile when a hardly noticeable pastry shop offers my tongue a pleasant surprise. A top local restaurant is, of course, also a must-go. I believe a nation's character is reflected in its cuisine. The fiery and vibrant Mexican, the tender and reserved Japanese, or the elegant and elevated French all tell stories through their finest cooking.

4.4　去特殊景点

I am a typical traveler. Now that the world is merging, especially as a big city dweller, I am able to access in my town, Beijing, everything from around the world. Our stores are filled with brands from all across the globe. Our restaurants serve food from Africa, Europe and America. Our colleges admit students of all races and ethnicities. The only thing I am missing and the only thing I can get from traveling are the places of interests. Some people may say that VR technology is gradually making travelling a redundancy[13]. This is not exactly true. It could happen one day, but right now, the "reality" it offers still has not captured[14] the authentic objects one hundred percent. This is why I have to go to those places in person.

[13] redundancy [ri'dʌndənsi] *n.* 多余，累赘

[14] capture ['kæptʃə] *v.* 捕捉 ▣ match

4.5　去热带沙滩

I prefer going to a tropical island and just sun bathing on the beach. I don't enjoy rushing through museums and theaters, or treading with sweat on a jungle path. When I'm on vacation, I like to just rest. My day often starts after 10 o'clock with a lovely brunch. Then I just enjoy a completely carefree afternoon on the beach. I could read for a while, order a massage, and then take a dive into the ocean for a good twenty minutes. I get to dominate my pace, and I choose not to speed.

05　Do you prefer traveling alone or with companions, and why?

真　题	题　型	年　份
Which of the following is the best way for a student to make new friends：joining a sports team, volunteering for a community activity, or traveling?	口语 第一题	2012/09/23
Some people like to write diaries or take photos to record what they've experienced when they're traveling；others don't do so. What's your opinion on it? Please explain in detail.	口语 第二题	2014/12/21
After high school, students should have at least one year to work or travel. It's better than attending university straight away.	独立 写作题	2015/01/31

5.1　独自旅行

I always travel alone. At least, I will always travel alone in the future. A lot of friendships are broken because friends choose to travel together. It is all because of the problem of planning. Unless the two are identical[1], they will have trouble planning together. Who makes the call?

[1] identical [ai'dentikl] *adj.* 相同的 ▣ the same

If one person is in charge, she had better hope it turns out great. Otherwise, the other will just bitch about the result and offers the same old "I told you so" speech. After the trip, they should count themselves lucky if they still talk to each other. Don't ask me how I know this. Let's just say it is not a pleasant story.

5. 2　跟朋友一起旅行

Friends make a bad trip fun, and a good trip unforgettable. They are the miraculous[2] finishing touch of a masterpiece. Practically speaking, a friend makes a trip a lot easier. When planning, it is hard to take everything into consideration, so a second opinion is especially important. When problems occur, a friend also offers a different perspective on how to deal with the issue. But we do not have friends travel with us just to deal with troubles. When we see great things, we love to share the joy, and that's what friends do. What's more, the trip becomes an indelible moment in the history of the friendship, and it makes it stronger than ever.

❷ miraculous [mi'rækjuləs]
adj. 奇迹的
🔲 magical

06 Do you spend a lot when you travel?

真　题	题　型	年　份
Some people prefer to spend lots of money on vacation; some people spend little money on vacation. Which do you prefer and why?	口语第二题	2014/10/11
It is better to spend money on traveling and vacation than to save money for the future.	口语第二题	2015/05/30
If you have some extra money, which would you prefer to spend it on? 1) some practical things, like clothes or electronics; 2) some experiences, like vacations and concerts	口语第一题	2015/10/31

6. 1　勤俭节约型

I have my way of budgeting when I travel. For starters, I always book hotels and vehicles beforehand. This way, I often get discounts, sometimes as much as 50% off. Also, I often book youth hotels, so I will share the cost with several others. As a result, I sometimes pay less than 10 dollars a night for hotel rooms. For transportation, as long as I take buses and subways, I won't overspend. For meals, fancy restaurants aren't necessarily good, so it is crucial to look for guides on the Internet beforehand. All the apps on restaurants provide so much information on what places are affordable. Overall, on a trip, I've mastered how to have a great experience while keeping my wallet tight.

6. 2　随心所欲型

I don't intentionally overspend, but I don't control my budget when I travel. Travelling is for leisure, so it is important not to be so calculating. Too much thinking just kills the mood. In fact, the cheaper prices of things often come at a cost. Cheap plane tickets are often accompanied by partial service and extremely early departure. Once I took a midnight flight just to save money, and the next day became a disaster. I was in no mood for sightseeing. A cheap hotel room can be the nightmare of a disastrous trip. I had the experience of staying in a dirty room while hearing sirens outside the window and a hooker next door. These failed experiences gave me a life lesson, That is, spend, or just don't travel.

07 Do you plan ahead when you travel?

真　题	题　型	年　份
Some people prefer to spend lots of money on vacation; some people spend little money on vacation. Which do you prefer and why?	口语第二题	2014/10/11
Some people like to write diaries or take photos to record what they've experienced when they're traveling; others don't do so. What's your opinion on it? Please explain in detail.	口语第二题	2014/12/21

（续）

真　题	题　型	年　份
It is better to spend money on traveling and vacation than to save money for the future.	口语 第二题	2015/05/30
If you have some extra money, which would you prefer to spend it on? 1）some practical things, like clothes or electronics；2）some experiences, like vacations and concerts	口语 第一题	2015/10/31

7.1　提前计划型

It is important to plan ahead. Online apps today offer so much advice. Taking a thorough examination might save you from potential troubles, and even disasters. It tells you where you can get things at a reasonable prices while with quality guarantees. More importantly, it informs you of where is safe and where is not. Also, it just saves you from troubles. Once I chose to go to（place name）all of a sudden, I went, and it was closed that day. I wasted 4 hours, 4 good hours that I wouldn't have had to waste had I just looked on its website.

7.2　计划个大概型

I would like to reserve a room for whimsy when I travel. A vacation is not a job, where everything has to be organized and systematic. A vacation should be a time when your mind is completely relaxed and your schedule flexible. If I cannot enter a gallery or if I don't line up before 8 o'clock, then I'd rather not go instead of rushing through the morning. Some people may recommend apps on the Internet for advice. Honestly, the Internet is filled with too much information, most of which is only half reliable at best, while the others are angry complaints based on random observations. I once went to a 5-star restaurant, only to feel completely disappointed and even nauseus in the end. In contrast, when I accidentally came across a tiny shop in the street corner, I tasted the best（food name）I've ever had in my entire life. The surprises and unpredictability are what set vacations apart from rigid jobs, and they are what I seek when I travel.

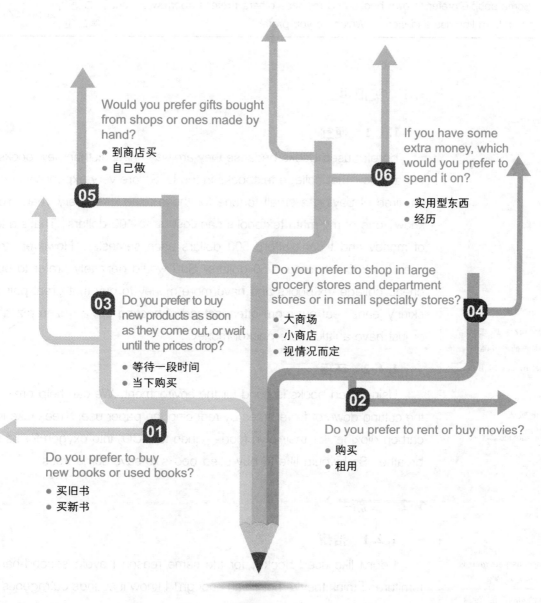

Would you prefer gifts bought from shops or ones made by hand?
- 到商店买
- 自己做

05

If you have some extra money, which would you prefer to spend it on?
- 实用型东西
- 经历

06

Do you prefer to shop in large grocery stores and department stores or in small specialty stores?
- 大商场
- 小商店
- 视情况而定

04

Do you prefer to buy new products as soon as they come out, or wait until the prices drop?
- 等待一段时间
- 当下购买

03

Do you prefer to rent or buy movies?
- 购买
- 租用

02

Do you prefer to buy new books or used books?
- 买旧书
- 买新书

01

消费

01 Do you prefer to buy new books or used books?

真　题	题　型	年　份
Some people prefer to own books and movies; others prefer to borrow or rent them from libraries and stores. Which do you prefer?	口语 第二题	2014/11/02

1.1　买旧书

1.1.1　便宜

I prefer used books because they are way cheaper than new books. We all know that college textbooks in the U. S. are very expensive and I am tired of paying a small fortune for those textbooks every year. You know, one of my math textbooks can cost up to 100 dollars! That's a lot of money and I can't afford 500 dollars each semester. However, the used book is only around 50 dollars. So I would definitely prefer to buy cheap college textbooks and have more money to buy that great pair of skinny jeans, eat out more often instead of heating up[1] a frozen pizza[2], or just have a little more pocket money[3].

1.1.2　环保

Using used books is good for the environment. We can help prevent the cutting down of fewer trees by reducing the paper use. Trees take in[4] carbon dioxide[5] for their own food — then turn CO_2 into oxygen for us to breathe! So I would like to buy used books to save some trees.

1.2　买新书

1.2.1　洁癖

I don't like used books, for the same reason I avoid second-hand furniture. I think they're not clean enough! I know it sounds outrageous[6]. It's just those stains[7], thumbprints and creases[8] make me so queasy[9]. Before I finally vowed to never buy second-hand again, I purchased a copy of Harry Potter from an online charity shop. When it arrived in the mail, I found that it had a lot of stains on some of the inside pages. It was so gross[10]! It looked like somebody had read the book while eating

① heat up 加热
② frozen pizza 速冻比萨
（超市卖的半成品）
③ pocket money 零用钱

④ take in 吸收
⑤ carbon dioxide 二氧化碳

⑥ outrageous [aut'reidʒəs] adj. 令人吃惊的
⑦ stains [stein] n. 污渍
⑧ crease [kri:s] n. 折痕
⑨ queasy ['kwi:zi] adj. 感到恶心的
⑩ gross [grəus] adj. 恶心的

a chocolate bar. So you see I just can't stand second-hand books.

1. 2. 2 特殊爱好

I must admit, I am addicted to[11] buying new books. Usually, I don't like to shop at all. Shopping for clothes is a little bit like torture for me. Shoes, jewelry, and bags just don't attract me at all. However, as for new books, it's like heaven. Whenever I am in a bookstore, I am like a kid in a candy store! My heart pumps faster. I still remember how excited I was when I got my brand new Harry Potter books. I just love the smell of new books and the way they look pristine[12] on a shelf.

⑪ be addicted to 沉溺于

⑫ pristine ['pristain] *adj.* 崭新的

1. 2. 3 不需要挑选

New books are easy to shop for. I can always find the latest and greatest edition, and I know that the book is in good condition without having to see it in person. Shopping for new books is much more convenient than hunting for their used counterparts[13]. All I have to do is log on[14] to Amazon, and I can have my books shipped to me without ever leaving the couch.

⑬ counterpart ['kauntəpɑːt] *n.* 起同等作用的人或物
⑭ log on 登录

02 Do you prefer to rent or buy movies?

真 题	题 型	年 份
Some people prefer to own books and movies; others prefer to borrow or rent them from libraries and stores. Which do you prefer?	口语 第二题	2014/11/02

2.1 购买

I'm a creature of repetition when it comes to movies, so I don't like renting movies. If I rent a movie from iTunes, I only get 30 days to start watching the rented movie and 24 hours to finish once I start. And once it expires[1], the film will be automatically withdrawn[2] by iTunes unless I rent it again. You know, I have watched *La La Land* at least 20 times.

❶ expire [ik'spaiə] *v.* 到期
❷ withdraw [wið'drɔː] *v.* 移开，拿走

I love how it encourages me — a 20-something, middle class girl pursues her dreams no matter what it takes. So now this movie has already become a kind of "comfort food" for me. Whenever I feel down, tired or ill, I like to turn to this emotional savior[3], instead of expending energy on finding a new and risky alternative[4]. So, of course I would like to buy it because I can watch it whenever I want.

❸ savior ['seivjə] *n.* 救星

❹ alternative [ɔːl'təːnətiv] *n.* 可替代的食物

2.2 租用

I prefer to rent movies because it can save me a lot of money. Some people may say the disadvantage of renting movies is that you can't keep it forever. However, for me, there are some videos I know I will only watch once and do not want to own. Good examples would be documentaries[5]. Also, there is a chance that if I buy a movie, it will not be good enough. Last time, I spent 20 dollars on the movie *Great Wall*. It was so boring that I almost fell asleep. The money I spent on it was definitely not worth it. However, if I rent it, the three dollar rent is not a big loss and I wouldn't have to eat instant noodles[6] for a whole week. Also, those rented movies take up a lot of space, and I have to put them on my shelves neatly, which takes a lot of energy and time.

❺ documentary [ˌdɔkjuˈmentəri] *n.* 纪录片

❻ instant noodles 方便面

03 Do you prefer to buy new products as soon as they come out, or wait until the price drops?

真 题	题 型	年 份
Would you buy the latest electronic gadgets, or would you rather wait?	口语第二题	2012/04/20
Some people prefer to buy innovative high-tech products like cell phones and computers when they first came out; others would buy them after the price has decreased. Which do you prefer? Explain why.	口语第二题	2014/11/29
Some people prefer to buy a product as soon as it is on the market. Other people prefer to purchase a product when it has been on the market for some time. Which do you prefer and why?	口语第二题	2014/12/06

3.1　等待一段时间

I prefer to wait for some time to buy innovative high-tech products because there is a chance that I can get some incredible deals. I remember when the iPhone 6 first came out, it was about 800 dollars. That was too expensive, and I couldn't afford it. However, one year later, when the next generation of iPhone was released, Apple cut the price of iPhone 6 by 100 dollars. The price drop was significant! So, it's obvious that I saved a lot of money this way. Also, I think it's wise to wait for some time and read some reviews before buying high-tech products. You may find that some devices have a broken power button[1] or very short battery life. So you can make a better decision about what to buy.

❶ power button 电源按钮

3.2　当下购买

I prefer to buy innovative products when they first get introduced to the market. I know it's more expensive, but my brain is wired to make me crave[2] new technology. I always want the newest and best thing on the market and I don't know why. I just assume[3] that the new version[4] must be better than the one before. For example, I can't resist buying the latest Apple product as soon as it's released. Usually, I watch the tech news to find out when updates are planned. When Tim Cook marketed the Apple Watch a year ago, he described it as "unbelievably unique and very special" and said it would be the "ultimate experience." Hearing this, I felt thrilled[5], and bought the watch for myself. I couldn't wait to see how this technological innovation would revolutionize[6] my life.

❷ crave [kreiv] v. 渴望
❸ assume [ə'sjuːm] v. 假定
❹ version ['vəːʃn] n. 版本

❺ thrilled ['θrild] adj. 激动的，狂喜的
❻ revolutionize [ˌrevə'luːʃənaiz] v. 使彻底变革

04 Do you prefer to shop in large grocery stores and department stores or in small specialty stores?

真　题	题　型	年　份
Some people prefer to shop in large grocery stores and department stores. Other people prefer to shop in small specialty stores. Which do you prefer? Explain why.	口语 第二题	2014/03/16

4.1 大商场

4.1.1 商品齐全

I prefer to shop in big shopping malls because I can get everything I need in one place. Shopping malls are usually in a grand building. There are several escalators that carry people to all levels. They contain a variety of fascinating stores, including Apple, Northface, Sephora, and Nike. So I do not need to bother to move from one physical location to another to buy the stuff I want. Also, I do not need to throw myself into the hassle[1] of driving in traffic jams. I can save a lot of time and get clothing, electronic devices, food, and makeup[2] in one place.

4.1.2 品尝美食

There is usually a food court[3] on the lower ground floor of the shopping mall. The food court features[4] international specialties[5], from the familiar to the exotic[6]. Last week, I grabbed a sandwich in a shopping mall's food court. I wasn't expecting anything amazing at first judging from the sandwich's rather homely[7] appearance, but that one was very delicious. That simple-looking sandwich was packed with quality ingredients. The thickly[8] sliced turkey tasted like it was fresh from the farm and the bread was warm and toasted. I have to say it's a great experience to eat some delicious food and take a rest after long time shopping.

4.2 小商店

I like small shops. I live in the suburbs, far from those fancy big shopping malls. Once, I wanted to buy myself a backpack. I knew I could get good deals in a shopping mall, but I just didn't want to waste my time on the commute[9]. So, I chose to buy the item from the nearest shop. Small shops are usually around residential areas. Indeed, the prices are a little bit expensive, but for me the most important thing is I don't need to drive to the shopping mall when I am very tired after eight working hours.

4.3 视情况而定

I think it depends. If I need to buy clothes, I head directly to[10] particular brand shops in my area since I am very brand loyal. Most of

① hassle ['hæsl] n. 困难，麻烦
② makeup ['meikʌp] n. 化妆用品
③ food court 美食广场
④ feature ['fiːtʃə] v. 以……为特点
⑤ specialties ['speʃəltiz] n. 特色菜
⑥ exotic [ig'zɔtik] adj.（常因来自遥远的他国而显得）奇异的
⑦ homely ['həumli] adj. 相貌平平的
⑧ thickly [θikli] adv. 厚地
⑨ commute [kə'mjuːt] n. 通勤
⑩ head to 前往

them are small shops. Their style is very unique and there is no way you can find them in big department stores. I really enjoy wandering from one small shop to another, selecting the clothes that catch my eyes. When it comes to family shopping day, I prefer going to big shopping malls. We can shop, eat, and watch movies all around the same place, which is very convenient.

05 Would you prefer gifts bought from shops or ones made by hand?

5.1　到商店买

Of course, I like gifts from shops. Most people like practical things, such as electronics, shoes, and designer clothing, and there is no real home replacement for those things. For example, last time my friend was going to a party and I knew she wanted a beautiful dress. Of course, I didn't have advanced sewing[1] skills to make her something beautiful. So I bought her a designer dress, which she liked very much. In addition, the price was very good too. It is a myth that people often say home-made gifts are cheaper. Today, between putting in our time, buying the materials, and improving at our craft[2], home-made gifts are often more expensive.

❶ sewing ['səuiŋ] *n.* 缝纫

❷ craft [krɑːft] *n.* 手艺，工艺

5.2　自己做

I like home-made gifts because they are customized[3] specifically for the receiver. They can convey[4] a sense of care and affection[5] for the recipient, which store-bought gifts often lack. They may have your name, initials[6], or certain colors that the gift giver knows the recipient[7] will love. For example, at my last birthday party, my boyfriend gave me a doll he made himself. I was surprised that he sewed my initials on the doll. I was moved that he spent hours making this. I thought it was so much more valuable than a store-bought gift.

❸ customize ['kʌstəmaɪz] *v.* 定制，定做
❹ convey [kən'vei] *v.* 表达
❺ affection [ə'fekʃn] *n.* 喜爱
❻ initial [i'niʃl] *n.* 首字母
❼ recipient [ri'sipiənt] *n.* 接受者

06 If you have some extra money, which would you prefer to spend it on?

真　题	题　型	年　份
If your friend wants to make a big purchase, but doesn't have enough money. What can she do to get enough money?	口语第二题	2015/09/17
If you have some extra money, which would you prefer to spend it on? 1）some practical things, like clothes or electronic products；2）some experiences, like vacations and concerts.	口语第二题	2015/10/31

6.1　实用型东西

6.1.1　实用

I think the best use of money is buying practical things. And spending money on things that you actually use will make you much happier. For example, I am a writer. I spend a ton of time sitting in a desk chair. Last time, I was going shopping, I bought a new chair that's insanely comfortable. Of course, I was pretty happy even if it doesn't seem like a "fun" purchase. And I can't gain this happiness from traveling and going to concerts.

6.1.2　减压

Shopping is the best stress reliever. As a computer programmer/ college student, I am under constant pressure. So, sometimes, I buy myself a pair of shoes or a bag as a reward[1], and I feel very satisfied. I know traveling sounds like a better choice to relax, but I have to work/ study. I just can't leave everything behind, shut my phone[2], and enjoy the vacation. That's why I prefer shopping for practical things, which give me instant gratification[3].

6.2　经历

6.2.1　旅游

It is true that buying a new iPhone or the first drive in a new car is

❶ reward [ri'wɔ:d] n. 奖励

❷ shut the phone 关机

❸ instant gratification 即刻的满足感

satisfying and thrilling[4], but that only lasts for a short while. The thrill always fades[5] and we find ourselves back in the same place seeking the next purchase to keep the feeling going. On the contrary, the joy and memories of experiences, such as traveling, can last a lifetime. So instead of buying a fancy dress, I would rather spend money travelling, especially to foreign countries. It opens up my horizons and allows me to see a different world. On a trip, I can truly enjoy the beauty of nature, feel the power of history, and embrace the shock of culture. So I do think the money spent on it is worth it.

④ thrilling [ˈθrɪlɪŋ] *adj.* 令人兴奋的

⑤ fade [feid] *v.* 逐渐变弱

6.2.2　音乐会

If I am asked to choose between buying new clothes and going to a nice concert, I'd choose the latter without doubt. The feeling of enjoying a great concert is way better than that of getting a nice-looking suit. Plus, the memory of a great concert can stay with you until the last moment of your life. But, by contrast, you probably will throw your clothes away after two years, even if they are very expensive, and even if you liked them. The experience of going to a concert stays forever with you, whereas clothes come and go.

Part 2

托福高分万能思路:
跟名师练 TOEFL 口语/写作

TOEFL 独立口语、
写作真题索引

TOEFL

独立口语、写作真题索引

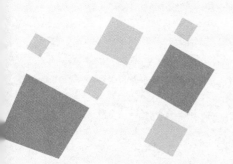

第一类 运动

真 题	题 型	年 份	话题索引
All students should attend social activities, such as joining a club or a sports team in school.	口语 第二题	2015/04/12	1 - 1
			1 - 5
			1 - 13
Do you agree or disagree with the statement that watching sports programs on TV is not a good use of time?	口语 第二题	2016/08/21	1 - 9
			1 - 10
			1 - 11
If the school received a barrel of money, what do you wish it would be spent on? A sports gym or a laboratory?	口语 第二题	2016/07/10	1 - 1
			1 - 12
If the school received a barrel of money, what do you wish it would be spent on? A sports gym, laboratory, or a scientific research facility?	口语 第一题	2016/01/24	1 - 1
			1 - 12
In their free time, young people (aged 14 - 18) spend time taking part in different activities, such as music lessons or competitive sports. Some young people divide their time between different kinds of activities. But other young people will spend most of their time focusing on just one activity that is important for them. Which approach do you think is better?	口语 第二题	2015/07/04	1 - 1
			1 - 2
			1 - 3
			1 - 4
			1 - 5
			1 - 13
Is watching sports programs a good use of time?	口语 第一题	2012/09/22	1 - 9
			1 - 10
			1 - 11
It's a good idea for first year students to join a sports team or any other kind of campus organization.	口语 第二题	2016/10/29	1 - 1
			1 - 5
			1 - 13
Many people spend a lot of time watching sports programs on TV or following their favorite sports teams, which can have negative effects on their lives.	口语 第二题	2016/08/21	1 - 9
			1 - 10
			1 - 11
Nowadays, children rely too much on technology, like computers, smartphones, and video games for fun and entertainment. Playing with simpler toys or playing outside with friends would be better for children's development.	独立 写作题	2016/02/28	1 - 1
			1 - 2
			1 - 3
			1 - 4
			1 - 5
			1 - 13

真　题	题　型	年　份	话题索引
Playing sports teaches people important lessons about life.	独立写作题	2015/06/14	1－1
			1－5
			1－13
Playing sports teaches people more important lessons about life.	独立写作题	2012/12/15	1－5
			1－13
			1－1
Some people prefer to do team sports; others prefer to do individual sports. Which do you prefer?	口语第二题	2013/09/29	1－1
			1－5
			1－7
			1－13
Some people prefer to watch a sports game from the audience seat; others prefer to be in the sports field and compete with others. Which do you prefer?	口语第二题	2013/10/20	1－1
			1－13
Some students prefer to join school clubs, such as sports teams, right after they enter college, while others wait until the second semester. What do you prefer?	口语第二题	2014/06/15	1－1
			1－13
Some think that natural talent and ability is more important for an athlete; others think that hard work is more important. What do you think?	口语第二题	2013/12/14	1－8
			1－10
The university will spend money on the dormitory to improve the student's quality of life. Which of the following do you think is best? 1) providing a room for quiet study; 2) building an exercise room; 3) providing a movie room	独立写作题	2016/09/25	1－1
			1－12
These days, children spend more time on doing homework or participating in organized activities related to school or sports. However, they should be given more time to do whatever they want.	独立写作题	2015/07/12	1－1
			1－2
			1－3
			1－4
			1－5
			1－13
To be successful in sports, which is more important? Talent or hard work?	口语第二题	2015/08/30	1－8
			1－10
Which new skill do you want to learn? Playing a musical instrument, flying a plane, or playing a new sport?	口语第一题	2013/01/14	1－1
			1－14

真　题	题　型	年　份	话题索引
Which of the following activities do you think is the most beneficial for a child's growth? Doing team sports, talking with others, or traveling?	口语第一题	2013/01/13	1 - 1
			1 - 2
			1 - 3
			1 - 4
			1 - 5
			1 - 13
Which of the following activities would you like to do on a weekend afternoon? Doing exercise, watching TV, or spending some time with family?	口语第一题	2012/10/28	1 - 1
			1 - 14
Which of the following do you prefer? Doing exercise every day, or only when you are free? Explain your choice in detail.	口语第二题	2012/10/14	1 - 1
			1 - 2
			1 - 3
			1 - 4
Which of the following is the best way for a student to make new friends：joining a sports team, volunteering for a community activity, or traveling?	口语第一题	2012/09/23	1 - 1
			1 - 2
			1 - 3
			1 - 4
			1 - 5
			1 - 13
Which of the following qualities do you admire the most（or would you be most interested in having?）Art skills, language skills or sports skills? Use details and explanations in your response.	口语第一题	2012/09/02	1 - 1
			1 - 14
Which of the following three activities would you most prefer to do on a weekend afternoon? Play a sport, visit a friend, or cook at home?	口语第一题	2012/07/28	1 - 1
		2012/08/19	1 - 1
Your city is planning to spend more on one of the following three projects. Which do you think is the most important? Expanding tourism, building city parks, or improving the public transportation system?	口语第一题	2012/03/18	1 - 1
			1 - 12
Your school used to offer three after-class activities：1）sports，2）art，3）volunteering，but this year, the school's extra money can only offer one activity. Which one do you choose and why?	口语第二题	2015/06/27	1 - 1
			1 - 12
		2015/07/11	1 - 1
			1 - 12

第二类　游戏

真　题	题　型	年　份	话题索引
Do you agree or disagree with the statement that playing video games is a waste of time?	口语 第二题	2014/08/16	2 - 1
Some people believe that video games could inspire young students' interest and make their study more efficient rather than distracting them and wasting their time, so young students should be allowed to play video games.	独立 写作题	2016/01/23	2 - 1
Some people play games for enjoyment；some people play games for winning. Which one do you prefer and why? Use specific reasons and examples to support your answer.	口语 第二题	2012/03/10	2 - 1
What are the advantages or disadvantages of children playing video games? Use details and examples in your response.	口语 第一题	2013/10/27	2 - 1
Your university will sponsor one of the following activities for students：an outdoor camp night, a music festival to experience the local culture, or a computer game contest in the dorm. Which do you think is the best and why?	口语 第一题	2015/09/17	2 - 1

第三类　音乐

真　题	题　型	年　份	话题索引
A friend of yours studies in a business school now, but he really likes playing a musical instrument, so he plans on dropping business school to study music. What suggestion would you give to this friend?	口语 第一题	2015/05/30	3 - 1
Choose between the following three that your school is planning to hold. 1）theater performance by student actors；2）concert by professional musicians；3）lectures by well-known professors	口语 第一题	2015/06/27	3 - 1
Some people like listening to music when they are going from one place to another, while other people are not fond of this. Which one do you prefer and why? Please include specific reasons and examples to support your answer.	口语 第二题	2015/10/31	3 - 1
			3 - 5
Some people prefer live music, while others prefer recorded music. Which do you prefer and why? Please include reasons and examples to support your response.	口语 第二题	2015/09/17	3 - 1
			3 - 5
			3 - 6
			3 - 10

真　题	题　型	年　份	话题索引
Talk about the kind of music you enjoy the least, and explain why you don't like it.	口语 第一题	2015/01/10	3 - 3
			3 - 4
			3 - 6
			3 - 7
			3 - 9
Which new skill do you want to learn? Playing a musical instrument, flying a plane, or playing a new sport?	口语 第一题	2015/03/07	3 - 1
			3 - 3
			3 - 4
			3 - 6
			3 - 7
			3 - 9
Which of the following three activities do you prefer to do with a group of people rather than alone: eat a meal, listen to music, or do homework?	口语 第一题	2016/12/11	3 - 1
			3 - 5
Your primary school is considering spending more time on teaching young students (aged 5 - 11) technology (like computers) than teaching them music and art.	独立 写作题	2016/09/10	3 - 1
Your university will sponsor one of the following activities for students: an outdoor camp night, a music festival to experience the local culture, or a computer game contest in the dorm. Which do you think is the best and why?	口语 第一题	2015/09/17	3 - 1

第四类　艺术

真　题	题　型	年　份	话题索引
Do you agree or disagree with the statement that it's important for students to study art and music in school? Explain your answer in detail.	口语 第二题	2014/04/19	4 - 1
It is more important for the government to spend money on art museums and concert halls than on recreational facilities such as swimming pools and playgrounds.	独立 写作题	2010/12/15	4 - 3

真　题	题　型	年　份	话题索引
Some people think that one needs to be talented to be an artist; others believe training and hard work are more crucial for someone to be an artist. Which do you think is more important? Give details and examples in your response.	口语第二题	2013/06/15	4 - 2
Some people think that one needs to be talented to become an artist; others believe that anyone could be an artist with years of practice. Which do you agree with? Explain why.	口语第二题	2012/02/24	4 - 2
Which of the following classes would you like to take? Math, painting science?	口语第一题	2016/12/03	4 - 1
Which one of the following classes would you choose? 1）science history；2）art history；3）European history	口语第一题	2016/09/10	4 - 4
Which one of the following history courses should be added? History of science, art history or modern history of the 20th century?	口语第一题	2016/01/23	4 - 4
Which one of the following two factors is more important to the success of an artist? Natural talent or hard work?	口语第二题	2016/02/27	4 - 2
Your city is going to build new places to attract more visitors. Among the following three options, which do you think is the best? 1）a local history museum；2）a modern art and film museum；3）a children's science museum	口语第一题	2016/09/10	4 - 3
Your primary school is considering spending more time on teaching young students（aged 5 - 11）technology（like computers）than teaching them music and art.	独立写作题	2017/07/15	4 - 1
Your school used to offer three after-class activities：1）sports, 2）art, 3）volunteering, but this year, the school's extra money can only offer one activity. Which one do you choose and why?	独立写作题	2015/11/08	4 - 1

第五类　影视

真　题	题　型	年　份	话题索引
Many people spend a lot of time watching sports programs on TV or following their favorite sports teams, which can have negative effects on their lives.	口语第二题	2016/08/21	5 - 3
Movies and television have more negative effects than positive effects on the way young people behave.	口语第一题	2016/05/28 2016/11/26	5 - 1 5 - 1

真　题	题　型	年　份	话题索引
Movies are worth watching only when they teach something about real life.	独立写作题	2015/04/12	5 - 1
One can learn about another person from the books and movies that person likes.	独立写作题	2015/09/17	5 - 5
Some people prefer to watch entertainment programs on television, while others prefer to watch educational programs. Which do you prefer and why?	口语第二题	2016/08/20	5 - 3
Some schools prevent students from putting a TV in the dormitory. What are the advantages and disadvantages of this policy? Please include specific reasons and examples to support your answer.	口语第一题	2015/05/09	5 - 4
The university will spend money on the dormitory to improve the student's quality of life. Which of the following do you think is best?1）providing a room for quiet study；2）building an exercise room；3）providing a movie room	口语第一题	2013/10/05	5 - 4
Which do you prefer? Watching a movie silently or chatting with others?	口语第二题	2015/08/22	5 - 5
Which of the following activities would you like to do on a weekend afternoon? Doing exercise, watching TV, or spending some time with family?	口语第一题	2015/01/31	5 - 5

第六类　书籍

真　题	题　型	年　份	话题索引
A club at your school plans to help one of the following groups of people：1）teach pupils reading and math；2）build houses for those who cannot afford housing；3）take care of the elderly. Which do you think is the best plan?	独立写作题	2016/03/19	6 - 1
			6 - 2
			6 - 8
			6 - 9
Among the following types of books, which do you dislike the most? Romantic books, science fiction, or biography?	口语第一题	2015/04/18	6 - 1
			6 - 2
			6 - 3
			6 - 4
			6 - 5
			6 - 6
			6 - 8
			6 - 9

真　题	题　型	年　份	话题索引
Do you prefer to buy new books or used books?	口语 第二题	2016/11/13	6－3 6－8 6－9
One can learn about another person from the books and movies which that person likes.	独立 写作题	2012/11/17	6－1 6－2 6－3 6－4 6－5 6－6 6－8 6－9
One can learn about another person from the books and movies which that person likes.	独立 写作题	2013/11/17	6－1 6－2 6－3 6－4 6－5 6－6 6－8 6－9
Students doing their own personal reading is as important as, or more important than reading assigned by teachers.	独立 写作题	2016/03/11	6－1 6－2 6－8 6－9
Which of the following is the most effective way of learning：studying from textbooks, having discussions with a group or reading articles written by others?	口语 第一题	2015/02/01	6－1 6－2 6－8 6－9

第七类　网络

真　题	题　型	年　份	话题索引
Describe one of the most popular websites in your country. Explain why it is popular, with details or examples.	口语 第一题	2015/06/27	7－1
Nowadays, students do many things like surfing the Internet and listening to music when they are learning. Do you agree or disagree that doing other things has a bad effect on learning?	独立 写作题	2015/09/19	7－2

真　题	题　型	年　份	话题索引
Talk about the advantages of online shopping. Give examples and details in your response.	口语第一题	2013/11/23	7 - 2

第八类　通信

真　题	题　型	年　份	话题索引
Classmates and partners can work together face to face to finish projects better than by sending e-mails.	独立写作题	2015/01/25	8 - 1
Do you agree or disagree with the following statement：cell phones have improved our life?	口语第二题	2015/03/07	8 - 3
Do you agree or disagree with the following statement：technological devices have brought distance between people? Please use details and examples in your response.	口语第二题	2015/10/25	8 - 4
Do you like talking to people face to face, sending text messages, or by emails?	口语第一题	2015/04/18	8 - 1

第九类　广告

真　题	题　型	年　份	话题索引
Advertisements make products appear better than they really are.	独立写作题	2015/03/28	9 - 1
Do you agree that advertisements have a great influence on what we buy?	口语第一题	2016/07/10	9 - 2

第十类　交通

真　题	题　型	年　份	话题索引
Do you think that bicycles will be replaced by more modern vehicles such as cars or buses?	口语第一题	2012/07/15	10 - 2
If you had to volunteer for a project, which one would you choose? Cleaning up the city, creating bicycle trails, or planting trees?	口语第一题	2013/07/14	10 - 2

真　题	题　型	年　份	话题索引
Some people prefer to own cars; others prefer to mainly use public transportation. Which one do you prefer?	口语 第二题	2013/03/30	10－1
What do you think we should do to decrease the usage of cars or other vehicles and solve the traffic problems?	口语 第一题	2012/07/28	10－2
What is the most useful action for people to help the environment in their local communities? 1）Plant trees and create parks; 2）Persuade local shops to stop providing plastic bags for consumers; 3）Increase access to public transportation（such as buses and trains）, and reduce the number of automobiles on roads.	独立 写作题	2016/09/03	10－2
Which transportation do you enjoy, bicycle, automobile or train?	口语 第一题	2014/02/22	10－1
Your city is planning to spend more on one of the following three projects. Which do you think is the most important? Expanding tourism, building city parks, or improving the public transportation system?	口语 第一题	2014/11/08	10－2

第十一类　环境保护

真　题	题　型	年　份	话题索引
Describe some ways to reduce air pollution.	口语 第一题	2012/05/26	11－4 11－5
If you were making a donation, which organization would you make your donation to, environmental protection group, city library, or animal shelter?	口语 第一题	2016/08/21	11－1
Many companies sell products or services but at the same time cause environmental damage. Some people say it can be stopped by asking them to pay a penalty, such as a higher tax, when they cause environmental damage. Others say there are better ways to stop them from harming the environment. What do you think is the best way to prevent the environment from deteriorating?	独立 写作题	2015/12/12	11－4
Nowadays, air pollution is a common problem in many places. What can people do to reduce air pollution? Include reasons and details to support your response.	口语 第一题	2015/05/09	11－4 11－5

真 题	题 型	年 份	话题索引
The most effective way for governments to encourage energy conservation is by increasing the price of gasoline and electricity.	独立 写作题	2013/10/25	11 - 4
The most important thing the government should do to improve health conditions is to clean the environment.	独立 写作题	2013/10/20	11 - 1
			11 - 2
What is the most important action for the government to tackle environmental problems? 1) fund researches on new energy sources such as solar and wind power；2) protect forests and natural wildlife species；3) pass and enforce laws to reduce the pollution	口语 第一题	2013/08/17	11 - 4
What is the most useful action for people to improve the environment in their local communities? 1) Plant trees and create parks； 2) Persuade local shops to stop providing plastic bags for consumers； 3) Increase access to public transportation（such as buses and trains），and reduce the automobiles on roads.	口语 第一题	2016/09/03	11 - 5
Which of the following community services would you be most interested in doing and explain why? Cleaning the city park, planting flowers and trees, or building a bicycle lane?	口语 第一题	2016/01/24	11 - 1
Which of the following three classes will you choose to fit into your schedule? 1) Musical History；2) World Economics；3) Environmental Science	口语 第一题	2015/11/14	11 - 1
Who has the biggest impact on reducing the environmental contamination, government regulation or individual efforts？	口语 第二题	2015/03/14	11 - 5

第十二类　动物保护

真 题	题 型	年 份	话题索引
Children can benefit in important ways from taking care of a pet.	独立 写作题	2015/07/04	12 - 2
If you were making a donation, which of the organizations would you make your donation to, environmental protection group, city library, or animal shelter?	口语 第一题	2015/03/28	12 - 1
			12 - 2
What do you think of having pets?	口语 第一题	2012/02/25	12 - 2

真　题	题　型	年　份	话题索引
What kind of activity do you think children do can cultivate a sense of responsibility? 1）Keep a pet；2）do house chores；3）help take care of their younger sisters or brothers. Use specific details and examples in your response.	口语第一题	2015/10/31	12 - 2
Which one of the following would you donate your money to? Choose one, and explain how you would use the money：community charity, environment protection, animal rescue.	口语第一题	2013/09/13	12 - 1
			12 - 2
Your friend is considering getting a pet. What kind of pet, and what advice would you give him?	口语第一题	2012/02/11	12 - 2

第十三类　医疗

真　题	题　型	年　份	话题索引
Do you agree or disagree with the following statement, experienced doctors are better than young doctors?	独立写作题	2016/09/25	13 - 1
Do you agree or disagree with the statement that government should encourage citizens to live healthier lifestyles?	独立写作题	2016/03/13	13 - 2

第十四类　外表

真　题	题　型	年　份	话题索引
Do you agree or disagree with the following statement：it is okay for people to use surgery to change their appearance?	口语第一题	2016/07/16	14 - 3
Do you agree or disagree with the statement that advertisements make products seem better than they really are?	独立写作题	TPO17	14 - 4
Some people believe it's better to wear formal clothes at work, while others believe it's better to wear casual clothes. Which do you prefer?	口语第二题	2016/03/26	14 - 1
Talk about the things you do that keep you healthy. Give examples and details in your explanation.	口语第一题	2013/11/22	14 - 2
The university dining hall is changing its food service to include more healthy food with lower calories. What do you think are the advantages and disadvantages of this change?	口语第一题	2013/10/12	14 - 2

真　题	题　型	年　份	课题索引
What suggestions would you give a friend who is starting a new job? Give examples and details in your response.	口语 第一题	2013/04/20	14－1
What suggestions would you give a friend who is starting a new job? Give examples and details in your response.	口语 第一题	2013/04/20	14－5
Which of the following activities would you like to do on a weekend afternoon? Doing exercise, watching TV, or spending some time with family?	口语 第一题	2012/10/28	14－2
Which of the following do you prefer? Doing exercise everyday, or only when you are free? Explain your choice in detail.	口语 第一题	2016/09/24	14－2
Your friend has bad eating habits. What suggestions would you like to give the friend?	口语 第一题	2012/03/18	14－2
Your friend is going to an important interview. What suggestions would you give to your friend?	口语 第一题	2015/03/07	14－1
			14－5

第十五类　朋友

真　题	题　型	年　份	话题索引
Competition between friends often negatively impacts friendships. Use specific details and examples to support your opinion.	独立 写作题	2016/07/01	15－3
Do you agree or disagree with the following statement? It is possible for friends to maintain their friendship even when they have disagreements over certain issues.	口语 第二题	2015/09/05	15－4
Getting advice from friends who are older than you is more valuable than getting that from your peers.	口语 第二题	2016/02/28	15－2
It is better to make friends with people who are intelligent than with these who have a good sense of humor.	口语 第二题	2016/12/10	15－2
It is often not a good thing to move to a new city or a new country because you will lose touch with old friends.	口语 第二题	2016/01/23	15－3
Nowadays, children rely too much on technology, like computers, smartphones, and video games for fun and entertainment; playing with simpler toys or playing outside with friends would be better for children's development.	口语 第一题	2015/06/14	15－1

真　题	题　型	年　份	话题索引
Some believe that we should spend more time far away from the people we care about benefit, because it is necessary for people to understand the importance of relationships, while others think being away from people we care about can damage our relationships with them.	口语 第二题	2015/11/15	15 - 3
When you have been friends with someone for a long time, it is important to continue your friendship with that person even if he or she does something you do not like.	口语 第二题	2013/03/30	15 - 3
Which one of the following invitations would you go to, a family dinner party, or a friend's party?	口语 第二题	2016/11/16	15 - 1
Which of your traits do your friends like the best? Kindness, cheerfulness, or intelligence?	口语 第一题	2015/07/11	15 - 2

第十六类　性格

真　题	题　型	年　份	话题索引
Do you agree or disagree with the following statement? If you want to be successful in running a business, being outgoing and friendly is very important.	口语 第二题	2016/08/21	16 - 1
Do you agree or disagree with the statement that people's personalities never change?	口语 第二题	201/03/16	16 - 3
Do you think you can learn a lot about a stranger from the first observation, or you have to know his personality for a long time?	口语 第二题	2016/03/13 2016/06/27	16 - 4 16 - 4
It is better to make friends with intelligent people than with people who have a good sense of humor.	独立 写作题	2015/06/27	16 - 2
Nowadays, children rely too much on technology, like computers, smartphones, and video games for fun and entertainment；playing with simpler toys or playing outside with friends would be better for the children's development.	口语 第一题	2015/06/14	16 - 1
Some people like to share their thoughts through publications like newspapers and blogs. Others prefer to only share them with friends. Which one do you prefer?	口语 第二题	2014/12/27	16 - 1

真 题	题 型	年 份	话题索引
Some people like to spend their spare time with family members and friends; some people like to spend it alone. Which do you prefer?	口语 第二题	2014/12/27	16 - 1
		2014/03/02	16 - 1
Some people prefer to buy a product as soon as it is on the market. Other people prefer to purchase a product when it has been on the market for some time. Which do you prefer and why?	口语 第二题	2016/09/03	16 - 2
Some people prefer to celebrate special occasions like birthdays with their friends; others prefer to be alone at such occasions. Which do you prefer? Use examples and details to support your response.	口语 第二题	2013/08/17	16 - 1
		2014/11/29	16 - 1
Some people prefer to finish assignments a long time before the due date, while others prefer to finish the assignment right before the deadline. Which one do you prefer and why?	口语 第二题	2016/09/25	16 - 2
Some students prefer to live alone or live with their friends when they study abroad. Other students prefer to live with a local family when they study abroad. Which way do you prefer and why?	口语 第二题	2012/07/22	16 - 1
		2014/05/25	16 - 1
When parents cannot afford time to accompany their children, they could choose to send their children to child-care centers, where many children are cared for together; or they could send their children to an individual caregiver. Which one is better?	口语 第二题	2015/11/08	16 - 1
When there's a challenge, would you prefer to face it alone, or would you rather seek help from others?	口语 第二题	2013/04/20	16 - 1
		2015/05/30	16 - 1
Which do you prefer? Watching a movie silently or chatting with others?	口语 第二题	2015/08/22	16 - 1
Which of the following activities do you think is more beneficial for a child's growth? Doing team sports, talking with others or traveling?	口语 第一题	2014/12/13	16 - 1
Which of the following activities would you do with friends rather than alone? Taking a walk, watching a movie or traveling?	口语 第一题	2012/10/28	16 - 1
		2013/11/16	16 - 1
Which of the following three activities do you prefer to do with a group of people rather than alone? Eat a meal, listen to music, or do homework?	口语 第一题	2012/08/19	16 - 1
		2012/08/25	16 - 1
		2016/12/11	16 - 1
Which of your traits do your friends like the best? Kindness, cheerfulness, or intelligence?	口语 第一题	2012/05/20	16 - 2
		2016/09/25	16 - 2

第十七类　年龄

真　题	题　型	年　份	话题索引
Do you agree or disagree with the following statement：people should be required to retire after the age of 65?	口语 第二题	2016/05/28	17 - 3
Do you agree or disagree with the following statement：it is easier to be an adult than it is to be a child?	口语 第二题	2015/11/14	17 - 1
Do you agree or disagree with this statement：a 16-year old is not mature enough to drive.	口语 第二题	2013/03/24	17 - 2
16-year-olds are old enough to drive a car.	口语 第二题	2013/06/08	17 - 2
Which of the following periods in life do you think is the hardest, being a kid, a teenager or an adult?	口语 第一题	2014/06/29	17 - 1
Which one of the following periods do you consider the most difficult one, childhood, teen period or adulthood?	口语 第一题	2016/08/20	17 - 1
		2016/08/21	17 - 1
Which stage of life is the most important, childhood, juvenile, or adulthood? Explain why.	口语 第一题	2012/06/15	17 - 1

第十八类　父母

真　题	题　型	年　份	话题索引
Do you agree or disagree with the following statement：it is more important to maintain relationships with family members than with friends?	口语 第二题	2016/03/11	18 - 3
Since the world has changed so much in the past fifty years, the advice our grandparents give us is not useful.	口语 第二题	2015/09/17	18 - 4
			18 - 5
The most important thing people learned is from families.	口语 第一题	2015/11/21	18 - 2
			18 - 4
What do you think is the most important thing that parents should teach their children? Please include details in your response.	口语 第一题	2016/04/23	18 - 2
What should parents do to help their children to succeed in school?	口语 第一题	2015/04/12	18 - 1

第十九类 老师

真 题	题 型	年 份	话题索引
A university should focus more on its facilities, such as libraries, computers or laboratories, rather than on hiring famous teachers.	独立写作题	2015/02/01	19 - 7
Describe a common mistake that experienced teachers often make.	口语第一题	2010/10/15	19 - 1
		2016/09/11	19 - 2
Do you agree or disagree that the success of a school depends on experienced teachers?	口语第一题	2016/01/24	19 - 7
Do you agree or disagree with the following statement: it's easier to teach children in primary schools than students in universities?	口语第二题	2016/07/10	19 - 5
It is generally agreed that society benefits from the work of its members. Which type of contribution do you think is most valued by your society: primary school teachers, artists or nurses?	口语第一题	2015/06/13	19 - 3
Leaving some time for group discussion in class is beneficial for study. Do you agree or not?	口语第二题	2015/01/25	19 - 1
			19 - 2
Many students are asked to evaluate their professors at the end of the semester. What are the advantages and disadvantages of this?	口语第二题	2016/07/16	19 - 4
Students doing their own personal reading is as important as, or more important than reading assigned by teachers.	口语第二题	2014/04/19	19 - 6
Teachers should be paid at least as much as doctors, lawyers, or business leaders are paid.	口语第二题	2013/11/19	19 - 3
When choosing research paper topics, some teachers give students the freedom to choose topics that interest them; others assign topics to students. Which do you think is better and why?	口语第二题	2013/06/08	19 - 6
Which of the following activities would you be more interested in doing? Teaching children, teaching adults to use computers, or cleaning the city park?	口语第一题	2013/01/12	19 - 5
Would you prefer an interesting professor with a strict grading policy or a boring professor with a loose grading policy?	口语第二题	2012/04/14	19 - 1
		2015/01/10	19 - 2

第二十类　合作

真　题	题　型	年　份	话题索引
Imagine if a professor wants students to learn as much as possible about a project in a short period of time. Is it better to let students work in a group or study alone?	独立 写作题	2016/11/13	20 - 1 20 - 2
		2016/11/19	20 - 1 20 - 2
Many schools require young children (aged 5 - 11) to work together in a small group instead of working alone for many of their activities.	独立 写作题	2016/10/16	20 - 1 20 - 3
Some people prefer to work independently; others prefer to work with others. Which do you prefer? Explain your answer in detail.	口语 第二题	2016/03/26	20 - 1
Some students like to learn by themselves; others prefer to share their ideas with others. Which one do you prefer?	口语 第二题	2013/11/22	20 - 1
Some students prefer studying with other students to prepare for an exam. Others prefer studying alone to prepare for an exam. Which way do you prefer and why? Include reasons and details in your response.	口语 第二题	2012/10/27	20 - 1
What is the most effective way to learn: taking notes, discussing with others or memorizing?	口语 第二题	2012/09/29	20 - 1

第二十一　学习

真　题	题　型	年　份	话题索引
Do you agree or disagree that students should take some additional courses so that they can get their credits more quickly?	口语 第二题	2016/03/19	21 - 2
Do you agree or disagree with the following statement: students should learn to draw or paint?	口语 第二题	2016/08/27	21 - 2
Some people prefer to work independently; others prefer to work with others. Which do you prefer? Explain your answer in detail.	口语 第二题	2016/03/26	21 - 3 21 - 7
Some universities require students to take foreign language classes, while others require students to take computer classes. Which do you think is more useful for students and why?	口语 第二题	2015/11/15	21 - 1
What's the biggest problem during the course of being a student? How do you usually deal with it?	口语 第一题	2016/03/11	21 - 7

真　题	题　型	年　份	话题索引
When do you think is the best time for one to learn a second language? Please use details to support your reasons.	口语第一题	2015/09/05	21 – 1
When you have trouble doing assignments, do you prefer to seek help from classmates or professors?	口语第一题	2015/07/12	21 – 7
Which do you prefer：starting a project as early as possible or waiting until the due time?	口语第二题	2016/09/25	21 – 4
			21 – 7
Which new skill do you want to learn? 1）playing a musical instrument；2）flying a plane；3）playing a new sport	口语第一题	2015/03/07	21 – 1
Which of the following classes would you like to take? 1）math, 2）painting，3）science	独立写作题	2016/12/03	21 – 1
Which of the following is the most effective way of learning：1）studying from textbooks；2）having discussions with a group；3）reading articles written by others? Please use specific reasons to support your idea.	口语第一题	2015/02/01	21 – 7
Which one do you prefer? Reviewing your notes after class and doing this throughout the whole semesters, or just reviewing at the end of the semester?	口语第二题	2015/06/27	21 – 7

第二十二类　学校

真　题	题　型	年　份	话题索引
A university should focus more on its facilities, such as libraries, computers or laboratories, rather than on hiring famous teachers.	独立写作题	2015/10/24	22 – 4
Do you agree or disagree with the following statement：all students should attend social activities such as clubs or sports teams in school?	口语第二题	2015/04/12	22 – 1
Do you think it is a good idea to let students keep pets in dorms?	口语第一题	2016/01/09	22 – 3
It is important to have rules about the types of clothing that people are allowed to wear at work and at school.	独立写作题	2013/08/24	22 – 3
Should universities allow their students to bring computers to class?	口语第一题	2015/06/14	22 – 3

真　题	题　型	年　份	话题索引
Some college students like to join clubs and enjoy club activities; others like to spend their time studying another course or doing schoolwork. Which one do you think is better and why?	口语第二题	2016/05/07	22 - 1
Some people think that it is an important part of children's education to go on field trips (e. g. museums). Others think a child's time is better spent in the classroom at school. Which do you prefer and why?	独立写作题	2013/10/05	22 - 1
Some schools prevent students from putting TVs in their dormitories. What are the advantages and disadvantages of this policy? Please include specific reasons and examples to support your answer.	口语第一题	2015/05/09	22 - 3
These days, children spend more time on doing homework or participating in organized activities related to school or sports. However, they should be given more time to do whatever they want.	独立写作题	2015/07/12	22 - 1
The university will spend money on the dormitory to improve the students' quality of life. Which of the following do you think is best? Providing a room for quiet study, building an exercise room or providing a movie room	独立写作题	2016/09/25	22 - 4
Which kind of extracurricular activity would you like to attend if you have the chance: writing essays for a student newspaper, joining a hiking club, or working in the dormitory discipline committee?	口语第一题	2015/11/08	22 - 1
Which one of the following should be done in order to improve the quality of life and study for the students? Repairing the swimming pool, building a new cafeteria, or improving laboratory equipment?	口语第一题	2016/03/13	22 - 4
Your school is planning to forbid the use of cell phones on campus. What do you think are the effects of the policy?	口语第一题	2016/05/29	22 - 3
Your school used to offer three after-class activities: 1) sports, 2) art, 3) volunteering, but this year, the school's extra money can only offer one activity. Which one do you choose and why?	独立写作题	2015/11/08	22 - 1
Your university will sponsor one of the following activities for students, an outdoor camp night, a music festival to experience the local culture, or a computer game contest in the dorm. Which do you think is the best and why?	口语第一题	2015/09/17	22 - 1

第二十三类　课外

真　题	题　型	年　份	话题索引
Do you think it's a good idea that some schools require students to finish 40 hours of community service each year?	口语 第一题	2016/05/07	23－1
If there is a community activity, would you like to play with children or do the gardening?	口语 第二题	2015/03/07	23－2
If you had to volunteer for a project, which one would you choose? Cleaning up the city, creating bicycle trails, or planting trees?	口语 第一题	2015/10/25	23－2
If you were to do a volunteer job in the community, which one of the following jobs would you choose? Clean up the park, plant trees, or build a bicycle lane?	口语 第一题	2016/06/04	23－2
Should schools require their students to participate in 40-hour-long community work?	口语 第一题	2015/09/05	23－1
Talk about an activity you participated in recently. Did everyone have a good time?	口语 第一题	2013/12/15	23－2
Talk about an interesting activity you recently participated in. Did everyone involved enjoy the activity? Give details and examples in your response.	口语 第一题	2013/12/14	23－2
Talk about one activity you will do in the near future and explain why.	口语 第一题	2013/12/07	23－2
The university is recruiting volunteers to help the community protect the environment. If you are recruited, which of the following three tasks will you choose to do? 1) pick up trash and litter on the street; 2) plant trees and flowers to green the town; 3) teach children about protecting the environment	口语 第一题	2013/10/12	23－2
What kind of activity do you think can help children cultivate a sense of responsibility? 1) Have a pet; 2) do house chores; 3) help take care of their younger sisters or brothers. Use specific details and examples in your response.	口语 第一题	2013/07/21	23－2
What should we do to help the elderly in our community?	口语 第一题	2015/08/22	23－2
Which kind of extracurricular activity would you like to attend if you have a chance? Writing essays for a student newspaper, joining a hiking club, or working in the dormitory discipline committee?	口语 第一题	2013/01/26	23－2

真 题	题 型	年 份	话题索引
Which of the following community services would you choose to do? Working with children, cleaning the city park, or planting a campus garden?	口语 第一题	2014/09/27	23－2
Which of the following hospital volunteer work would you be interested in doing? Talking to patients, reading to patients, or taking care of their families?	口语 第一题	2014/12/6	23－2
Which of the following would you choose to do in summer vacation? Working at the front desk of a public library, painting in a community art center, or being a life guard in a community swimming pool?	口语 第一题	2012/07/15	23－2
		2016/09/25	23－2

第二十四类 工作

真 题	题 型	年 份	话题索引
After high school, students should have at least one year to work or travel. It's better than attending university straight away.	独立 写作题	2016/03/13	24－1
Do you agree or disagree with one of your friends, who is planning to work part-time while studying on campus?	口语 第一题	2016/11/26	24－1
Do you agree or disagree that people should work for some time before they find a permanent job?	口语 第二题	2014/03/01	24－1
Do you think it's a good idea for students to work for a year before entering university?	口语 第一题	2013/09/29	24－1
It is generally agreed that society benefits from the work of its members. Which type of contribution do you think is most valued by your society, primary school teachers, artists or nurses?	口语 第一题	2015/12/05	24－3
It is important to have rules about the types of clothing that people are allowed to wear at work and at school.	独立 写作题	2013/08/24	24－5
Some people believe it's better to wear formal clothes at work, while others believe it's better to wear casual clothes. Which do you prefer?	口语 第二题	2014/11/29	24－1
Some people believe that it is important for young people to have a part-time job as a work experience, while others think they should spend more time on their studies. What is your opinion and why?	口语 第二题	2012/04/20	24－1
			24－1
Some people prefer to work in an office; others prefer to work at home. Which do you prefer?	口语 第二题	2014/03/15	24－2

真　题	题　型	年　份	话题索引
Talk about a positive experience you recently had working with another person. Explain why this experience was important to you.	口语第一题	2013/03/24	24 − 4
When you are at work, which of the following factors do you think is the most important to you? Having flexible schedules, having friendly coworkers, or having a helpful boss?	口语第一题	2015/03/14	24 − 4
Which would you choose：a higher pay job with longer hours or an average pay job with normal work hours? Explain your choice, using specific reasons and details.	独立写作题	2016/07/09	24 − 4
Your friend is planning to work for a year before entering university. Give your opinion about his plan.	口语第一题	2013/10/20	24 − 1

第二十五类　历史

真　题	题　型	年　份	话题索引
All university students should be required to take history courses no matter what their field of study is.	独立写作题	2015/01/07	25 − 1 25 − 3 25 − 4 25 − 5
If you are a teacher of a tutor group and you are going to take students on a study trip, where would you take them to? A science museum, a local farm, or a theatre performance?	口语第二题	2015/10/25	25 − 1 25 − 3 25 − 4
		2016/05/29	25 − 1 25 − 3 25 − 4
It is more important for the government to spend money on art museums and concert halls than on recreational facilities such as swimming pools and playgrounds.	口语第二题	2015/11/28	25 − 6
		2015/10/10	25 − 6
Some people think that it is an important part of children's education to go on field trips (e. g. museums). Others think a child's time is better spent in classrooms at school. Which do you prefer and why?	口语第二题	2016/03/27	25 − 1 25 − 3 25 − 4
		2016/06/07	25 − 1 25 − 3 25 − 4

真　题	题　型	年　份	话题索引
Visiting museums is the best way to learn about a country.	独立写作题	2014/09/29	25－1
When you're visiting a city you've never been to, how would you like to tour around? A. sign up for a well-organized trip；B. visit history museums；C. walk along the streets	口语第一题	2016/05/11	25－1
Which of the following classes do you think can attract the most students?1）sound engineering；2）history of rock music；3）film studies	口语第一题	2016/12/11	25－1 25－2
Which of the following is the best way to learn about a city? Joining an organized trip；visiting the museums；taking walks in the streets of its cities?	口语第一题	2016/05/22	25－1
Which of the following three classes will you choose to fit into your schedule? 1）Musical History；2）World Economics；3）Environmental Science	口语第一题	2015/11/14	25－1 25－2
Which of the following ways is the best to get to know Italian culture? 1）watching Italian movies；2）learning Italian cooking；3）attending Italian lectures or history classes	口语第一题	2012/07/22	25－1 25－2
Which one of the following classes would you choose? 1）science history；2）art history；3）European history	口语第一题	2012/06/17	25－1 25－2
Which one of the following history courses should be added? History of science, art history, or modern history of the 20th century?	口语第一题	2016/01/23	25－1 25－2
Your city is going to build new places to attract more visitors. Among the following three options, which do you think is the best? A local history museum, a modern art and film museum, or a children's science museum?	口语第二题	2016/10/10	25－6

第二十六类　政府

真　题	题　型	年　份	话题索引
Government, rather than of individuals, should cover Internet fees.	口语第一题	2015/11/28	26－1.3
Internet is as important as other services, such as building roads, that government should provide Internet access to all the citizens at no cost.	独立写作题	2016/04/23 2016/05/22 2016/07/03	26－1.3 26－1.3 26－1.3

真　题	题　型	年　份	话题索引
In times of an economic crisis, in which area should governments reduce their spending? 1) arts, 2) Scientific research, 3) Parks and public gardens	独立写作题	2015/09/14	26 - 1.2
			26 - 1.4
			26 - 1.5
It is more important for the government to spend money on art museums and concert halls than on recreational facilities such as swimming pools and playgrounds.	口语第二题	2015/11/28	26 - 1.1
		2015/10/10	26 - 1.1
People can solve important problems by themselves or with the help from their family members, so there's no need for the government to help them.	独立写作题	2016/05/29	26 - 1.4
		2016/05/07	26 - 1.4

第二十七类　城市

真　题	题　型	年　份	话题索引
Describe two cities you visited before and tell the differences.	独立写作题	2014/12/06	27 - 1
Do you agree or disagree with the following statement: it is important to learn the history of the city you live in?	口语第二题	2016/07/10	27 - 3
Do you agree or disagree with the statement that people from small towns are kinder and more helpful than people in big cities?	口语第二题	2015/03/28	27 - 1
If you had to volunteer for a project, which one would you choose? Cleaning up the city, creating bicycle trails, or planting trees?	口语第一题	2015/10/25	27 - 2
If your friend is moving to another city, what would be your suggestion for him? Give details and examples for your explanation.	口语第一题	2015/01/10	27 - 3
If you were making a donation, which of the organizations would you make your donation to: environmental protection group, city library, or animal shelter?	口语第一题	2016/08/21	27 - 2
One of your friends just moved to a new city. What suggestions do you have to help him fit in?	口语第一题	2015/12/05	27 - 3
Some people prefer to take a vacation in cities; others prefer to spend their vacations in the countryside. Which do you prefer? Explain why.	口语第二题	2014/11/23	27 - 1

真　题	题　型	年　份	话题索引
When you're visiting a city you've never been to, how would you like to tour around? A）sign up for a well-organized trip；B）visit history museums；C）walk along the streets	口语第一题	2013/03/17	27－3
Which of the following activities would you be more interested in doing? Teaching children, teaching adults to use computers, or cleaning the city park?	口语第一题	2013/01/12	27－2
Which of the following community services would you be more interested in doing and explain why：cleaning the city park, planting flowers and trees, or building a bicycle lane?	口语第一题	2012/10/19 2016/06/04	27－2 27－2
Which of the following community services would you choose to do：working with children, cleaning the city park, or planting a campus garden?	口语第一题	2012/10/14	27－2
Which of the following is the best way to learn about a city? Joining an organized trip, visiting the museums, or taking walks in the streets of the city?	口语第一题	2012/09/22	27－3
Which of the following volunteer activities do you think is the most beneficial to the environment, cleaning the city, planting trees or recycling?	口语第一题	2012/07/22	27－2
Your city is going to build new places to attract more visitors. Among the following three options, which do you think is the best? A local history museum, a modern art and film museum, or a children's science museum?	口语第一题	2012/03/24	27－3
Your city is planning to spend more on one of the following three projects. Which do you think is the most important：expanding tourism, building city parks, or improving the public transportation system?	口语第一题	2012/03/18	27－2

第二十八类　饮食

真　题	题　型	年　份	话题索引
Describe a memorable experience in a restaurant or cafe.	口语第一题	2015/09/17	28－5
Do you prefer to cook home or eat outside?	口语第二题	2012/04/20	28－2

真　题	题　型	年　份	话题索引
For getting a better understanding of nutrition and health, your school decides to open cooking classes；do you think this is a reasonable decision?	口语 第二题	2016/09/10	28－3
If one of your friends wants to run a restaurant, what is your opinion or advice on food and location?	口语 第一题	2016/10/11	28－4
People will spend less time cooking and preparing food in twenty years than they do today.	独立 写作题	2015/03/25 2015/03/07	28－3 28－7
Some people prefer to eat at fast food restaurants；others prefer to eat at regular restaurants. Which do you prefer? Explain your answer in details	口语 第二题	2014/11/15	28－2
Some people prefer to prepare meals at home；others like to eat out in restaurants. Which do you prefer? Explain with details and examples.	口语 第二题	2014/10/26	28－2
The university dining hall is changing its food service to include more healthy food with lower calories. What do you think are the advantages and disadvantages of this change?	口语 第一题	2013/10/12	28－6
Which of the following ways is the best to get to know Italian culture? 1）watching Italian movies；2）learning Italian cooking；3）Attending Italian lectures or history classes	口语 第一题	2012/07/22	28－3
Your school is planning to provide healthy low-calorie food only. What are the advantages and disadvantages?	口语 第一题	2012/02/05	28－6

第二十九类　旅游

真　题	题　型	年　份	话题索引
After high school, students should have at least one year to work or travel. It's better than attending university straight away.	独立 写作题	2015/01/31	29－1 29－5
Do you agree or disagree with the following statement：traveling to new places should be a pleasant memory instead of a time-consuming and energy-burning task?	独立 写作题	2016/05/22	29－1
If you have some extra money, which would you prefer to spend it on? 1）some practical things, like clothes or electronics；2）some experiences, like vacations and concerts	口语 第一题	2015/10/31	29－1 29－6 29－7

真　题	题型	年　份	话题索引
It is better to spend money on travel and vacation than to save money for the future.	口语第二题	2015/05/30	29－2
			29－6
			29－7
Some people like to write diaries or take photos to record what they've experienced when they're traveling; others don't do so. What's your opinion on it? Please explain detail.	口语第二题	2014/12/21	29－5
			29－7
Some people prefer to take a vacation in cities; others prefer to spend their vacation in the countryside. Which do you prefer? Explain why.	口语第二题	2014/11/23	29－3
			29－4
Some people prefer to go straight to their destination while traveling, others prefer to spend more time looking around on the way. Which do you prefer?	口语第二题	2014/11/9	29－3
			29－4
Some people prefer to spend lots of money on vacation. some people would spend little money on vacation. Which do you prefer and why?	口语第二题	2014/10/11	29－6
			29－7
When going on vacations, some people prefer to go camping in tents; others prefer to stay in hotels. Which do you think is better?	口语第二题	2013/06/08	29－2
			29－3
			29－4
When traveling, do you prefer to stay in one place for a long time or spend less time but visit more place? Explain your answer in detail.	口语第二题	2013/04/20	29－3
			29－4
Which do you prefer? Traveling to foreign countries when you are young or when you are older? Give specific reasons or examples to support your decision.	口语第二题	2013/03/03	29－4
Which do you prefer with the same rate of pay, an interesting and challenging job with less vacation time, or a job with more vacation time but less fun?	口语第二题	2013/03/16	29－1
Which of the following is the best way for a student to make new friends: joining a sports team, volunteering for a community activity, or traveling?	口语第一题	2012/09/23	29－5
While traveling, some people prefer to go to new places; others prefer to visit familiar places. Which do you think is better? Explain why.	口语第二题	2012/04/28	29－3
			29－4

第三十类　消费

真　题	题　型	年　份	话题索引
If you have some extra money, which would you prefer to spend it on? 1) some practical things, like clothes or electronic products; 2) some experiences, like vacations and concerts	口语第二题	2015/10/31	30－6
If your friend wants to make a big purchase, but doesn't have enough money. What can she do to get enough money?	口语第二题	2015/09/17	30－6
Some people prefer to buy a product as soon as it is on the market. Other people prefer to purchase a product when it has been on the market for some time. Which do you prefer and why?	口语第二题	2014/12/06	30－3
Some people prefer to buy innovative high-tech products like cell phones and computers when they first came out; others would buy them after the price has decreased. Which do you prefer? Explain why.	口语第二题	2014/11/29	30－3
Some people prefer to own books and movies; others prefer to borrow or rent them from libraries and stores. Which do you prefer?	口语第二题	2014/11/02	30－1 30－2
Some people prefer to shop in large grocery stores and department stores. Other people prefer to shop in small specialty stores. Which do you prefer? Explain why.	口语第二题	2014/03/16	30－4
Would you buy the latest electronic gadgets, or would you rather wait?	口语第二题	2012/04/20	30－3